CONSUMING
CATASTROPHE

CONSUMING CATASTROPHE

Mass Culture in America's Decade of Disaster

TIMOTHY RECUBER

TEMPLE UNIVERSITY PRESS
Philadelphia • Rome • Tokyo

TEMPLE UNIVERSITY PRESS
Philadelphia, Pennsylvania 19122
www.temple.edu/tempress

Copyright © 2016 by Temple University—Of The Commonwealth System
of Higher Education
All rights reserved
Published 2016

Library of Congress Cataloging-in-Publication Data
Names: Recuber, Timothy, 1978– author.
Title: Consuming catastrophe : mass culture in America's decade of disaster /
   Timothy Recuber.
Description: Philadelphia : Temple University Press, 2016. | Includes
   bibliographical references and index.
Identifiers: LCCN 2016018610 | ISBN 9781439913697 (cloth : alk. paper) |
   ISBN 9781439913703 (paper : alk. paper) | ISBN 9781439913710 (e-book)
Subjects: LCSH: Disasters—Press coverage—United States. | Disasters—Social
   aspects—United States. | Mass media and culture—United States. | Mass
   media—Social aspects—United States. | United States—Civilization—21st
   century.
Classification: LCC PN4888.D57 R43 2016 | DDC 070.4/49973931—dc23
LC record available at https://lccn.loc.gov/2016018610

♾ The paper used in this publication meets the requirements of the American
National Standard for Information Sciences—Permanence of Paper for Printed
Library Materials, ANSI Z39.48-1992

Printed in the United States of America

9 8 7 6 5 4 3 2 1

CONTENTS

Acknowledgments		*vii*
Introduction: *A Decade of Disaster*		*1*
1	A History of Catastrophe: *Media, Mass Culture, and Authenticity*	*23*
2	The Limits of Empathy: *Hurricane Katrina and the Virginia Tech Shootings*	*58*
3	The Authenticity of Fear: *September 11 and the Financial Crisis*	*98*
4	Memory as Therapy: *September 11, Hurricane Katrina, and Online Commemoration*	*128*
	Conclusion: *The Deepwater Horizon Oil Spill and Disasters Still to Come*	*163*
	References	*181*
	Index	*205*

ACKNOWLEDGMENTS

I have been tremendously fortunate to spend the past eight years thinking and writing about disasters and their media representations, all while supported by talented advisers, generous colleagues, and loving friends and family. I owe them all much more than these brief acknowledgments, but at the very least I want to bear witness to their benevolence.

I began graduate school at the University of Maryland in the fall of 2001 and woke to news of the September 11 attacks the morning after moving into my first apartment with Jenna Kryszczun, who is now my wife. We moved to Brooklyn in late August 2005, as I had decided to pursue a doctorate at the Graduate Center of the City University of New York, and we got our television hooked up just in time to see the first images of people stranded on rooftops in an inundated New Orleans after Hurricane Katrina. As we experienced these and the other disasters covered in this book, Jenna was by my side at every turn, helping me make sense of this turbulent, tumultuous world. She has supported me in every imaginable way throughout this project—as a critic, a proofreader, a benefactor, and a promoter—and without her this book simply would not have been possible.

At the Graduate Center, Stuart Ewen helped me conceive of this project in its earliest stages and kept me focused on the bigger picture throughout. John Torpey provided thoughtful and encouraging comments on my work, as well as invaluable professional guidance. Sharon Zukin helped shape and sharpen my theorizing with her keen insights. My work and career have benefited greatly from the influence and friendship of all three. Others at the Graduate Center who aided my efforts include Patrick Inglis, who commented on an early draft of a chapter, and Kristen Van Hooreweghe and Elizabeth Bullock, who helped me clarify ideas over drinks in our Greenpoint neighborhood. While I was at the Graduate Center, the New York Public Library generously provided space in its Wertheim Study for me to pursue much of my preliminary research.

My colleagues at Queens College supported me as I was finishing my doctorate and writing the earliest draft of this book, and for their help and encouragement, Jason Tougaw, Ken Nielsen, and Judith Summerfield deserve many thanks. In addition, were it not for the care and stewardship of my intellectual career at its earliest stages provided by my mentors at the University of Maryland—Lory "Tomni" Dance, Bill Falk, George Ritzer, and the late Richard Harvey Brown—I would not be a sociologist or an academic of any kind.

I have learned a great deal about the craft of writing from my colleagues at the Princeton Writing Program (PWP), where I have taught for the past five years. Ali Aslam and Rebekah Massengill provided valuable feedback on drafts and proposals related to this project. I have benefited from the talents of my fellow lecturers in many discussions, workshops, and presentations at the PWP offices, and I have been especially fortunate to be able to teach courses such as my "Witnessing Disaster" seminar to so many bright, young first-year Princeton students. Their interest in and dedication to this topic have continually inspired my own.

Parts of Chapter 4 are derived from my article "The Prosumption of Commemoration: Disasters, Digital Memory Banks, and Online Collective Memory," *American Behavioral Scientist* 56, no. 4 (2012): 531–549. I thank the anonymous reviewers of that essay and the reviewers of two of my preliminary essays that also fed into this book: "Disaster Porn!" *Contexts* 12, no. 2 (2013): 28–33, and "The Terrorist as Folk Devil and Mass Commodity: Moral Panics, Risk, and Consumer Culture," *Journal of the Institute of Justice and International*

Studies 158 (2009): 158–170. I am also grateful to the reviewers of this book for their generous and enthusiastic suggestions and to Micah Kleit for his skilled editorial guidance.

While I have immersed myself for years in tales of disaster and destruction, I have been constantly surrounded by the love of my wife, my parents, my brother and brother-in-law, my friends, and especially my children—Margot and Simon. They remind me every day of the good and beauty in this world. By understanding disasters and their mass mediation, it is my hope that we can work to protect that beauty, promote the common good, and create a more just future for all.

CONSUMING CATASTROPHE

INTRODUCTION

A DECADE OF DISASTER

The World Trade Center towers burned and crumbled to the ground on live television as millions watched in awe, horror, and anguish. They watched alone or with loved ones, at home or at work, on television or online. Some stayed online and shared their thoughts, recollections, and fears with anonymous others. Some donated money, gave blood, volunteered their time. Some bought American flags, patriotic bumper stickers, memorial T-shirts and trinkets. Some bought bigger, safer cars; home security systems; even parachutes designed to save executives in skyscrapers from similar attacks in the future. And some made speeches, pushed policies, passed legislation that steered the country's recovery and shifted the national character in the new, post-9/11 reality.

So, too, did millions watch as New Orleans was flooded four years later, its poorest neighborhoods destroyed, its poorest residents stranded on rooftops and in a poorly organized mass shelter at the Superdome. They were, once again, horrified, saddened, angered. Again, these distant spectators sat glued to the television, or went online, or donated time or money, or bought music or T-shirts to benefit Hurricane Katrina recovery efforts. Some even purchased rooftop escape hatches to help them avoid the fates of those who were trapped in attics and consumed by floodwaters, should a similar disaster occur in the future. And again the government responded, though belatedly and ineffectively, as the country struggled to come to terms with the destruction of one of its major cities and cultural centers.

A year and a half later, millions again tuned in to breaking news coverage as an alienated and unstable student at Virginia Tech shot and killed thirty-two of his fellow students, and himself. They watched shaken and shocked students stagger out of classrooms into a pool of cameras and microphones. They watched two days later as portions of the shooter's deranged and violent multimedia manifesto were broadcast on major television news programs. They gave money to scholarship funds, bought the school's athletic apparel as a show of solidarity, and checked in on social networking sites with students at Tech and other universities. And Virginia politicians began a massive inquiry into what went wrong and what could have been prevented, while broader national debates about gun control and mental health were reflected in the speeches of pundits and politicians, though never in any subsequent federal legislation.

A year and a half after that, the sudden collapse of venerable investment bank Lehman Brothers signaled the beginning of another disaster, a massive global recession erasing billions in wealth and causing waves of evictions and unemployment across the country. Millions watched the less spectacular but frequently ominous footage of white-collar workers carrying boxes out of their emptying offices or heard the fearful pronouncements from news anchors and politicians about a potential meltdown of the global economy. Even the normal, twenty-four-hour-a-day coverage of the presidential race between John McCain and Barack Obama was superseded by a series of revelations about the insolvency of large financial institutions. This disaster ultimately resulted in the passage of highly controversial bank bailout legislation and other, smaller economic stimulus measures, none of which successfully reignited the American economy in the ways their creators had hoped. Meanwhile, Americans began to radically change their spending habits, out of either fear or necessity, as companies attempted to shift their marketing and advertising strategies to match the new frugality of panicked, economically insecure consumers.

In the first decade of the twenty-first century, Americans watched as mass media, consumer culture, big business, and national politics both shaped and were shaped by the September 11 terrorist attacks in 2001, Hurricane Katrina in 2005, the Virginia Tech shootings in 2007, and the financial crisis of 2008. Although each of these disasters was the focus of extensive news coverage, political debate, and popular culture, efforts to rebuild have been slow, at best, and often ineffective, particularly at instituting the safeguards necessary to prevent similar calamities in the future. The financial crisis has not resulted in meaningful prosecution of bankers or strong legislation to prevent future financial collapse. The shootings at Virginia Tech did not spur new gun control laws. Hurricane Katrina has only exacerbated the racial and class inequality that made the government's poor response so problematic in the first place. Even the massive post-9/11 security and surveillance apparatus has not seemed to decrease the sense of threat posed by terrorism. Although such failures have not gone unnoticed, they also have not sustained the high levels of concern that these disasters initially generated. Why is this? Why do we care so much about the live broadcasting of mass tragedies and give so much money to disaster relief efforts, only to quickly accept that the work is done, that the problem is over? Why, despite so many admonitions to *never forget*, do we seem to do just that—at least when it comes to the big, long-term solutions that disaster prevention tends to require?

Part of the explanation certainly lies in the narrow and formulaic ways that we engage with disasters and tragedies today and the kinds of outcomes that such engagement both constrains and enables. Although these were all very different disasters with vastly different death tolls, economic costs, cultural effects, and political ramifications, they followed surprisingly similar paths through public consciousness. These paths included an initial flurry of attention in which they dominated the media landscape in a highly spectacular and emotional fashion; followed by a broad response from a wide range of producers, advertisers, entrepreneurs, and politicians; then a slow tapering off of public attention and emotional investment, coupled with a backlash over the media coverage or mass consumption of the events themselves.

The January 26, 2011, issue of the satirical newspaper *The Onion* captured the backlash concerning September 11 in an article entitled "Congress Honors 9/11 First Capitalizers." It described the passage of a fictional "9/11 First Capitalizers Act," designed to honor those "who sensed the direness of the moment and immediately sprang into action on that terrible day, exploiting it for personal profit" ("Congress Honors 9/11 First Capitalizers" 2011, 1). Included in this group were "not only those who rushed to Ground Zero immediately to sell merchandise, participate in photo ops, or advance an ideological agenda, but also those who profited from afar by producing jingoistic songs and TV specials, or mentioning 9/11 in stump speeches as a way of scaring people into voting for them" ("Congress Honors 9/11 First Capitalizers" 2011, 7). Although the article singled out some real-life "capitalizers" such as the country musician Toby Keith, the filmmaker Oliver Stone, Halliburton's chief executive David Lesar, and George W. Bush, it also described a forty-eight-year-old woman named Linda Banks "who continues to trot out her maudlin, self-serving story of where she was on 9/11 every single time she sees an opportunity" ("Congress Honors 9/11 First Capitalizers" 2011, 7). The article closed by stating that a special plaque would be erected on the National Mall "containing the names of all 12,554,310 Americans who eventually capitalized on the tragedy" through "advertising, partisan rhetoric, forgettable novels, defense contracts, and all-around cheap, manipulative sentimentalism" ("Congress Honors 9/11 First Capitalizers" 2011, 7).

Although the "9/11 First Capitalizers Act" is a fabrication, the criticism behind this satire is quite real. Many commentators have been bothered by the roles of mass media and consumer culture in the American public's response to the September 11 attacks, and the political uses to which that response was ultimately put. Some, such as social theorist Frederic Jameson, argued that the public's emotional reaction to 9/11 constituted a kind of "utterly insincere" hysteria (Jameson 2002, 297). Others, such as the film critic Anthony Lane, were troubled by the degree to which viewers' responses to the spectacle of the attacks mimicked everyday forms of cinema spectatorship. He asked, "Where have you heard those expressions most recently—the wows, the whoohs, the holy shits—if not in movie theatres, and even on your own blaspheming tongue" (Lane 2001, para. 2)?

Whether aimed at the news media, real estate developers, Hollywood producers, souvenir vendors, government officials, or American consumers, these types of ethical, aesthetic, and political condemnations formed a countercurrent to the tide of mainstream public opinion immediately after September 11. As the decade continued, subsequent disasters generated similar processes of mediation, consumption, and, some would say, exploitation, which were often the subject of similar rebukes. Just as many held that tourism at the Ground Zero site was a morally dubious activity, so, too, did people come to perceive travel to New Orleans after Hurricane Katrina as a potentially ghoulish act. As one disaster recovery volunteer with the Federal Emergency Management Agency (FEMA) recalled on a website devoted to the storm, "It was not without reservation that I went to St. Bernard parish. I felt like—I was a voyeur in their neighborhood." This charge of voyeurism, this unease about viewing intimate details of others' suffering from a safe distance, appeared again in 2007 after the shootings at Virginia Tech. NBC News was flooded with criticism online and in print after it decided to air parts of the shooter Seung-Hui Cho's digital manifesto, and some victims and their families canceled their scheduled television appearances on the network as a result (A. Johnson 2007). Writing in *Advertising Age*, the media columnist Simon Dumenco assailed the news networks for their crass "Massacre at Virginia Tech" graphics, arguing, "We've come to the point at which murderous psychopaths and TV news executives are of the same mind when it comes to human tragedy: It's a branding opportunity" (Dumenco 2007, 34). It seems that when otherwise normal forms of commerce, entertainment, politics, or mass communication take disasters as their subjects or inspiration, they often rankle the sensibilities of many Americans.

Yet many more engage in precisely these types of activities each time a disaster strikes. Even *The Onion* recognized this situation by asserting that more than twelve million people had "capitalized" on the events of 9/11 in some fashion and thus deserved the sarcastic inclusion of their names on an honorific plaque. If watching a disaster on television or visiting a disaster site makes one a voyeur, if reacting to a disaster emotionally is insincere, if using a disaster to make a political point is exploitative, and if creating a product, service, or work of art that responds to a disaster is simply a way to capitalize on tragedy, then very few Americans have escaped the past decade ethically untarnished. The simple fact is that most Americans, and many others across the globe, rely on mass media and consumer culture to provide the resources through which we experience, understand, and respond to pain, tragedy, and loss—even, or perhaps especially, when they occur on such a massive scale.

In the wake of this decade of disaster, each of us has had to negotiate a stunning variety of images, texts, products, and services that address the harrowing realities of multiple crises and catastrophes. These negotiations, and the moral condemnations that sometimes accompany them, suggest that the norms concerning appropriate personal, commercial, and political responses to disasters are in the process of shifting and that a consensus on these matters is only beginning to emerge. Norms are the codes of conduct that delineate culturally acceptable behavior and that mark certain ways of seeing the world as legitimate or appropriate. "Just as sets of mutually consistent norms help regulate behavior, so sets of inconsistent or rapidly shifting norms . . . are often regarded as a symptom, if not a cause, of social unrest" (Hechter and Opp 2001, xi). Such unrest—or, at least, widespread unease—was evident almost immediately after September 11: one poll taken two weeks after the attacks found that 53 percent of Americans were very or somewhat worried that they or someone in their family "might become a victim of a terrorist attack" (Pew Research Center for the People and the Press 2001c). Two years later, 75 percent of Americans felt that the world had become a more dangerous place (Pew Research Center for the People and the Press 2003). In 2009, 58 percent of Americans still felt that way (Pew Research Center for the People and the Press 2009). By the end of the decade, in addition to these fears about terrorism, Americans' financial security had also been shaken: a full 70 percent of Americans had experienced a problem related to their job or personal finances (Pew Research Center for the People and the Press 2010b). It makes sense, then, that a period in which Americans from all walks of life had their sense of personal safety and economic security shaken would expose rifts and fractures in normative structures concerning not only disasters but also the larger role of mass media and consumer culture in American life.

This work explores the interwoven fabric of news, entertainment, advertising, commodities, and other services through which Americans came to experience disasters in the first decade of the twenty-first century. Within this fabric are threaded several important norms concerning the appropriate emotional, commercial, and political responses to disasters. These are often complementary, though occasionally contradictory, but taken together they explain the contemporary appeal of disaster consumption. Although many Americans are bothered by the consumption of catastrophe, many more actively participate in it—and, perhaps more accurately, those two groups need not be seen as mutually exclusive. Instead, individuals today are tasked with navigating the shifting cultural standards concerning forms of disaster spectatorship and consumerism that they may experience as morally appropriate, personally therapeutic, or, in extreme cases, ethically repugnant.

This book argues that disasters stand out from the rest of mass media and consumer culture because of their connection, however tenuous, to *the real* and because of the emotional power that such a connection generates. Typical elements of mass culture get disrupted by disasters, as do the cynical and ironic perspectives of audiences and consumers. Instead, the texts, products, websites, and other mediated experiences that stem from disasters are marked as different from the rest of popular culture by the traces of real loss and real pain that they signify. These traces, when clearly identifiable via certain aesthetic and performative cues, signal to audiences and consumers that it is OK, and even laudable, to be moved emotionally. In fact, this has become a norm or obligation—to allow oneself to empathize with distant victims of disasters and tragedies.

For instance, five days after the terrorist attacks of September 11, 2001, the *New York Times* discussed the details about the lives of the victims that had begun to emerge. "We are just now getting to know these people, the missing and the dead. Their stories carry a weight no one expected because they are such ordinary stories" ("The Faces Emerge" 2001). One sees in this ordinariness an important marker of authenticity, one that allows readers to forge a specific kind of emotional connection to these victims. As the *Times* put it:

> No person is interchangeable with another, but we all understand how interchangeable these . . . stories might have been if the timing of the attacks and the ultimate collapse of the towers had been different. The dividing line between those who made

it out and those who didn't is inexplicable. We are also learning how to recognize in the tales the obituaries tell, and in the profiles of the victims we see on television, how interchangeable we might have been with those who died. Their lives resembled ours more closely than we can let ourselves imagine. ("The Faces Emerge" 2001)

Despite the rhetorical flourish that this is all "more than we can let ourselves imagine," such imagination is precisely what the quote encourages from its readers. Indeed, the passage makes the case that these victims' stories are valuable because of the sort of personal, empathetic reflection they engender. While such engagement with the suffering of others is not necessarily, as some critics would have it, insincere or voyeuristic, the irony of disaster consumption resides in the fact that the catastrophes and crises experienced as the most real, the most harrowing, the most authentic contain the greatest potential for steering or manipulating public opinion. Indeed, the most seemingly authentic disasters ultimately can have the most inauthentic political ends. At the very least, the harrowing spectacle of mass-mediated disaster provides no guarantee that institutions will take the appropriate measures to safeguard us from future calamities. Far from it.

Instead, the assumption that consuming catastrophe allows us to learn from these tragedies and improve ourselves and our society as a result is often shattered when the next disaster strikes. For example, another *New York Times* editorial took the occasion of the four-year anniversary of the September 11 attacks to ponder Hurricane Katrina's recent devastation. "It took a day or two after Hurricane Katrina hit the Gulf Coast to understand that it could affect our feelings about what happened at the World Trade Center, at the Pentagon and in rural Pennsylvania" ("Revising 9/11" 2005). Lamenting the fact that "everyone did not behave well" and "the federal government was less prepared than it had been" before 9/11, the authors were forced to revise the "tidy story arc" about 9/11 in which "mistakes were made, but we would learn from them, and wind up stronger and better prepared" ("Revising 9/11" 2005).

This shock at the repetition of disasters, this disappointment at the lack of lessons learned, is a common feature of disaster media.

After the Virginia Tech shootings in 2007, comparisons to the mass shootings at Columbine High School in 1999 were, of course, commonplace. As the *Times* once again exclaimed, "Sympathy was not enough at the time of Columbine, and eight years later, it is not enough" ("Eight Years after Columbine" 2007). Yet sympathy and empathy are often all that we, as distant spectators of others' misfortune, have to give.

The book thus tells the story of how authenticity came to be a crucial element in the mass-mediation of disaster; how the authenticity of disasters works in tandem with the rise of empathy as a cultural norm; how empathy is connected to other emotions, such as fear and trust; how this focus on empathy for suffering others gets channeled toward the individualistic rather than the communal; and how this individualism makes disasters amenable to the manipulation of elites and reactionary forces. Ultimately, it argues that the *ineffability* of disasters—their stubborn refusal to provide a full understanding, or a complete catharsis, to their distant spectators—makes them a particularly powerful force in contemporary American mass culture. In fact, this quality encourages a kind of *empathetic hedonism*, in which the desire to understand the suffering of others is pursued doggedly, though always necessarily unsatisfactorily. But how did we arrive at this point?

The contemporary consumption of disaster is itself the product of a history of shifts in ways of knowing and responding to the suffering of others. The invention of the printing press first made tales of misfortunes suffered by distant others available to mass audiences, and discourse on the appropriate moral and political responses to such suffering has been a feature of social life since at least the Enlightenment. But the speed, frequency, and intimacy of our exposure to others' suffering has increased exponentially with the growth of consumer culture and the rapid development of a host of mass-media technologies. Today, audiences and consumers engage with disasters and tragedies through television news programs, reality television shows, documentary films, and digital archives, as well as the myriad other commodities that cater to some aspect of disasters—comic books with patriotic themes, T-shirts or records that benefit disaster-related charities, home and office security devices designed to protect against future disasters, and social networking sites devoted to sharing one's grief over a mass tragedy, to name a few examples. Thus, to fully understand the consumption and mediation of recent disasters such as September 11, Hurricane Katrina, the Virginia Tech shootings, and the 2008 financial crisis, one must explore the very development of the modern public sphere, as well as its recent transformations.

Disaster sociologists might find the grouping together of these events problematic inasmuch as the social disruption and social changes in communities affected by these disparate events have varied greatly (see Quarantelli and Dynes 1977). But the farther one moves away from victimized communities, or the more distant and mediated one's experience of a disaster becomes, then the more likely it becomes that these events will be experienced through similar cultural frameworks. Although the processes by which communities respond to and cope with disasters have been expertly investigated by sociologists such as Kai Erikson (1976, 1994), Eric Klinenberg (2002), Thomas Drabek (2010), and many others, the effects of disasters on national audiences who experience them only through media images and mass commodities remain less thoroughly explored within this sociological subdiscipline.

Scholars outside the traditions of disaster sociology have debated the effects of disasters as generators of media, consumption, and capitalism. Mike Davis (1999) has critiqued the denials about real disasters and inequality that are embedded in fantastic disaster-themed media, focusing on the especially disaster-prone city of Los Angeles. Marita Sturken (2007) has examined the ways in which kitsch consumerism helped construct a "culture of comfort" that depoliticized the national traumas of the Oklahoma City bombing and the September 11 attacks. E. Ann Kaplan (2005) has coined the term "empty empathy" to describe the emotions generated by harrowing images of war and disaster when the news media fails to adequately contextualize them. Kevin Rozario (2007) has highlighted the historical development of an American perspective on disasters in which they are seen as opportunities for both spiritual renewal and capitalist expansion. And the current neoliberal manifestation of this perspective may be the "shock doctrine" described by Naomi Klein (2007), in which elites in business and government depend on, and in some cases engineer, crises and catastrophes to shock the public into accepting aggressive and exploitative privatization schemes. Yet her account neglects the fact that, rather than shocked public acquiescence to elite schemes and frameworks, disasters often trigger spontaneous outpourings of nationalist sentiment, expressed through diverse forms of mass media and mass consumption, in support of many expansions of neoliberal governance.

One form of mass media has long been a focal point for these types of debates: the photograph. A deep discomfort with photographs of suffering emerged as early as 1945, when images of World War II and the Holocaust began to be labeled "pornographic" (Dean 2004). The effects of such so-called pornographic imagery were often believed to be a kind of deadening or flattening of audience engagement. John Berger has suggested that photographs of conflicts such as those in Vietnam or Northern Ireland became commonplace only once newspaper editors realized that their supposed radicalizing effect was "not what it was once presumed to be" (Berger 1991, 38). But if their effects on audiences were limited, such photographs nonetheless left their producers and consumers open to charges of exploitation. In *On Photography*, Susan Sontag argued that to photograph a moment of pain or trauma was "to be in complicity with ... another person's pain or misfortune" (Sontag 1990, 12). Later, Arthur and Joan Kleinman reminded readers that "images of trauma are part of our political economy. Papers are sold, television programs gain audience share, careers are advanced, jobs are created, and prizes awarded through the appropriation of images of suffering" (Kleinman and Kleinman 1996, 8).

These arguments certainly present a moral dilemma for the consumers of such images, who may be sympathetic to others' suffering but wary of exacerbating or exploiting it. Yet these critiques of photography, and the larger media culture in which it is embedded, may be overestimating the ill effects of mass-mediated pain. Sontag herself came to revise her position on these matters, writing that "such images cannot be more than an invitation to pay attention, to reflect, to learn" (Sontag 2003, 117). She went on to provide an interesting rationale for criticisms such as her earlier ones: "The frustration of not being able to do anything about what the images show may be translated into an accusation of the indecency of regarding such images, or the indecencies of the way such images are disseminated—flanked, as they may well be, by advertising for emollients, pain relievers, and SUVs. If we could do something about what the images show, we might not care so much about these issues" (Sontag 2003, 117). These remarks offer an alternative take on consumer culture's relation to suffering and disaster and the ethical condemnations surrounding them. Seen in this light, the consumption of catastrophe signifies less of a flattening of interest or emotion than a frustration with distant audiences' fundamentally limited possibilities for understanding and action. No matter how intimate their images, or how spectacular their broadcasts, disasters remain immeasurably complex, and others' suffering remains, in a way, inscrutable to its distant observers.

Nonetheless, as the phrase "consuming catastrophe" suggests, I believe that *consumption* is an appropriate rubric with which to assess and understand the predominant ways of experiencing crisis and catastrophe today. Raymond Williams (1985, 78) has pointed out that the earliest English uses of the word "consume" came with negative connotations of destruction, using up, or wasting. In this sense, the consumption of disaster refers not only to the fact that disaster-related products, services, and media are increasingly available for purchase but also to the fact that the heavily mediated experience of disaster in a consumer society involves using up the raw material of human tragedy, devouring the spectacular, tragic, and even the mundane aspects of catastrophes. Although the suffering they caused may persist, and the work of rebuilding may remain undone, once disasters lose their novelty or their resonance, one can expect to see fewer reminders of them on the evening news, in TV or magazine advertisements, and on the shelves of stores.

The raw material that gets consumed in this process of covering, packaging, and consuming a disaster is its authenticity. The contemporary usage of authenticity is generally fraught with contradictory interpretations, but I take authenticity to refer to the *perceived* quality of being unique, genuine, or, for lack of a better term, real. Although the difference between authentic and inauthentic sometimes seems natural—a home-cooked meal with locally produced ingredients seems more authentic than a meal at a fast-food chain, just as live news footage of a flooded New Orleans seems more authentic than a Hollywood disaster film—authenticity ultimately refers to subjective, aesthetic distinctions rather than to any quality intrinsic to commodities, texts, or images. It is a social construct, but one that reveals much about American values, desires, and fears. Disasters tend to attract large numbers of viewers and consumers based on the perception that they are much more real than the rest of what is available in contemporary media culture. Each disaster strikes us as new and immediate, creative in its unique pattern of destruction. Yet each also strikes primal emotional chords and reminds us of ancient calamities. What is more, we know that disasters affect real people and real communities and that 'but for the grace of God' we could be victims of a similar fate.

In consumer culture today, such perceived authenticity is incredibly valuable and highly sought after by all sorts of companies precisely because it can inspire powerful emotional responses from otherwise jaded or detached audiences. For instance, the management consultants Jim Gilmore and Joe Pine have published a widely read guide entitled *Authenticity: What Consumers Really Want* that teaches companies how to "manage the perceptions of real and fake held by the consumers of your enterprise's output—because people increasingly make purchase decisions based on how real or fake they perceive various offerings" (Gilmore and Pine 2007, xi). Scholars such as Sarah Banet-Weiser (2012) have tracked the results of this increasing commercial focus on the somewhat nebulous notion of authenticity. Her research confirms that "in the US, the 21st Century is an age that hungers for anything that *feels* authentic, just as we lament more and more that it is a world of inauthenticity, that we are governed by superficiality" (Banet-Weiser 2012, 3).

How, then, to study such consumption of authenticity? This book focuses on the texts that are consumed during and after disasters, especially those associated with factual media, including news, documentary films, reality television programs, and digital archives. At times throughout the book, these sources will be supplemented with discussions of other products, services, and experiences associated with disasters, but the main analytic focus of each chapter is on a small sample of media texts. After an initial chapter focusing on the history of disaster-related media, each subsequent chapter compares texts from two different disasters in the hope of drawing out the common themes between them and highlighting the differences among them.

The aim of this approach is to identify the larger meanings and prevailing cultural norms at work in disaster-related mass culture. Certainly, any particular text will generate some alternative readings as individual audience members decode it in oppositional or idiosyncratic ways (see S. Hall 1980). Still, at a minimum, one can say that media texts reflect the ideas, norms, and values at work in the culture that produced them. The fact that a number of news broadcasts, films, advertisements, television shows, and websites reflect the same small set of norms and values across a variety of different disasters tells us at least that these ideas were meaningful influences on the lives of many viewers and consumers. As such, analyzing the texts through which Americans experienced the disasters of the past decade can tell us about the norms that guided these experiences.

Of course, too many texts were produced around the four major disasters covered here to allow for a comprehensive sampling of them. Even a single disaster such as September 11 generated so much media that a vast array of scholarship has been devoted just to analyzing the mass media and popular culture around it (see, e.g., Chermak, Bailey, and Brown 2003; Heller 2005; Izard and Perkins 2011). But focusing only on September 11 has the potential to reinforce some flawed conventional wisdom about the uniqueness of that disaster relative to any other tragic or catastrophic events; this is often expressed as the idea that September 11 "changed everything." By contrast, situating September 11 in a long history of mass-mediated disasters, then comparing it with the disasters that immediately proceeded it, exposes the larger normative structures at work around many different instances of mass mediated suffering, and the continuities between these cases.

This book uses several text-based methods of inquiry to uncover these continuities. Chapter 2 employs close reading of the narratives at work in four different texts—two news broadcasts, a documentary film, and a reality television program. "Narrative texts are packed with sociological information" (Franzosi 1998, 517), and a close reading of these four texts shows how narratives about suffering, misfortune, and violence get told in ways that are meaningful but also problematic. Chapters 3 and 4 use the methods of discourse analysis to investigate television news broadcasts and users' submissions to digital archives, respectively. In both cases, my analysis focuses on the ways the texts offer "cues in the process of interpretation" (Fairclough 1989, 24). What scholars engaged in the somewhat overlapping practices of content analysis, discourse analysis, or "ethnographic content analysis" (Altheide 1996) all have in common is the use of documents to systematically "understand the process and meaning of social activities" (Altheide 1996, 10). The study of texts and discourses can reveal "how ways of talking in a society simultaneously reflect, constitute, and reproduce social organization . . . cultural beliefs . . . and norms about everyday living" (Grimshaw 2001, 752). It can even expose the ways "more powerful groups in society can influence less powerful groups through cultural models" (Gee 1999, 66). These are the central concerns of this book.

As mentioned, the wide variety of disasters covered here, and the incredible number of texts representing these disasters that might be studied, mean that any sampling of texts will necessarily be quite partial. There is no scientific way to ensure that the sample analyzed here is representative of the whole. However, in this book, as is common with discourse analytic methods, I have attempted to keep my interpretations closely aligned with those of the texts' authors. I have also attempted to present to the reader many direct quotations from the texts being analyzed. Both of these elements serve as checks on the reliability of discourse analytic work such as this (see Potter 1996). Still, rather than traditional social science notions of generalizability based on random sampling and large sample sizes, the types of qualitative and textual interpretation in this book might best be understood as aiming for "transferability." The term "implies that the results of the research can be transferred to other contexts and situations beyond the scope of the study" (Jensen 2008, 887). The way researchers typically establish transferability is to "describe the context of the case/situation in sufficient detail, so that the receiver has an appropriate base to make a judgment" (Hellström 2008, 327). Indeed, "it is the responsibility of the inquirer to provide sufficient base to permit a person contemplating application in another receiving situation to make a judgment of similarity" (Lincoln and Guba 1985, 360). My approach, then, has been to provide a chapter's worth of historical context in order to situate the present cases. Within each chapter, I have aimed to provide enough background information on the disasters and the texts analyzed to convince readers that the themes and meanings I uncover are present across these cases and even potentially in cases that have not been studied here.

Such attention to historical context helps reveal that the public appetite for mass-mediated disasters, and the taste for disaster representations that are both undeniably real and spectacularly unfamiliar, are important if somewhat overlooked elements of modernity itself. For instance, although the ancient destruction of Pompeii left behind only a single eyewitness account, the rediscovery and excavation of the city in the eighteenth century helped inspire a host of commodities, from silverware and pottery mimicking ancient styles to novels dramatizing Pompeii's last days. Coupled with a devastating earthquake in Lisbon, Portugal, in 1755, these disasters helped steer Enlightenment thought toward new understandings of natural disasters that were secular, scientific, and even occasionally romantic. Subsequent technological developments in mass production and communication continued to stoke public appetites for tales and artifacts of disaster, but the twentieth-century critique of modern culture as conformist and inauthentic really set the stage for disasters to achieve their contemporary status as uniquely valuable carriers of authenticity. Walter Benjamin believed that new forms of mass-producible media, such as photography and film, had eliminated the authentic existence in a particular time and place characteristic of the "aura" of older forms of art (Benjamin 1969), while other members of the Frankfurt school assailed the mass deceptions of the burgeoning "culture industry" of the 1940s (Horkheimer and Adorno [1944] 2002). But Benjamin's earlier writings on the topic portrayed the aura as a sort of specter of reality that haunted its photographic reproductions (Duttlinger 2008; see also Benjamin 1999). Thus, one may understand the aura of disaster as the haunting traces of the real still captured in its many representations. These traces attract a consumer culture in thrall to such authenticity yet are also always already in decay as media coverage and mass commodification begin to transform the disaster into spectacle, kitsch, morality play, or political platform.

Much of mass-media spectatorship and mass consumption today involves an exercise in determining the authenticity or genuineness of people, products, or experiences—be they reality television stars (Andrejevic 2004; Rose and Wood 2005), tourist sites (Grayson and Martinec 2004), automobiles (Leigh, Peters, and Shelton 2006), ethnic handicrafts (Wherry 2006), jeans and sneakers (Botterill 2007), or urban neighborhoods (Zukin 2008, 2010). In this same sense, audiences and consumers are tasked with assessing the authenticity of disaster-related texts and commodities and balancing potentially inauthentic aspects, such as their mass-produced, for-profit nature, against the seemingly undeniable kernel of real loss and pain with which they have been imbued. The results of those assessments of authenticity tend to determine the level of socially acceptable economic, emotional, or political investment in these texts and products. Judging from the sheer amount of disaster-related media and consumption that is discussed in this book, it appears that although there are a variety of competing standards concerning the authenticity of disaster-related media and products, there is certainly no blanket, normative prohibition against the consumption of catastrophe. For instance, watching the digital videos created by the Virginia Tech killer Seung-Hui Cho on network television news offered an authentic, uncensored glimpse into the mind of an alienated young killer for some viewers or, perhaps, a chance to understand and prevent future school shootings, while for others the broadcast smacked of a sensationalist ratings grab that resulted in the glorification of a murderer. In any case, such ethical debates concerning disaster mediation tend to coalesce today around the theme of authenticity and the appropriate emotional responses to such authentic depictions of suffering and pain.

This process of assessing the authenticity and trustworthiness of media texts also helps audiences and consumers determine their levels of apprehension over looming risks and future threats. The "risk society" first envisioned by Ulrich Beck (1992) and Anthony Giddens (1990, 1991) appears to operate affectively as much as rationally and often in a kind of retrospective fashion. Rather than being informed of potential disasters and then acting preventatively, governments, media, and consumers often seem to only really appreciate a threat that has already materialized as a spectacular catastrophe.

Social responses to such disasters thus tend to look backward, in an almost nostalgic panic, with the aim of preventing a recurrence of the same disaster rather than proactively anticipating new and different ones. The deployment of media frames—persistent discursive principles that structure social reality and create shared cultural meanings (Reese 2003)—can inspire widespread public acceptance of government risk claims in the wake of a disaster or engender fierce political opposition to official policy proposals. In either case, public understandings of risks and their possible prevention in the future both rely on and shape normative codes concerning the spectacles of real suffering generated by mass-mediated disasters. Trust in the risk assessments of government officials, technical experts, media icons, and other authority figures is thus a heavily mediated and highly emotional process.

This affective component of disaster representation, mediation, and consumption has been somewhat neglected by mainstream sociology. For instance, sociologists who study disasters have long disputed the conventional wisdom that mass panic is the usual public response to disasters, especially on the ground in affected communities (Quarantelli 2001; Tierney 2007). But while it is true that disaster-struck communities tend to exhibit a whole host of positive, pro-social responses, it does not mean that mass-media accounts of disaster may not inspire panic in distant spectators who are less directly affected. Divorced from the kinds of sustaining, ad hoc, local communities that maintain order and provide support during and in the immediate aftermath of disasters (see Solnit 2009), those who merely consume distressing stories and images at a distance may be more likely to take drastic measures or respond with overwrought emotional displays. Of course, mass media today tend to operate in crisis mode at all times, even over seemingly trivial matters (McRobbie and Thornton 1995), making the shock and immediacy of disaster-related stories an overly familiar style of communication, and thus potentially contributing to the onset of what has come to be known as "compassion fatigue" (Moeller 1999). However, American audiences of disasters have demonstrated over the past decade that distant or unaffected spectators are likely to feel that they too have been vicariously traumatized and thus enfranchised to participate in mass-mediated rituals of commemoration, or to claim the social and political status of victim (see Kaplan 2005; Savage 2006).

Such vicarious emotional connections to disasters and their distant victims are increasingly common today, and one of the most powerful, emergent norms in this regard is the obligation to show empathy toward those directly affected. Media texts have particular ways to present the suffering of others, designed to draw out these reactions, which engender a kind of *empathetic gaze* rooted in reality television but now transcending that genre. This stylized or idealized empathy for the suffering of distant others is rehearsed today even in non-disaster-related media programming, but it is particularly prevalent when large-scale tragedies result not only in live television news broadcasts but also in the many commemorative events and product sales that are supposed to benefit those distant others. Consuming such experiences and products marks one as a moral person with the capacity to understand the pain of others. Unlike classical forms of Enlightenment sympathy, however, in which detached spectators sought to actually alleviate the suffering of unfortunate others whose causes they found worthy, the empathy on display when one buys a Virginia Tech T-shirt or a record that benefits New Orleans musicians, or when one watches television programs devoted to these disasters, seems to be as much about self-improvement as about the improvement of the conditions of those who are less fortunate. This can be thought of as a kind of *empathetic hedonism* inasmuch as there is pleasure to be gained in attempting to imagine what others are feeling—even if those feelings are painful. This is not to say that such consumption is not driven by sincere concern for disaster victims, but simply that mass culture tends to direct such concern toward viewing habits and consumption practices that help the self-image of the viewer or purchaser at least as much as they help any disaster-stricken communities.

The consumption of disaster thus encourages a kind of "political anesthesia" (Szasz 2007) that reduces one's ability to recognize the collective solutions to problems, as well as one's willingness to work toward them. As Andrew Szasz (2007, 4) puts it, "A person who buys some products because those products promise to shield them from trouble is not at that moment a *political* actor. He or she is, instead, in the modality of a *consumer*." While that distinction may be too sharp, the authentically threatening quality of disasters does often nurture a paradoxically fantastic desire to secure the safety of oneself and one's family through private acts of consumerism. These fantasies are often backward-looking; they envision the next disaster as a similar chain of events that, having recently happened, is actually unlikely to happen again due either to officialdom's new awareness of the problem or simply to the remote odds of two similar disasters happening in such close succession. Of course, in the current American political moment of ascendant neoliberal governance, such individualistic strategies of preventative consumption may constitute the only measures being taken on one's behalf.

These atomizing tendencies of consumerism have even fed back into norms surrounding creative new forms of online experience. Rather than promoting a simple one-way consumption of information, the Internet increasingly encourages various types of digital content co-creation, which are often referred to as *prosumption* because they blur traditional distinctions between producers and consumers. New forms of media witnessing that rely on raw, incidentally recorded footage of disasters and tragedies may at times disrupt elite news framing strategies (Frosh and Pinchevski 2014; McCosker 2013). And new sites of collective memory such as digital archives and online memorials similarly empower consumers to become active, creative collaborators in the process of memorializing disasters. Yet despite the communal nature of many online efforts at commemoration, the messages collected there are frequently exercises in therapeutic self-help, in which the act of reading or writing a message serves as a form of psychic healing for oneself rather than for the community of other contributors. Such digital forms of commemoration can also end up encouraging a kind of nationalistic pride concerning the nostalgic or heroic aspects of disaster responses, while abetting a national forgetting of a disaster's more shameful elements and the persistent social inequalities that such disasters often magnify.

This book seeks, then, to develop a model of disaster consumption that holds true across diverse types of contemporary crises or catastrophes. In this model, a disaster and the texts and commodities it generates stand out from the normal flow of mass media and popular culture because they are generally perceived as more authentic. This authenticity allows otherwise skeptical consumers to invest genuine emotion in the media coverage of the disaster, as well as in subsequent acts of consumption devoted to displaying patriotism, securing one's home, expressing empathy, enacting therapeutic self-help, or any of the other goals and motivations of disaster consumerism. It also encourages many of the kinds of economic or political "capitalizing" described earlier in this Introduction. As time passes and images and commodities from the disaster become increasingly commonplace, one sees a disaster's authenticity itself become increasingly consumed or used up. In this period, with its aura of sacredness diminished, critical, oppositional, or ironic responses to the disaster become more socially acceptable, and the risk claims and emotional reactions that the disaster had inspired become subject to retrospective scrutiny. This has certainly been the case with September 11—writers at *Time* and *Vanity Fair* declared an end to the "age of irony" in the weeks following the attacks (Nunberg 2001), but less than a decade later, satirical pieces such as *The Onion*'s were fairly commonplace. Still, a trace of that reality, an aura, tends to haunt disaster texts and commodities long after those tragic events have dulled in our memories.

That is not to say, however, that all disasters are perceived as equally authentic. Implicit in the very act of witnessing others' suffering—or, at least, in the use of the term "witnessing" to describe some kind of direct or mediated experience of suffering—is a value judgment on what kinds of experiences, media, and rhetoric are more truthful, objective, or genuine (J. D. Peters 2001). Although there is always a degree of uncertainty about the veracity of any testimony, John Durham Peters reminds us that society tends to privilege "being there" over simply watching an event unfold via live media transmission or visiting the site where an event transpired in the past. When one merely watches the recording of an already transpired event, he argues, "the attitude of witnessing is hardest to sustain" (J. D. Peters 2001, 720). While the description of a hierarchy of witnessing and spectatorship is a useful starting point, the research in this book suggests that even recordings of disaster or disaster-related souvenirs can be weighted with much the same historicity as actual disaster sites and genuine artifacts. Such a connection to real human suffering, in fact, is another way to understand what makes disaster-related media and commodities appear genuine in the first place. For this reason, our understandings of these phenomena need to move beyond the assumption that a spectator's spatial or temporal distance from an event necessarily limits the authenticity of his or her experiences and emotions.

The geographical distance of spectators is, after all, largely immaterial when they are subject to the kinds of "disaster marathon" (Blondheim and Liebes 2002; Liebes 1998) television coverage in which normal routines and programming are dropped in favor of a spontaneous focus on calamitous events across multiple channels and platforms. The communication scholars Elihu Katz and Tamar Liebes argue that media coverage of disasters and accidents has become more influential today than coverage of staged "media events" such as coronation ceremonies and athletic contests. However, they suggest that these newly ascendant disasters are "disruptive" forces, "out of the reach of establishment control" (Katz and Liebes 2007, 164), in contrast to the "integrative" influence of staged and ceremonial media events. This book suggests otherwise. At least as far as distant audiences and consumers are concerned, the most seemingly disruptive, destructive, shocking, and unprecedented disasters may exert the most integrative, unifying influence, and provide the most leverage for elites looking to profit from the apparent chaos. And that fact makes them all the more dangerous.

1

A HISTORY OF CATASTROPHE

*Media, Mass Culture,
and Authenticity*

The emotional effects of tragic works of art have been a source of debate at least since the ancient Greeks. Plato feared the irrational emotions stirred up by tragic poetry, while Aristotle argued that such works brought about a necessary emotional release, or catharsis, that left audiences at ease in its aftermath. Much later, the English literary critic A. D. Nuttall (1996) suggested that viewing tragedies gave audiences pleasure because it allowed them to prepare themselves for the real horrors they might one day confront and the psychic anguish those horrors might cause. However, all of those notions of tragedy had one thing in common: the tragedies in question were fictional. As Nuttall (1996, 83) put it, "Traditionally, most of the answers offered to the question 'Why does tragedy give pleasure?' have been founded on the essential unreality of tragic drama, on our implicit awareness that what we are looking at is a representation and not the thing itself."

The tragedies that we view today—the big ones that bring us together around television sets, that keep us glued to smart phones and computer screens, that monopolize the newspaper headlines, that inspire grand monuments as well as cheap memorabilia—are all too real. The history of mass media is, among other things, one of increasingly timely and intimate exposure to disasters, catastrophes, and other real-life misfortunes, and a state of uncertainty about the appropriateness of viewing others' suffering has been a consistent feature of modern life. Thus, the stakes are higher today than they were for the ancient Greeks as they puzzled over the appeal of a literary genre. Our fascination with the fates of the others whom we so frequently view or read about as they suffer through disasters is both more understandable and more ethically dubious precisely because we know or presume that the pain we see is genuine, not simulated. And yet that has not dissuaded the ever growing numbers who have come to consume catastrophes in the modern era. Disasters have remained an important topic for media and consumption in part because they speak to a host of modern anxieties about the self, individuality, reason, emotion, progress, authority, and community.

There have, however, been important changes to the ways that publics have come to know of tragic or catastrophic events over the past three centuries. Four related phenomena have combined in that time to create the current cultural climate toward disaster: a gradual loss of confidence in various public and private arenas of authenticity, be they art, mass communication, or individual sentiment; a growing awareness on the part of the press, the advertising industry, and governments of the need to address this lack of confidence in their dealings with the public; developments in mass communication that have increased the speed, clarity, and variety with which consumers receive information and entertainment; and the growing exposure to distant, suffering others that results from those developments.

This chapter provides a historical overview of the mass mediation and consumption of modern disasters and the norms about authenticity and emotional expression that have developed around the misfortune of others. From the discovery of Pompeii's ancient ruins in 1748 to the earthquake in Charleston, South Carolina, of 1886; the sinking of the *Titanic* in 1912; the assassination of John F. Kennedy in 1963; the space shuttle *Challenger* disaster in 1986; and the death of Princess Diana in 1997, this chapter looks at the ways disasters have shaped and been shaped by modern mass culture. Despite the tremendous changes in mass media and consumer culture over the hundreds of years covered here, some common features of disasters' mediation and consumption have persisted. I argue that disasters have been, and remain today, such powerful forces in mass culture precisely because of their undeniable connection to *the real*. Modernity has broken down a whole host of traditions and institutions, and as it has called into question the authenticity of our selves and our connections to others, disasters have offered a chance to really feel for suffering others and to publicly demonstrate that feeling. As modernity has made death a less frequent and less visible presence in daily life (see Ariès 1974; Becker 1973), disasters remind us of the real fragility of human existence and the vicarious excitement of survival in the face of catastrophe. As modernity has made publics increasingly wary of, and savvy about, the staged and simulated character of mass culture, disasters have generated media texts and cultural products that feel more genuine and more trustworthy than others. All of this depends on a claim to the real that sets disasters apart from other subjects of mass media and consumption.

Of course, this claim to reality is not necessarily "real" in and of itself. Rather, it is contingent on cultural and aesthetic codes that change over time with the emergence of new media technologies as they alter common-sense beliefs about what sorts of things in a mass-mediated social world are still genuine. In this way, a televised news report from the site of a disaster, or a moving documentary about its aftermath, or the handwritten note left behind by one of its victims, or a blog post written on its first anniversary may all be said to contain a kind of authenticity that allows audiences to grieve as if they were also affected, to fear as if they may still be, or to exalt that they were not. However, that trace of the real is frequently watered down through the persistent reproduction of images, stories, and products that accompany many disasters, to the point that media devoted to even the deadliest or most catastrophic events eventually lose much of their perceived authenticity. Still, the minute traces of the real associated with disaster-related images and commodities can be enough to inspire all sorts of emotional responses, political decisions, and life choices. Consuming catastrophe gives us the exhilaration of coming close to real pain and real death but always from the safety of some mediated distance.

In this way, disasters can be said to have a kind of "aura," similar to Walter Benjamin's (1969) term for the unique and absorbing presence of classical works of art. Although Benjamin sometimes suggested that this aura had been destroyed by modern, mass-produced art forms such as photography and film, his earliest work contained a less restrictive view of the term (see Duttlinger 2008; Hansen 2008). This book argues that, indeed, the aura of disaster persists even as it is mass produced. That aura stems from the connection to real pain and suffering at the heart of disaster-related texts and commodities. Such a connection draws viewers in; it invites and even demands their contemplation. It has done so since the earliest shipwreck narratives were printed in the sixteenth century, and it continues to do so today. Yet the aura of disaster produces a kind of distance from the audience, as well. It absorbs viewers but is always just out of reach. As distant spectators we never truly know what it is like to survive an earthquake, or to escape a terrorist attack, or to be trapped in a flooded city, no matter how vividly or in how timely a fashion these events are communicated to us.

Thus, throughout history, disaster-related media and culture have revealed as much about the *ineffability* of others' suffering as they have about the ever increasing frequency and intimacy with which we are exposed to it. This just-out-of-reach sense of the real meaning or genuine experience of mass-mediated disaster helps explain how disasters generate more and more consumption, spurring us to more reading, listening, viewing, purchasing, and downloading of disaster-related texts and products. Such a quality has made disasters and disaster consumption a potent force inspiring communal sentiments across great distances and among diverse peoples since the dawn of modernity. It also makes disasters powerful tools in the hands of elites looking to steer a frightful, angry, or mourning public in useful or profitable directions.

Pompeii, Lisbon, and the Emergence of the Public Sphere

On August 24, 79 C.E., the eruption of Mount Vesuvius destroyed the ancient cities of Pompeii and Herculaneum. While hundreds and perhaps thousands of people died in those cities and the surrounding villas and towns as a result of the eruption, only one eyewitness account has survived to the present day. Almost thirty years after the events, the Roman historian Tacitus asked his friend and student Pliny the Younger to write about the death of his uncle, Pliny the Elder, during the eruption of Vesuvius as source material for Tacitus's own historical work. Although the portion of Tacitus's *Histories* covering these events has not survived, Pliny the Younger's two letters on the subject have (Moser 2007). While these accounts were undoubtedly read by some Romans at the time, nothing that might be called consumption of this catastrophe occurred on a large scale in its immediate aftermath. The Roman Senate authorized some efforts to recover vaults and other valued property from the ruins of Pompeii to finance disaster relief for survivors, but the cities remained mostly buried and faded from memory until their rediscovery more than 1,600 years later (Pellegrino 2004; Stewart 2006).

Like the ancient art and artifacts that for centuries they held secret, the ruins of Pompeii and Herculaneum exhibit a classical sense of the aura. Only a handful of copies of the one surviving eyewitness account existed in various European monasteries for many centuries (Moser 2007). There is a temporal gap between the calamitous events that unfolded there and the contemporary observer of the ruins that cannot be bridged; it is "the unique phenomenon of a distance, however close it may be," as Benjamin (1969, 222) might describe it. In Pompeii, evidence of life and death intertwine. Amid graffiti on the side of a brothel and footprints left by children outside a school, one finds ghostly figures trapped in their death poses. But even these are not actual human remains. Rather, they are plaster and cement impressions made by filling pockets of ash where human remains had once been. One can know Pompeii and Herculaneum only through the traces scattered around its ruins, traces that invite the kind of deep contemplation associated with high art. Pompeii absorbs the visitor and returns his gaze, as Mark Twain put it when describing his visit in 1875:

> [I] went dreaming among the trees . . . of this city which perished . . . till a shrill whistle and the cry of "All aboard—last train to Naples!" reminded me that I belonged to the 19th century, and [that I] was not a dusty mummy, caked with cinders and ashes, 1,800 years old. The transition was startling. The

idea of a railroad train actually running to old dead Pompeii, and whistling irreverently, and calling for passengers in the most bustling and business-like way, was as strange a thing as one could imagine, and as unpoetical and disagreeable as it was strange. (Quoted in Pellegrino 2004, 147)

Twain's description suggests the unique power of this place to evoke contemplation, not only of what happened there centuries ago, but of one's own time and place as well.

That is not to say, however, that the experience of Pompeii remains as it was on the day that the ruins were first discovered. When Pompeii and Herculaneum were finally unearthed between 1738 and 1748, they emerged in a context in which mass media and mass consumption were growing social phenomena. The sites quickly became tourist destinations for wealthy Europeans, thanks to numerous published descriptions of their excavation. Victorian architects adopted the Roman styles found at Pompeii and Herculaneum in buildings as diverse as Washington's Capitol Building, California's Getty estate, and Buckingham Palace's "Pompeiian Room." Thomas Jefferson designed silverware based on what he had seen recovered from the sites during a visit to Italy. Josiah Wedgwood's popular ceramics reproduced frescoes and sculptural scenes found in Herculaneum's Villa of the Papyri (Pellegrino 2004; Stewart 2006). This resurgence of interest in Ancient Rome also led to a renewed awareness of Roman law and philosophy among men such as Jefferson, George Washington, and Benjamin Franklin, resulting in the heavy Greco-Roman influence on American political philosophy (Pellegrino 2004).

The eighteenth century's fascination with Pompeii and Herculaneum coincided to a large extent with the devastation in 1755 of Lisbon, Portugal, by a powerful earthquake. Three main shocks and the resultant tsunami and fires combined to kill between 10,000 and 15,000 out of a population of 275,000 (Kendrick 1956). The discovery of Pompeii and Herculaneum followed by the Lisbon earthquake served to shake the religious and philosophical foundations of all of Europe (Davis 1999), thanks especially to the ways in which print media responded to the seemingly apocalyptic Lisbon tragedy. Many tracts and sketches were printed describing the terrifying ruins of Lisbon, and eyewitness accounts of the disaster were spread across the continent through newspapers and pamphlets. These helped to create "the illusion of proximity and unity among the peoples of different European nations" (Araújo 2006, para. 1) and led many central Europeans to convince themselves that they had also felt the earth shake on the day of the earthquake.

A mass-mediated public sphere began to emerge in which new, modern ideas about the causes and meanings of natural disasters appeared to challenge traditional or superstitious beliefs. Lisbon had been widely perceived as a pious city, and the long-standing religious view that natural disasters represented God's vengeance failed to hold sway for many educated Europeans. Instead, Enlightenment thinkers such as Voltaire, and later Immanuel Kant, used the earthquake to argue against the philosophical optimism of the past and to encourage explanations of seismic activity that were scientific rather than supernatural (Dynes 1998). Much has been made of the way the Lisbon earthquake helped to usher in Enlightenment thought, but what is less frequently emphasized is the way in which early forms of mass consumption helped steer this process. Voltaire's novel *Candide*, a continuation of themes explored in his "Poem on the Lisbon Disaster," used the Lisbon earthquake and other tragedies to emphasize a more skeptical view of divine Providence. It sold 20,000–30,000 copies in the first year it was published, despite its denunciation by the Catholic Church (Mason 1992). News of the tragedy reached Europeans not only through Voltaire's philosophical writings but also through the somewhat sensational accounts disseminated by the press. Just as with the rediscovery of Pompeii and Herculaneum, the public's desire to be informed dovetailed with its desire to be entertained or to vicariously experience what life had been like during (in the Lisbon case) or before (in the case of the ancient cities) a natural disaster. In both cases, forms of consumption emerged to stoke and satisfy those desires.

The Lisbon earthquake has been called the first modern disaster, not only because it was part of an Enlightenment effort to supplant religious explanations of natural phenomena with reasoned, scientific ones. The ability of elites to capitalize on the earthquake through standardized urban planning and aggressive rebuilding marked another fundamentally modern response to disaster, exhibited for the first time in Lisbon. Portugal's secretary of state, the Marques de Pombal, used the disaster as an opportunity not only to modernize the city's structures but also to cement his own power and reputation. He engineered the execution of a rival, Gabriel Malagrida; expelled the Jesuits from Portugal; and essentially ruled Portugal until the king's death in 1777 (Kendrick 1956; Rozario 2007). Furthermore, a third current of modern thought pulsed through the debates around the Lisbon quake: anti-modern backlash. Rousseau argued that Voltaire's views on Lisbon robbed survivors of the comforts of Providence. He also argued, in what Russell Dynes (2000) contends is the first social science view of disaster, that reckless buildup of overcrowded urban areas caused the terrible effects of the earthquake, not God or nature.

Despite the increase in mass-produced accounts of disasters such as the Lisbon earthquake, the experience of disasters in the eighteenth century maintained much that might traditionally be described as authentic. Only those present at the precise time and place knew the real effects of the Lisbon earthquake or any other disaster. The resulting destruction and ruins were also really knowable only to those who lived near or traveled to that place to see the aftermath. Reproduced drawings and printed firsthand accounts certainly did become available after the fact, but with nothing near the immediacy that later mass-media technologies would allow. Indeed, despite the growing public appetite for depictions of catastrophe, disasters retained their unique presence in time and space, their ability to elicit a kind of contemplative spectatorship, and their stubborn, tantalizing refusal to reveal all their secrets to distant viewers.

Mass production of printed materials thus allowed for the dissemination of accounts of the suffering of others to an expanding number of readers, but to truly experience the kinds of sympathetic identification with sufferers lauded by Enlightenment thinkers, one still had to imagine oneself in the role of the sufferer (Adam Smith [1790] 2009; see Boltanski 1999). The Romantic movement associated with Jean-Jacques Rousseau provided the imaginative, emotional inspiration behind both the rising levels of consumer desire that accompanied developments in mass production of the late eighteenth and early nineteenth centuries and the increasing relevance of the suffering of others in the development of modern mass communication. For Rousseau, compassion consisted of man's "innate repugnance to see his kind suffer" (Rousseau 1997, 152). As a basic emotional response, such feeling for the plight of others was "so Natural that even the Beasts sometimes show evident signs of it" (Rousseau 1997, 152). Yet this commiseration with the situation of suffering others varied "in proportion as the Onlooking animal identifies more intimately with the suffering animal" (Rousseau 1997, 153).

Philosophers such as David Hume and Adam Smith also extolled the virtues of sympathy, although their definitions varied. Hume conceived of sympathy mainly as the communication or transfer of an emotion from one individual to another, a process of coming to feel what another feels (Mercer 1972). "As in strings equally wound up, the motion of one communicates itself to the rest; so all the affections readily pass from one person to another, and beget correspondent movements in every human creature" (Hume 1874, 335). Smith viewed sympathy as an act of imagining oneself in another's place: "The compassion of the spectator must arise altogether from the consideration of what he himself would feel if he was reduced to the same unhappy situation, and, what perhaps is impossible, was at the same time able to regard it with his present reason and judgment" (Adam Smith 1869, 12). Among the general literate public, the eighteenth century's cult of sensibility privileged "susceptibility to tender feelings" and "an ability to enter into the sufferings of others" (C. Campbell 1987, 140).

Thus, while governments began to see disasters as objects of scientific knowledge and opportunities for enlarged development or expanded powers, modern consumers came to view them as chances to experience emotion and to reaffirm their own sincerity. The powerful emotional character of this emerging system of mass consumption ensured that disasters would remain a popular topic for the press and other entrepreneurs. Jürgen Habermas's image of a "private people come together as a public" to engage authorities in reasoned debate "over the general rules governing relations in the basically privatized but publicly relevant sphere of commodity exchange and social labor" (Habermas 2001, 27) remains the dominant conception of the eighteenth-century public sphere. Yet his account neglects many of the kinds of affective or non-rational communication that have always constituted an important part of public discourse (see Bickford 2011; Crossley 1998; Petersen 2011; Vetlesen 1994). As we have seen, the bourgeois public sphere that emerged in the eighteenth century was not limited to the sorts of everyday economic and political discussions most commonly associated with Habermas's theory: disasters, crises, misfortunes, and the suffering of distant others were central topics of discussion there, although these literate publics frequently disagreed about the moral and ethical acceptability of such macabre subjects (see Boltanski 1999). As new media technologies developed in the nineteenth century that made accounts of others' suffering an increasingly frequent and vivid presence within social life, such disagreements were magnified.

Sensationalism and Shock

Newspapers changed a great deal in the nineteenth century, thanks to declining paper costs, new color printing technologies, enhancements in the speed of delivery, and the invention of the electric telegraph (J. Campbell 2001). The telegraph made long-distance communication at nearly instantaneous speeds, far surpassing the pace of an actual letter carrier, a reality. Gathering news via telegraph allowed newspapers to achieve previously unthinkable levels of timeliness. Before then, information about an event such as the Revolutionary War was discovered by the press through no method more organized than the haphazard arrival of private letters and official or semiofficial messages (Mott 1962). The telegraph changed all that, but initially, at least in the United States, inexpensive daily newspapers such as the *New York Sun* were the only papers to really use it. Selling on the street rather than by subscription, and for a reduced price, meant the penny press had to print news that was more timely and eye-catching than that of its more up-scale competitors. The penny press focused on crimes and scandals, leading to widespread criticism by the establishment press of the 1830s. Still, by the 1880s this focus had become typical of most major papers in cities such as New York, and use of the telegraph to relay information to newspaper publishers was commonplace (Schudson 1978).

One of the first major American disasters to be relayed to the public with the aid of the telegraph was the 1886 earthquake in Charleston, South Carolina. The powerful quake damaged a majority of the buildings in Charleston and killed more than a hundred people, while the rest of the city's inhabitants fled to the streets. More than forty thousand people were still sleeping outside a week after the quake, as severe aftershocks continued ("Three Shocks Yesterday" 1886). The initial earthquake was felt as far away as Boston, Milwaukee, and Bermuda (T. Steinberg 2000). The morning after, telegraph linemen were dispatched to repair the lines and return telegraph service to the city. In less than a day, the lines were repaired, and reports of the disaster went out across the region and the country (L. C. Hall 1902). A week later, a telegram concerning the possible geological causes of the earthquake was sent over the newly laid transatlantic cable and read at the British Science Association in London ("Three Shocks Yesterday" 1886).

Rather than simply learning the facts about the destruction, some Americans sought a more intimate experience of the earthquake. George LaGrange Cook sold copies of nearly two hundred different photographs depicting the destruction of Charleston to curious consumers (Teal 2001), though the taste for such photos had perhaps already been stoked—or, at least, the taboo against them had been mitigated—by Matthew Brady's gruesome pictures of Civil War battlefields (see Sontag 2003). Visitors traveled to Charleston from all over the East Coast to see for themselves the spectacular devastation (T. Steinberg 2000), but unlike the disaster tourism surrounding ancient sites such as Pompeii, Charleston's tourists descended on the city mere days or weeks after the disaster struck.

Just as some had viewed the Lisbon earthquake as a chance to improve on the city's backward provincialism (Dynes 1998), the business community of Charleston emphasized that the earthquake was a chance to renew the city, to wash away "decadence" and attract rural merchants to the "newest old city in the Union" (Doyle 1990, 171). Still others saw the quake as a chance to reassert white supremacy in the face of post–Civil War gains made by blacks and, especially, post-earthquake gains made by black tradesmen, who saw a windfall during the city's early reconstruction. In response, within three years

Charleston's leading moderate white politician had been murdered, and its white citizens had passed laws legalizing segregation and disenfranchising black voters (Williams and Hoffius 2011).

Public interest in disasters was certainly not created by the telegraph, however, nor was it apparent only within journalism. Disaster had also become a recurrent theme in works of fiction in the early nineteenth century, as in Jean-Baptiste Cousin de Grainville's *Le Dernier Homme* (1805) and the subsequent work that it inspired, Mary Shelley's three-volume epic *The Last Man* (1826). Both novels presented apocalyptic scenarios of human extinction (Davis 1999). Edward Bulwer-Lytton's dramatic novel *The Last Days of Pompeii* enjoyed phenomenal success in 1834, when another eruption by Vesuvius preceded its publication by only a few months (Simmons 1969). It remains one of the most popular disaster novels of all time (see Davis 1999). But the press took the bulk of the early criticism for the seemingly growing public appetite for bad news. As early as 1800, William Wordsworth bemoaned the daily and hourly reports of "extraordinary incidents" that were commonplace in modern urban living, and Baudelaire made similar complaints in 1863 about the glut of newspaper reporting on wars, crimes, and other horrors (quoted in Sontag 2003).

By the mid-nineteenth century, the thirst for timely news of disasters that had begun to reveal itself a century before in the widely consumed accounts of Lisbon, and probably even a century before that with the publication of shipwreck narratives (see Huntress 1974), was associated with the telegraph's ability to transmit information almost instantaneously. But the accusation of journalistic "sensationalism" that emerged in this period did not refer primarily to the speed with which news was delivered. According to Michael Schudson, such criticisms of the press focused instead on the style in which the news was displayed. "Sensationalism meant self-advertisement . . . anything about newspaper layout and newspaper policy, outside of basic news gathering, which is designed to attract the eye and a small change of readers" (Schudson 1978, 95). In addition to the standard tales of crime and misfortune, this penchant for self-advertisement was reflected in the aesthetic experiments of newspapers with larger fonts for headlines, imaginative illustrations and photographs, and bold layouts in which one story took over the whole front page (J. Campbell 2001). Newspapers became consumer goods, as concerned with advertising themselves and increasing their ad revenues as with reporting the day's events. Progressives also seized on this growing taste for the sensational in a variety of "muckraking" books, newspaper exposés, and magazine articles. Although these texts assembled a large national audience around important political issues, they hinted at a growing susceptibility to spectacle among the public (Ewen 1996). The label "sensationalist" also had implications for news consumers; it suggested that readers' or spectators' interests in a particular calamity were maudlin or voyeuristic, concerned with tawdry emotions or vicarious thrills rather than reasoned deliberation of facts.

Enthusiasm for natural disasters continued to grow among the American public at the dawn of the twentieth century, and Americans often found themselves reveling in tales of fires, hurricanes, and earthquakes. Even many survivors of such calamities declared the experiences exhilarating (Rozario 2007). Stores in New York sold a booklet that served as a key to the fire department's bell system; it allowed curious onlookers to find their way to the scene of a fire just by listening to the fire bells (Schudson 1978). Other novel forms of disaster consumption were developing, as well. From 1904 to 1911, various Coney Island amusements centered on reenactments of famous disasters such as the Johnstown, Pennsylvania, flood of 1889; the Galveston, Texas, hurricane of 1900; the volcanic eruption of Mount Pelée in Martinique in 1902; and a ride in which firefighters had to save people trapped in simulated New York tenement fires (Sandy 2001; T. Steinberg 2000). The film industry has also been involved in the depiction of disaster almost since its inception. One early British film, *The Launch of the H.M.S. Albion* (1898), captured the real-life drowning of thirty-four people when a landing collapsed during the ship's launch. It became the subject of much controversy when another film producer at the scene wrote an editorial against its exhibition. While documentary footage of real disasters remained a rarity for some time thereafter, real-life catastrophes remained the inspiration for many films. Bulwer-Lytton's dramatic account of Pompeii's destruction was the most filmed novel of the early years of cinema, with four movie versions made between 1903 and 1919, although they were not American productions (Davis 1999). The American film industry began to depict disasters as well, and the American Biograph Company even produced a fake documentary on the San Francisco earthquake and fire of 1906 by building a miniature city out of cardboard and setting it ablaze (Rozario 2007).

The invention and widespread popularity of radio telegraphy and motion pictures at the beginning of the twentieth century, coupled with the steady rise of consumer culture in general, would seem to have threatened the disaster's unique presence in time and space. What might have come to replace this aura, according to Benjamin, was "shock." Aesthetic experience in the age of mechanically reproduced art such as cinema replaced the contemplative immersion of classical art with a disorienting form of almost tactile experience. The constant flicker of images that simulate motion in the cinema, and the various edits between those sets of images, provided Benjamin with an analogue to modern urban living. "The spectator's process of association in view of these images is indeed interrupted by their constant, sudden change," he wrote. "This constitutes the shock effect of the film" (Benjamin 1969, 238). In one note on the "Work of Art" essay, Benjamin compared this shock effect to a man on a street in city traffic and argued that "the film is the art form that is in keeping with the increased threat to his life which modern man has to face. Man's need to expose himself to shock effects is his adjustment to the dangers threatening him" (Benjamin 1969, 250n19). He also drew comparisons between the sensory shock effect of new communication technologies and the moral shock effect of Dadaist artwork, with its obscene collages and crude, anti-art stance. The critique of sensationalism combines precisely these two forms of shock: sensory and moral. As new technologies of mass communication make possible new forms of human sensory experience, they also allow the dissemination of new kinds of information that many find unsettling or offensive. The effect is a kind of disorientation, "an experience of estrangement which then requires recomposition and readjustment" (Vattimo 1992, 51). But although aura and shock are often set in opposition to each other, with shock being the sensationalist antidote to the aura's more careful form of spectatorship, many important twentieth-century disasters demonstrate a kind of coexistence between these two aesthetic concepts.

The *Titanic* as Archetype of Disaster Consumption

One of the most famous disasters in history, the sinking of the *Titanic*, first shocked the American public via the new technology of wireless telegraphy. At the beginning of the twentieth century, more and more ships were equipped with this early form of radio in the hopes of preventing maritime disasters (Barnouw 1966). On April 15, 1912, a twenty-one-year-old telegraph operator stationed at the Wanamaker's department store in New York heard a faint signal coming over the wireless with the message, "S.S. Titanic ran into iceberg. Sinking fast." The operator, David Sarnoff, gave the information to the press, alerted other ships he could reach, and established communications with the *Carpathia* after that ship had picked up the *Titanic*'s survivors. Sarnoff stayed at his post until a complete list of survivors had been relayed seventy-two hours later; by that time, the Wanamaker's store was filled with policemen holding back a crowd of reporters, friends and relatives of passengers, and curious onlookers (Barnouw 1966; Heyer 1995). The event made Sarnoff famous and launched an illustrious career in which he went on to head the Radio Corporation of America (RCA) and found the National Broadcasting Company (NBC), although many now suggest that parts of that story are exaggerated or apocryphal (see "Sarnoff, David" n.d.).

The *Titanic*'s almost mythic place in history is taken for granted today, but it is worth reiterating that the sinking of the unsinkable ship was enshrined in popular culture through myriad forms of mass consumption occurring with an unprecedented rapidity relative to previous disasters and catastrophes (Heyer 1995). A seemingly endless flow of commentary and reflection began almost as soon as radio waves containing word of its impending sinking reached the shore. New York newspapers initially speculated on whether the ship had truly sunk or was simply being towed back to shore by the *Carpathia*—initial wireless reports were unclear on this matter. For instance, the April 15 issue of the *Syracuse Herald* ran the headline "Titanic's Passengers All Rescued" above a giant drawing of passengers in lifeboats in a choppy sea, with the *Titanic* looming large in the background, a broken steam pipe its only visible sign of damage (Groom 2012). By contrast, the *New York Times* made its journalistic reputation partly through its coverage of the *Titanic*, which the paper correctly surmised had sunk when rival publications were still cautiously optimistic. In its widely praised coverage, the *Times* examined a variety of hypothetical scenarios concerning the crash and rescue and published speculative opinions gleaned from interviews with maritime experts to tell *Titanic*'s story before the *Carpathia* had even returned (Heyer 1995).

But the story of the *Titanic* was told, and sold, to the public through more than just newspapers; survivors' accounts, novels, poems, plays, songs, and films relayed the tale to an enthralled audience. The actress Dorothy Gibson, a real-life *Titanic* survivor, wrote and starred in a short silent film in which she retold the story of her escape and rescue to a group of actors portraying her family. The film was shot in a week and debuted less than a month after the *Titanic* had sunk. Literary figures such as Joseph Conrad, George Bernard Shaw, Arthur Conan Doyle, and Thomas Hardy published a series of responses to the great tragedy (Heyer 1995). Even the blues legend Leadbelly performed a song that told a fictional tale about the African American boxer Jack Johnson being prevented from boarding the doomed ocean liner by its racist white captain.

In many ways, the *Titanic* catastrophe has become a kind of archetype of disaster consumption. Today, new technologies continue to be used to increase the speed with which information about disasters is transmitted to the public. News agencies continue to blend speculative elements with factual news reporting. Firsthand accounts from survivors are still emphasized, and eye-catching images are given as much prominence as the stories themselves. Novels, plays, films, and other kinds of pop culture still dramatize or fictionalize the spectacular events surrounding catastrophes. And strong emotional reactions from audiences remain important, and expected, in the consumption of contemporary catastrophes.

As such, it is tempting to see the consumption of the *Titanic* tragedy solely as an example of the media's increasing penchant for shock, spectacle, and sensationalism. Critics such as Neil Postman (1985) adopt such a view of all media since the invention of the telegraph, which he argues first placed immediacy over content and led publics and journalists to eschew careful exposition in favor of a "peek-a-boo" world of various short-lived events and sensations. In this view, the decline of the aura of the written word precludes any meaningful engagement with the social world in general. But there are also important ways in which the *Titanic* disaster maintains a kind of profound and mysterious connection to the real, even with its hyper-mediated and over-consumed legacy. The ship's mythic place in modern culture as a cautionary tale about technologically induced hubris has imbued it with a kind of ritualistic power. Moreover, the ship's brief and tragic history has retroactively endowed the few photographs of it with a kind of haunting, otherworldly quality. The same can be said for other *Titanic* memorabilia, and especially for the sunken ship itself, which remained lost until 1985. Thus, although the wreckage of the *Titanic* has since been scoured by both treasure hunters and Hollywood directors, as in James Cameron's 3D IMAX film *Ghosts of the Abyss* (2003), Postman's argument rings hollow here. If the development of electronic communication technologies has stifled certain possibilities for reasoned exposition—a dubious claim in and of itself—it has also made possible new forms of identification and emotional connection with an ever increasing number of distant others, and it has done so in ways that are not limited to the literate upper classes. Today, anyone can purchase authentic pieces of coal recovered from the wreck, or reproductions of the *New York Times* headlines from its sinking, or original *Titanic* stock certificates and at least potentially use these products to reflect more deeply on the disaster, its continued significance, and the lives of those who perished there.

Media Panics and the Inauthentic

This democratizing aspect of mass communication and consumption has had its own critics, however, especially in relation to disasters. As early as 1841, the journalist Charles Mackay had compiled a historical account of various "popular delusions" resulting from the gregarious, suggestive nature of mankind (Mackay [1841] 1980). But with the growth of mass democracy and the popular press, this penchant for delusion became more problematic. Gustave Le Bon viewed such behavior as a tendency toward mob mentality and argued that the throngs of lower-class voters had become a dangerous, irrational element of democratic society (Le Bon [1895] 1960). Psychologists such as Sigmund Freud and Wilfred Trotter built on and critiqued Le Bon's analysis; Trotter saw the "herd instinct" as a natural function of human evolution, while Freud saw mass suggestibility as the result of powerful libidinal ties formed between group members and certain leaders who functioned as ego ideals for the rest of the group (Freud [1921] 1959; Trotter [1919] 1953). Following Freud, the implications of mass irrationality for governments and markets became important concerns of men such as John Dewey, Walter Lippmann, and Edward Bernays. Although Dewey championed the decision-making ability of the people, Lippmann believed that enlightened social scientists and technocrats had to steer public policy away from the frivolity of the masses, while Bernays accepted the public's irrationality and developed psychological techniques of persuasion for use in the emerging field of public relations (Ewen 1996).

The supposed irrationality of the masses was on display in 1938 when Orson Welles's "War of the Worlds" radio broadcast convinced millions of Americans that an alien invasion was under way. In *The Invasion from Mars* (1940), the social psychologist Hadley Cantril performed an extensive survey of radio listeners to try to determine what kinds of social and economic factors affected their responses to the simulated catastrophe. The study, which argued that those who panicked in the face of the broadcast lacked "critical ability," has been highly influential in subsequent sociological debates concerning mass panic during disasters, although its methodology has more recently been called into question (Quarantelli 2001). Although nineteenth-century newspapers had frequently featured outlandish hoax stories, which they would later reveal as false to the amusement of their readership (see Goodman 2008), Welles's broadcast directly called into question the authenticity of human emotions generated by mass media. By mimicking the aesthetic features of a real news bulletin while making the actual content of the news an almost obvious fabrication, Welles exposed the possibility that audiences were responding to the style of news stories rather than their content—the spectacle of mediation itself rather than the gravity of actual events.

This insight has been further explored in the "moral panic" literature in sociology, which emerged from Stanley Cohen's (1980) investigation of public fears in 1960s Britain about violent youth gangs known as "mods" and "rockers." One of Cohen's core insights, and one that has been confirmed in subsequent studies of panics concerning communists (Ungar 1990), Satanists (Victor 1991), and homosexuals (Heatley 2007), is that the threat to the social order posed by these stigmatized groups was actually very small, but the news media had given them a disproportionately large amount of coverage, thereby inflaming an exaggerated and irrational sense of threat around them.

The belief in the public's susceptibility to irrationality in the face of crisis has added weight to concerns over mass conformity more broadly. With the rise of fascism and the growing sophistication of mass propaganda in Germany and the United States, the post–World War II period has borne witness to a further loss of trust in the authenticity of mass communication and the genuineness of the emotional responses it solicited (Ewen 1996). The shock of new media technologies became associated not only with a sort of inflamed sensationalism but also with trauma, with a benumbing of individual consciousness in the face of the overwhelming machinery of modernity and its instruments of persuasion.

The postwar period also revealed an increasing discomfort with explicit images of war and human suffering. Writing in 1945, James Agee first described newsreel footage of the battle of Iwo Jima as pornographic because "we have no business seeing this sort of experience" (quoted in Dean 2004, 21). The label "pornographic" was soon applied to images of the Holocaust, as well, although, as Carolyn Dean has noted, the critique behind such a label has not been always been clear: "Does it encourage us to identify with victims or with perpetrators? Does it excite us or numb us or both" (Dean 2004, 18)? Nonetheless, this strain of critique has persisted to the present day in the epithet "disaster porn" that is frequently lobbied at contemporary disaster-related media, even those devoted to fictional disasters (Recuber 2013).

Of course, America in the midst of postwar suburbanization has also been romanticized as a period of stability and calm. This era did see fewer of the deadly domestic disasters that plagued the United States around the turn of the twentieth century: the Galveston hurricane of 1900 killed 6,000–15,000 people, and the San Francisco earthquake and fire of 1906 killed 3,000–6,000, while no subsequent American natural disaster of the twentieth century claimed nearly as many lives. Still, the very unnatural disaster of World War II had provided the United States with the economic engine and political will to promote this period of growing consumer culture in the first place (see L. Cohen 2003). At the same time, the country's triumphalist "victory culture" would not last long, with the emergence of the threat of nuclear confrontation with the Soviets, increasing military entanglement in the Vietnam War, and the national tragedy of John F. Kennedy's assassination (Englehardt 2007).

The Kennedy Assassination as a New Archetype

The gradual ascendance of television journalism also changed Americans' experience of tragedies and disasters. To many observers, the power of film and television to disseminate news and, by extension, to create spectacle was not fully realized until the 1960s. "John Kennedy defeated Richard Nixon on television; Lee Harvey Oswald was shot on television; presidents dissembled, protestors protested, in front of cameras, indeed with their eyes fixed upon cameras" (Stephens 1988, 282). The Kennedy assassination and the events that surrounded it became seminal moments in American history, and they provided a dramatic turning point in the mass-mediated consumption of tragedy and disasters. Film and television not only brought the story of Kennedy's assassination in increasing detail to an immense audience but also became part of that story themselves.

John F. Kennedy, the "television president," was widely believed to have won the 1960 election because of his understanding of that emerging medium. Just as his skillful embrace of TV helped legitimize his presidential candidacy, it also led in some ways to television's legitimization as an instrument of political discourse. Even many television journalists considered TV news an inferior counterpart to print media at the beginning of Kennedy's ascent to the presidency (Zelizer 1992). But the assassination in Dallas on November 22, 1963, cemented the position of television as the primary news-disseminating apparatus in American life. Most of the press initially on-site in Dallas were corralled in two busses at the time of the assassination, so the coverage of the shooting began not as it happened but immediately afterward. Only one Associated Press (AP) photographer witnessed and photographed the event: James Altgens stood only fifteen feet away when the president was shot, close enough to nearly be struck by fragments of Kennedy's head, and shocked enough to miss the moment of impact, despite having already focused his camera (Lubin 2003). Still, his photo of a Secret Service agent climbing over the back of Kennedy's limousine was transmitted to AP twenty-five minutes after the shooting and ended up on the front page of thousands of newspapers across the globe the next day. By contrast, Walter Cronkite had already interrupted CBS's regular television broadcast ten minutes after the shots were fired to inform the audience of the attack on the president's motorcade. More than half of the nation—and as many as 68 percent, by one estimate—had heard news of the shooting before Kennedy was even pronounced dead (Stephens 1988; Zelizer 1992). As a point of contrast from almost a century earlier, President Abraham Lincoln was shot on a Thursday evening and died that Friday morning, but with the telegraph and the newspaper delivering the news, it took most of Friday and into Saturday for the country to become fully aware, and the national period of mourning really began on that Saturday, April 15, 1865—a day and a half later (Harper 1951; Lewis 1957).

In any case, although print and radio journalists worked alongside and together with television journalists in the harrowing hours and days following the assassination, television inserted itself into the story more prominently than other media. Two days after Kennedy's death, Jack Ruby emerged from a crowd of reporters, photographers, and cameramen to shoot the suspected assassin Lee Harvey Oswald as Oswald was being transferred to county jail. This marked the first time that a real homicide was carried on live television (Zelizer 1992), and it occurred in the midst of three days of non-stop television news coverage of the aftermath of the assassination. Such an abandonment of normal TV format has remained, in the years following, a signal of very important news (Gans 1979). The culmination of the coverage was Kennedy's funeral, which 93 percent of Americans viewed live on television (Zelizer 1992). This also seems worth contrasting with Lincoln's case a century earlier: the train carrying his body back to Springfield, Illinois, drew thousands of onlookers at each of the twelve cities in which it stopped (Harper 1951), but there was, of course, no way for the rest of the nation to act as live participants in this mourning ritual.

Kennedy's assassination inaugurated an era in which the tragic, disastrous, and catastrophic would frequently be caught on camera and often broadcast live on television. The ascendance of television news and the increasing ubiquity of TV, film, and video cameras in contemporary life have not only enabled such frequent broadcasts of macabre events but also created the expectation that such events should and will be televised. Twenty-four-hour news networks, which appeared first in 1961 on the radio and on television in 1980, require an even greater surfeit of events to cover, and bleak or tragic news stories are rarely in short supply. "With the vast pool of occurrences available to modern news organs, our ancestors' need to be alert to potential threats is now satisfied by daily, hourly immersions in a selection of tragedies so unrelievedly black that the world itself, always grim when viewed through the news, may appear to actually have darkened" (Stephens 1988, 291). While it is hard to argue that the amount of disaster, tragedy, and misery in the world has grown, the quantum of such misfortune to which we may be exposed, and the speed and intimacy with which such exposure occurs, certainly have increased.

The Kennedy assassination produced some iconic images that have remained central parts of American history and culture, such as John John's salute to his father's passing funeral procession, Vice President Lyndon Johnson's somber swearing-in next to Jackie Kennedy aboard Air Force One, or Lee Harvey Oswald's pained grimace during his own assassination. But what roles do such images play in American culture today? In one sense, iconic photographs of tragedies and death have become taken-for-granted aspects of daily, mass-mediated life. David Lubin (2003, xi) argues that "these images are so famous that they have in a sense become invisible."

Yet the "aesthetically familiar forms" of iconic images allow them to help us confront "basic contradiction[s] or recurrent cris[es]," according to Robert Hariman and John Louis Lucaites (2007, 29). By capturing troubling or traumatic events in conventional forms of photojournalism or framing them with time-honored themes of heroism or sacrifice, iconic photos have served as powerful resources for American civic discourse (Harriman and Lucaites 2007). Thus, the ubiquity of Kennedy-related mass culture allows the trauma of his assassination to be reframed in the familiar terms of heroism and sacrifice, rather than as simply tragic or unjust, and made real for subsequent generations who were not alive to witness it.

Yet in another way the mystery of Kennedy's death persists through media, as well, embodied in the single, twenty-six-second piece of celluloid known as the Zapruder film. The Zapruder film was once a heavily guarded, enigmatic, almost sacred artifact. Although it was recorded on the date of the assassination in 1963, the public did not get its first nationally televised view of the Zapruder film until 1975. *Life* magazine had purchased the film from Abraham Zapruder shortly after the assassination for the sum of $150,000, and three copies of the initial negative were made, with one going to the magazine, one to Zapruder, and one to the Secret Service. For more than a decade after that, the film appeared only as a selection of still frames in the pages of *Life* or to small audiences with special clearance, such as government investigators or the jury in Jim Garrison's trial of Clay Shaw, famously depicted in Oliver Stone's *JFK* (1991). However, bootleg copies of the film began to appear in the hands of conspiracy theorists and in college lecture halls not long after its creation. A photo technician named Robert Groden had covertly made a copy of the film when working on it for *Life* in 1968 and had optically enhanced it to provide clearer details of the shots hitting the president. This higher-resolution version was finally shown to the nation on *Good Night America* by Geraldo Rivera in April 1975, causing "a national sensation" (Granberry 2013; see also Lubin 2003; Simon 1996).

The history of the Zapruder film suggests that even the modern, mechanically reproduced medium of film can create objects with the cloistered or secret qualities of classical art forms such as painting and sculpture. Though just twenty-six seconds long, the film appeared only in still fragments, or to small bands of authorized elites, or in underground settings organized by bootleggers for the first decade of its existence. Like a statue in a cella, or a covered Madonna, the

Zapruder film gained its uniquely powerful status precisely because it remained hidden from public view. And like the religious relics exhibited at irregular intervals for only brief periods of time by churches in the Middle Ages (see Ewen and Ewen 2006; Man 2002), a grieving nation believed that the Zapruder film might contain healing powers—in this case, the power to heal the wounded trust in government that rampant conspiracy theories revealed. It also required a kind of religious faith—not in God or government but in the power of film, and vision more generally, to capture truth (Simon 1996). As an inversion of the cult of the beautiful associated with classical art, these twenty-six seconds of celluloid were believed to contain truth precisely because of their stark, unadulterated recording of a brutal murder. This same claim to truth or authenticity explains much of the appeal of disaster consumption today.

Once the film was publicly televised and *Life* relinquished its copyright claims, this faith in visual truth was tested by numerous reinterpretations based on careful forensic measurement, further technological enhancement, and continued frame-by-frame dissection. An audio recording made from Dallas police radio broadcasts at the time of the shooting was also eventually added to the mix and pored over by acoustics experts and assassination buffs (Simon 1996). But in the end, the film offered proof of theories involving multiple-assassin conspiracies as well as a lone gunman, depending on who analyzed it. Over time, the reproduction and dissemination of these images, which had been long delayed, managed to modify the public perception of the Zapruder film. But it did not destroy its arresting power.

The Zapruder film today maintains a kind of unique presence in American popular culture despite, or perhaps because of, its ubiquity. Now easily accessible to anyone with an Internet connection, and thus no longer containing the aura of some hidden artifact, the images have their own haunting and mysterious essence nonetheless. Currently, six different versions of the film have been viewed more than a million times each on YouTube, with the most popular version closing in on four million views. The film is no longer distant from the public, but it continues to captivate with its stubborn obfuscation of truth, its mysterious ability to hide the real story seemingly in plain sight. The film haunts us today as the frustratingly indecipherable key to solving a mystery, an unintelligible whisper from beyond the grave. Its frequent reproduction in magazines, television programs, forensic reenactments, documentaries, and Hollywood movies—and the iconic status that such reproductions reinforce—has not resolved its mysteries. Clare Birchall has argued that "the fact that the Zapruder film 'proves' so many conflicting versions of events says something about the inherent instability of film as factual record" (quoted in Rose 2013, para. 10). Audiovisual media's simultaneous claim to truth and amenability to interpretation have inspired similar conspiracy theories around more recent disasters such as the September 11 attacks as well (Rose 2013). Thus, the Zapruder film speaks above all else to the ineffability of disaster and tragedy. Even when it is captured on film, or broadcast live, or commemorated, or consumed, the pain of others is always difficult to fully grasp. Yet this difficulty does not dim its appeal to consumers.

As Art Simon put it, "Perhaps no set of imagery has toured the cultural landscape as much as that referring in some way to the death of JFK" (Simon 1996, 1). JFK commemorative coins, Christmas ornaments, pocket watches, utensils, and apparel are sold in many places, including the John F. Kennedy Presidential Museum and Library, and works of art such as Andy Warhol's series of "Jackie" prints from 1963 to 1964 and Oliver Stone's movie *JFK* attest to the wide influence of the assassination throughout the culture industry over a long period of time. Thus, as with the *Titanic* tragedy, the JFK assassination has been spun off and packaged for mass consumption in a variety of forms. Imagery surrounding the assassination has even been reappropriated to shock or transgress, as in the 1992 concert poster by Frank Kozik that altered the image of Lee Harvey Oswald at the moment of his own assassination to look like the photograph of a rock-and-roll band. In it, a wincing Oswald appears to be singing into a microphone, Jack Ruby holds a guitar, and a keyboard player stands behind them.

But how can consumption of such crass, cheap, or kitschy memorabilia really have anything to do with authenticity? I want to suggest that even this kind of consumption may maintain an indexical trace of the real, the disastrous, and the traumatic. The nature of modern consumerism suggests that even these sorts of objects may maintain a slight but unbridgeable sense of distance or mystery. These traces of real pain and tragedy constitute the aura of disaster consumption. At the very least, such commodities' connections to real tragedies allow consumers to imagine them as authentic. Since consumption is partly based on consumers' imagined relationships with the things they consume, then the connection to the real at the heart of disaster consumption is "real in its consequences," to borrow from the sociologist W. I. Thomas's famous maxim. Moreover, the perceived authenticity of disaster images and products allows consumers to engage in deeper emotional and imaginative relationships with these commodities—one's fear, grief, anxiety, and empathy are more appropriately expressed in even the most outlandish forms of consumerism when such consumerism is connected to a real-life disaster or tragedy. Through such affective connections, one is able to join in a real or imagined communion with other spectators, victims, and even the dead.

In sum, the assassination of JFK marked the ascendance of a new set of relationships between aura and disaster, just as the sinking of the *Titanic* did a half century before that. Disasters have become more and more likely to be captured on film, radio, and television as they happen. The power of live, televised news broadcasts, showcased in the events surrounding the assassinations of Kennedy and Oswald and at Kennedy's funeral, has marked a push toward increasing use of live news and, eventually, the first of what are now many twenty-four-hour TV news networks. And with the growth of media technology at the consumer level, "citizen journalists," as they are called today—and of which Abraham Zapruder may have be the prototypical case—are often the ones who actually capture the most shocking, powerful, or iconic images of disaster. Accompanying these developments have been an increasing commercialization, recycling, and reproduction of disasters in consumer culture and a growing audience who also feels itself upset, moved, or even traumatized by the vicarious, mediated experience of disaster. In this sense, the disaster as a multimedia event may be the seat of its aura—not so much one image as the sum total of these shots, their blending or composite into general motifs across individual recollections and collective memory (see Dahmen and Miller 2012). Thus is born the contemporary model of disaster consumption: artifacts and images from the moment or scene of the disaster maintain a haunting aura, an authentic quality derived from the unfathomable magnitude or significance of the tragedy that they represent, and yet such authenticity makes a disaster the subject of constant reproduction and consumption that attempts to trade on its significance for power and profit.

Using the Kennedy assassination as the model for contemporary disaster consumption does, however, expand the definition of "disaster": while Kennedy's death was certainly a tragedy of immense weight and significance, is it really the same as the large-scale destruction of life and property that we usually associate with the term "disaster"? I believe that it is, although not, perhaps, for communities that are actually affected by a disaster. In terms of popular culture, individual tragedies and large-scale disasters are presented and consumed in very similar ways. The past thirty or forty years, in fact, have revealed an expanding definition of victimhood and trauma. For instance, television talk shows encourage guests to construct narratives of the self that are framed by suffering or distress. This suffering is usually caused not by earthquakes or wars but by the personal relationships and entanglements of everyday life (Illouz 2003). In such a culture, it is no surprise that "victim stories" have become a common feature of most television news broadcasts, since they play on the recognition that our daily lives are subject to horrible disruptions at a moment's notice (Langer 1992). Thus, an odd equivalence exists between mass disasters and individual tragedies: both remind audiences of the ever present possibility of their own victimization, and both can produce the same kind of vicarious emotional responses in viewers. Both also allow for the creation of larger communities around specific misfortunes and increase our opportunities to feel for the distant others whom those misfortunes have befallen.

The Space Shuttle *Challenger*, Princess Diana, and Mass-Mediated Mourning

In today's hyper-mediated pop culture landscape, even those who simply view images of traumatic events can lay claim to being traumatized themselves (see Kaplan 2005). The idea of vicarious, media-induced trauma amounts to an expansion of the aura to include televised live events. That is, after all, the basis of the national exercises in mourning surrounding the Kennedy assassination or a later tragedy such as the explosion of the space shuttle *Challenger* in 1986. Although far fewer people died in the *Challenger* explosion than in the *Titanic* sinking, the tragedy dominated popular culture and the national consciousness in much the same way. However, the *Challenger* exploded on live TV in front of millions of children who were watching the launch during school hours in connection with the "Teacher-in-Space" program. An estimated 40 percent of late elementary and secondary school children in the United States witnessed the launch live on TV, and 95 percent of Americans had watched some of the *Challenger* explosion on television by the end of the day (Zinner 1999). Indeed, the footage was repeated on television so much that it seemed inescapable. As one *Time Magazine* writer described it, "Over and over, the bright extinction played on the television screen, almost ghoulishly repeated until it had sunk into the collective memory" (quoted in Hariman and Lucaites 2007, 251). This kind of endless looping of disaster footage was perhaps even more intense, and at least equally traumatizing, to television audiences in the wake of September 11.

Within hours of the *Challenger* explosion, President Ronald Reagan—another leader known for his skillful use of television—set the tone for mourning with a nationally televised speech. The Teacher-in-Space program had been his proposal, and the charismatic "teachernaut" Christa McAuliffe had already been introduced to the nation through a series of interviews in the run-up to the launch. In his speech, Reagan reaffirmed his faith in the space program in a way that "model[ed] childlike deference to the state rather than rational assessment and democratic deliberation" (Hariman and Lucaites 2007, 266). Of course, like the many other "pseudo-events" (see Boorstin 1987) of dubious importance with which public culture is populated today, the Teacher-in-Space program was designed specifically as a public relations mission. In an irony likely to be repeated in many future tragedies, the heavy public relations efforts leading up to the launch contributed extra attention to the mission's disastrous outcome. Nonetheless, Reagan's speech after the *Challenger* disaster helped reassert the legitimacy of the National Aeronautics and Space Administration (NASA) in spite of its costliness and the high risks involved (Hariman and Lucaites 2007).

Still, as with Kennedy's assassination, a government investigation ensued, focusing eventually on defective "O-rings" and the culture of groupthink pervading NASA. But one somewhat overlooked aspect of the investigation was the fate of the crew members' bodies. The live footage of the fiery explosion made it seem as if the shuttle and crew members had been incinerated in midair. But, in fact, the crew compartment had hurtled in a three-minute-long free-fall into the ocean, where it was later recovered. NASA's original transcript of the voice recorder omitted the pilot Michael Smith's final "Uh oh," and NASA only later revealed that some of the crew members had actually used their emergency air packs during the descent, suggesting that some of the shuttle passengers may have been alive and conscious as they fell to Earth—a fact that neither NASA nor the government's investigators were willing to admit (Larabee 2001). Many Americans saw NASA's official position as part of a cover-up, and news agencies sued under the Freedom of Information Act to get access to the crew's voice recordings (Zinner 1999). They hoped the recordings would capture the truth about the tragedy in ways similar to the public's hopes about the Zapruder film.

Thus, even images with the kind of haunting, tragic aura of the *Challenger*'s midair explosion leave doubt as to their veracity and the authenticity of the responses of the viewing or consuming public. What really happened beyond what we can see and hear on television? How much is it appropriate to grieve for people one has never met? Is it legitimate to feel that one has been traumatized simply by watching a catastrophe unfold on a screen? And how much can we even trust what we see on the screen? After all, the harrowing images of the *Challenger*'s explosion revealed little about the bureaucratic and technological causes behind the tragedy and even confused the whereabouts of the crew members' bodies. If these images maintain an aura today, it is due to the mysteries they conceal, the unfathomable last seconds of the crew members that one cannot help but ponder, the grief of family and friends watching from the ground, and the communal experience of instantaneous loss suffered by so many that day. All of this remains embedded, at least in traces, in the well-worn images of the ship's explosion and the various forms of commemoration that continue to summon them. As with most mass-consumed catastrophes, nothing can fully answer these questions, but people are often drawn together as they consider them.

In an age of niche marketing and political fragmentation, the ability to call forth such strong emotions from such wide audiences is rare. As Charles Taylor (1991, 117) put it, "A fragmented society is one whose members find it harder and harder to identify with their political society as a community. This lack of identification may reflect an atomistic outlook, in which people come to see society purely instrumentally. But it also helps to entrench atomism, because the absence of effective common action throws people back on themselves." While not necessitating any individual action, the affective strength of disaster pulls people together; it reaffirms the bonds of community, nation, and humanity that are often viewed as being in decline. In fact, image-based media can often do this in ways that print media cannot, by "providing resources for thought and feeling that are not registered in the norms of literate rationality that constitute the discourse of political legitimacy in Western societies" (Hariman and Lucaites 2007, 14).

The general scarcity of such communal sentiment in modern nation-states makes the aura of disaster so valuable. In the United Kingdom, the death of Princess Diana in 1997 provided another striking example of this. Diana's death "led to more newsprint, and her funeral to a bigger global television audience, than had any previous event" (Davies 1999, 3). Hundreds of thousands of people made pilgrimages to Kensington Palace in London and elsewhere across the British Isles (Davies 1999, 3). One million copies of Andrew Morton's 1992 biography of Diana were reprinted and distributed to bookstores, and even across the United States vendors sold Princess Diana T-shirts, posters and other memorabilia near the sites of spontaneous Diana shrines (Haney and Davis 1999, 233). This combination of real-life suffering and mass-mediated celebrity has much in common with the aesthetics of reality television, which was beginning its cultural ascent at this moment (see van Zoonen 1998, 115). Some have also argued that this widespread form of communal grieving showcased a shift in British values from the traditional "stiff upper lip" to a more emotional set of social conventions with less deference for authorities and greater multicultural aspirations (Jeleniewski Seidler 2013; Turnock 2000).

Yet the massive crowds at various public sites of mourning across London may reflect more of "a compulsion to attend, to 'feel the mood,' to see for [ones]self" (Turnock 2000, 72) than the deeply shared sense of mourning that was often interpreted and encouraged by the press. As one critic explained, "This involved interviewers going on about how sad it all is until the interviewee started to blub and the camera zoomed in on tears. . . . Such manipulation by interviewers of their subjects then provided a warrant for a *new* news item about the depth of grief of ordinary people for someone they had never met. After three days of this anyone not already near to tears felt there was something wrong with them" (Harris 1999, 100).

Disasters thus provide a powerful means of steering public sentiment. Princess Diana's death became, at the very least, a boon to television ratings and newspaper and book sales. Before that, President Reagan had used his televised address to the nation after the *Challenger* explosion to deflect attention from political and bureaucratic mistakes and reaffirm American faith in technologically mediated progress. Even as far back as the Lisbon earthquake of 1755, one finds elites using disasters as the justification for the disenfranchisement of a maligned minority group. It should not have been surprising, then, when all of these themes came back into play around the terrorist attacks of September 11, 2001. But for such elite efforts to bear fruit, they must resonate with their audiences. The ineffability of disasters is key in that regard.

Conclusion: The Ineffability of Disaster

As we have seen, disasters lay claim to a kind of authenticity that has, at its core, the reality of their victims' pain. Yet physical pain, as Elaine Scarry (1985, 4–5) argued, "resists objectification in language" and thus "whatever pain achieves, it achieves in part through its unsharability." Indeed, the pain of others is "at once that which cannot be denied and that which cannot be confirmed" (Scarry 1985, 4). While her focus was on physical, embodied pain, not its emotional or psychological variants, this perspective is the final key to understanding the appeal of disaster consumption and spectatorship. Just as Scarry speaks of the "inexpressibility" of one's own physical pain, one can consider the incomprehensibility of *others'* pain. All pain—or, at least, all testimony about pain—impels its recipients to try to understand but leaves them uncertain about how well they have done so.

This sort of uncertainty is a fundamental part of mass communication itself. In *Speaking into the Air*, John Durham Peters (1999, 177) explained that even as modern technologies of recording and transmission have enlarged the possibilities for mass communication, they "multiply the opportunities for mishaps and breakdowns." For Peters, modern communication is animated by "the dream of spirit-to-spirit contact unimpaired by distance or embodiment," but at the same time it is marked by the sense that "all action, especially all communicative action aimed at coming into conjunction with another soul, is action at a distance" (J. D. Peters 1999, 178). In this view, communication is always imperfect, always subject to some unbridgeable distance between phenomenological experience and the thought or utterance that expresses it. That distance is then multiplied as utterances are transmitted to others. The potential to communicate with others thrills us, but there is always doubt left over in the wake of our communication. This is especially true in times of uncertainty and distress: "The common world may be habitual and sound, but breakdown allows all the primal uncanniness to return. In a blackout, or the telephone's suddenly going dead, or the static caught between stations, we discover the gaps, not the bridges" (J. D. Peters 1999, 205). Rather than discouraging us from engaging with disasters, however, the incomprehensibility of others' pain and the veracity gap in others' testimony about that pain are precisely the sort of features that make disasters such powerful resources for the imagination and, thus, for mass consumption.

Colin Campbell's (1987) work on the psychosocial roots of modern consumerism reminds us that modern consumers have come to focus not on the immediate, sensate pleasures of goods but on an imaginative relationship based on the emotional anticipation of those pleasures. In modern consumerism, "if a product is capable of being represented as possessing unknown characteristics then it is open to the pleasure-seeker to imagine the nature of its gratifications. . . . [In this way . . . greater desire is experienced for the unknown than the known" (C. Campbell 1987, 86). Indeed, such desire and pleasure are "constituted in a subjective imagining of consumption's meanings for the self" (Dunn 2008, 46). Imagination not only heightens the pleasures of the act of consumption. It also enables us to feel certain ways about ourselves based on what we consume.

At the same time, Campbell (1987, 86) argues that the actual experiences of consumption "are unlikely to compare favorably" with those encountered in one's own imagination. For Campbell, a cycle of enchantment, disenchantment, and re-enchantment explains the psychosocial appeal of mass consumption (see also Ritzer 1999). "The consummation of desire is thus a necessarily disillusioning experience" that prompts a turn back to fantasy and imagination, so "the dream will be carried forward and attached to some new object of desire such that the illusory pleasures may, once more, be re-experienced" (C. Campbell 1987, 86). As such, the actual consumption of commodities never quite lives up to their imagined pleasures. Campbell believes that this ethic of "autonomous, self-illusory hedonism" can explain the exploding desire for consumer goods that allowed the Industrial Revolution to succeed and that continues to animate the hyper-consumption of Western populations today.

It also ties together the themes that run throughout this chapter: the rise of mass media and mass consumption, the growing normative encouragement to imagine the pain and suffering of distant others, and the privileged place of disasters as carriers of authenticity. Modern mass consumption—at least beyond the satisfaction of the basic necessities of life—depends on this gap between what is imagined and what is actually experienced. This is much the same as the act of mass communication, in which the excitement of exchanging information and experiences is always subject to doubt over their veracity. In both cases, the mass audience for these processes turns this epistemological quandary into a social problem, as huge numbers of audiences and consumers are driven to keep reading, listening, viewing, and consuming, spurred on as much by the desires that remain unfulfilled as by those that are actually satiated. This helps explain, for one thing, why the earliest moments of disaster news—in which information is often unreliable—are so widely watched anyway. Our desire to know what's going on, to understand the risks, and to appreciate what others are suffering is inflamed by the uncertainty pervading what we actually find out.

We arrive, then, at a psychosocial model that explains the appeal of disaster media and commodities. In this model, the ineffability of disaster is its chief appeal to distant spectators. Disasters are novel and highly emotional phenomena. They happen to everyday, relatable people. They expose our own potential vulnerabilities. They pose moral dilemmas. And yet they offer few answers. They are complex. They spin tangled webs of culpability. Victims lose everything and survivors escape unscathed seemingly at random. All of this uncertainty means that—unlike basic needs for food, shelter, and other, simpler kinds of information—disaster media and culture spur more and more spectatorship and consumption precisely because the promise of *understanding* always necessarily remains partially unfulfilled.

And so each new disaster strikes us as eerily or heartbreakingly reminiscent of others but also offers the hope of finally learning the right lessons—or, at least, finally understanding the awful complexity of such tragedies. The traces of real pain and loss at the heart of disaster-related media appear to confirm this. Benjamin (1999, 510) found this transcendent aura in early photographs, where "the beholder feels an irresistible urge to search such a picture for the tiny spark of contingency, of the here and now, with which reality has (so to speak) seared the subject." One sees the same traces of the here and now, the same seared markers of reality, in the Zapruder film or the footage of the *Challenger* explosion. That same trace of reality, that aura of disaster, is also apparent in the incredible array of images from September 11, as well as in certain footage of flooded New Orleans streets and stranded rooftop survivors during Hurricane Katrina. The haunting traces of catastrophes in consumer culture and their stubborn refusal to reveal their secrets speak to the diminishing yet still unbridgeable distance between others who suffer and those who consume that suffering. This is the aura of disaster.

As such, the central problem of contemporary disaster consumption is not the inauthenticity of disaster consumption or of those engaged in it, but the ability of cultural and political elites to frame a narrow range of emotional or political responses as the only appropriate ones. The consumption of catastrophe is most threatened—or, perhaps, most threatening—when dominant interests are able to channel the wide range of emotions that surround disasters into a few politically or economically useful contexts. The aura of disaster is not only a source of deep emotion for audiences and victims; it is a contested terrain, a site of struggle for control over the fleeting essence of reality itself. But as this book shows, at least during the first decade of the twenty-first century that contest tended to heavily favor elite interpretations and definitions.

Since the Enlightenment, the importance of genuine emotional responses to the suffering of others has been a subject of public discussion and debate. In the intervening centuries, the contours of that debate have changed alongside new developments in media technology and new styles of consumer culture, but always some belief in the possibility of an authentic public reaction has obtained, even if that possibility seemed a diminishing one. This remains true today, at a time when consumer culture puts a premium on authentic selfhood despite the doubt cast on the entire notion of authenticity by modern and postmodern critics of media culture (see Featherstone 1991; Goulding 2000). Disasters partially resolve this problem by providing, at least in extreme cases, cultural products with an undeniable relation to reality, regardless of their mediation or reproduction. Emotional investment in such cultural products has become accepted and even expected precisely because of this connection to real loss, mass suffering, and unjust death—though the outcome of such investment is liable to encompass a wide range of responses. Disasters, after all, are complicated; they tend to transcend simple designations of cause and effect or blame and victimhood, and they generate multiple meanings based on the context in which they are experienced, viewed, or consumed. Nevertheless, disasters always demand our attention, emotion, and contemplation. They cast a shadow over their distant spectators, haunting them with the lingering ghosts of collective traumas. This aura remains in the traces and fragments left behind in a disaster's wake, not only in the physical landscape, but also in the landscape of media and consumer culture. And it is this trace of authenticity that allows spectators to believe that they can truly empathize with a disaster's distant victims simply by consuming its media representations, as the next chapter demonstrates.

2

THE LIMITS OF EMPATHY

*Hurricane Katrina and
the Virginia Tech Shootings*

When Hurricane Katrina made landfall in Louisiana, Paula Bealer watched on television from 350 miles away. Despite the fact that she and her family had safely evacuated, she began to weep. This weeping continued in the weeks following the storm, as she described in an essay written for the website Helium, "I grieved intensely for those that were lost in the hurricane as though they were my own loved ones. I cried tears of pain for the homes and all the family mementos lost in the devastation. I cried for businesses that people worked so hard to establish just to have them washed away so quickly. I felt the weariness of the rescue workers who despite all their efforts were unable to save everyone" (Bealer 2007, para. 3).

Coleman Collins, a former basketball player at Virginia Polytechnic Institute and State University (Virginia Tech), experienced the tragic shootings on his campus in somewhat similar terms. He watched the television coverage from the safety of his girlfriend's house while making phone calls and using Facebook to figure out whether anyone he knew had been harmed. In an entry on ESPN's TrueHoop blog, he explained:

As it turned out I didn't know anyone personally. People always give off a sigh of relief when I tell them this. . . . How could I explain that because I didn't know anyone who was killed that day, that everyone I know was killed that day? There will be people that read this who personally knew victims. Trust me, I can't compete with your pain, but God . . . I didn't know I could feel that way. I think they call it empathy. So yeah, that was the day I realized what empathy was. (Collins 2010, para. 7–8)

Bealer also described her experience as one of empathy. She lauded this powerful sentiment and wrote, "As intense of an emotion as empathy is, I never regret being able to feel it. In my opinion, empathy is an emotion that connects us to each other. How else would we begin to understand the pain of others without actually feeling it" (Bealer 2007, para. 13)?

Of course, her question need not be taken rhetorically. The pain of others has not always been apprehended in the ways that American culture encourages us to experience it today. Disasters have obviously always evoked strong emotions in those they have directly affected, as well as in those who have watched from afar or who have learned of them after the fact; bearing witness to the misfortunes of others has always had the potential to generate a feeling of commiseration and a desire to help those unfortunate others. But the precise nature of this feeling and the socially appropriate forms of help have changed over time. As disasters have assumed a prominent role in contemporary popular culture, and as the news media have developed the ability to transmit footage of mass catastrophes across the globe almost instantaneously, the norms surrounding emotion and the spectatorship of suffering have adapted and evolved. Alternative "structures of feeling" (Williams 1977) and new "emotional regimes" (Reddy 2001) have appeared to challenge the prevailing norms and rituals governing emotional expression in today's heavily mediated and consumed experience of disasters.

When contrasted with Enlightenment ideals of emotional expression, and even with more recent examples of mass-mediated emotion in the wake of tragic events, American mass culture in the first decade of the twenty-first century encouraged a more intimate form of spectatorship focused on an in-depth understanding and vicarious experience of the emotional pain of others. Certainly, all media bring the experiences of others closer to us and thus can surely be experienced as intimate or in-depth. For instance, an iconic war photograph such as "Accidental Napalm" intimately exposed viewers to the intense suffering of a Vietnamese child. Similarly, a radio broadcast such as Herbert Morrison's infamous narration of the explosion of the Hindenburg captured in the subtle, audible details of his voice the despair of witnessing that tragedy. Nonetheless, recent technological developments such as camcorders and smart phones have the potential to do more than even this. They can bring us the innermost thoughts of disaster victims, recorded as the disaster unfolded in the midst of their struggle to survive. They can even reveal the last words of a mass murderer, spoken directly to his own camera and broadcast across the globe a mere two days after his murderous rampage ended in suicide. In such texts, and in more mundane forms of contemporary media, a new empathetic way of looking is both encouraged and implicated. Scholars such as Alison Landsberg argue that such media engagement can force audiences to empathize with others who are radically different from themselves and might therefore encourage "more radical forms of democracy aimed at advancing egalitarian social goals" (Landsberg 2009, 221). But is the empathetic, mediated engagement with disasters necessarily so democratic or egalitarian?

This chapter examines the cultural products that emerged from Hurricane Katrina and the Virginia Tech shootings, paying specific attention to the codes surrounding emotional expression that they exhibit. After a general overview of the consumption and mediation of both disasters, the chapter focuses on four particular media products that exemplify current trends. A close reading of the September 1, 2005, broadcast of CNN's *Anderson Cooper 360 Degrees* (*AC 360*) and the documentary *Trouble the Water* (2008) provides evidence about specific features of the consumption of disaster during Hurricane Katrina, while the *NBC Nightly News* broadcast from April 18, 2007, and an episode of the Biography channel's show *I Survived*, which dealt with the Virginia Tech shootings, offer similar evidence concerning that tragedy's mediation.

These two news broadcasts were chosen because of their particular cultural importance in the unfolding of these disasters, and the two other texts were selected because of the ways they exemplify the empathy-generating power of factual media and disaster narratives. For instance, Anderson Cooper's highly emotional performance in this particular broadcast was called "a breakthrough for the future of television news" (Van Meter 2005, para. 1). Similarly, the exclusive broadcast of the Virginia Tech killer Seung-Hui Cho's package of self-made footage on *NBC Nightly News* was largely unprecedented. As the *Washington Post* explained, "Until the package arrived at NBC, the story had almost started following what might be considered a template for national tragedies, a series of stages that has become dismayingly familiar: the initial shock; reaction to the event; essays on historical perspective that keep the story in the forefront of news; and, finally, criticism of the media for how the story has been played—or, more likely, overplayed. The Virginia Tech tragedy was clearly about to enter that last phase when the prototype was shattered, and in a uniquely 21st-century way" (Shales 2007, para. 12–13). The *I Survived* series has been lauded for its focus on "real people and candor" and for the unique and inspirational nature of the "raw humanity" it portrays in its stark depictions of near-death experiences (Courson 2009, para. 1–2). Finally, *Trouble the Water*'s emotional focus on real people and the authenticity of their encounters with disaster has led critics to proclaim that "only the most heartless of individuals would fail to empathize with the victims" ("'Trouble the Water' Examines Katrina Aftermath" 2008, para. 9).

In these four programs, aesthetic and technological cues about the authenticity of media texts served as de facto evidence of the personal, emotional authenticity of their producers and audiences, as well as the performances of the subjects on screen. Moreover, these cultural products announced a change in notions of spectatorship relative to classical discussions concerning the moral ramifications of the suffering of others. Whereas classical notions of sympathy required one to act or speak out on behalf of the suffering other, these texts evinced a shift away from sympathy and toward empathy as the moral responsibility of the spectator. This chapter argues that as mass mediation has increased the amount of attention paid to tragedies and catastrophes, and as therapeutic culture has placed increasing value on emotional intelligence and the ability to adapt to multiple roles or identities, and as reality television has cemented intimate new styles of viewing others' emotional lives, a new *empathetic gaze* has emerged. This empathetic way of relating to narratives of others' suffering, which prioritizes simply understanding what others are going through, has developed as a kind of alternative to an older, sympathetic moral requirement that more explicitly linked such understanding with concrete action to help alleviate the suffering of others. The narratives examined here still "create a particular kind of social world, with specified heroes and villains, deserving and undeserving people and . . . the construction of social problems" (Bennett and Edelman 1985, 157). Yet this chapter argues that the empathetic way of looking at social problems may steer us away from the kinds of long-term actions that such problems often require.

In sum, the four texts analyzed in this chapter all rely on a way of looking at others' suffering that is designed to induce empathy in spectators. The presence of this empathetic gaze points to the growing normative value placed on empathizing with others' suffering in contemporary American culture at large. This emergent norm and the forms of mass culture that embody it encourage spectators to try to really *feel* what others have felt, to vicariously experience the pain of others. But by lauding this kind of deep, intimate engagement with the suffering of distant others, and the concurrent performance of having been moved by it, the empathetic gaze places less importance on correcting the social and political conditions that facilitated such suffering in the first place.

Charity, Mass Media, and Mass Consumption

Although the U.S. government and residents of the Gulf Coast had been informed by meteorologists and news services for two to three days about Hurricane Katrina's impending landfall in the region, the storm that hit New Orleans on August 29, 2005, found a city unprepared. The storm caused an estimated $81 billion worth of damage in the area (Nordhaus 2006) and resulted in the deaths of at least 1,836 people. As the deadly aftermath of the storm came into focus, officials such as President George Bush and Michael Brown of the Federal

Emergency Management Agency (FEMA) emphasized, as many officials had done after September 11, that no one could have imagined this kind of devastation, despite the fact that weather forecasters had accurately predicted the strength of the storm and that the weakness of the city's levees and its vulnerability to hurricanes had been well established in the mainstream press and in FEMA's own reports. Mayor Ray Nagin's late evacuation plans also made no allowance for public transportation, thereby leaving the city's poor or otherwise immobile residents essentially on their own, while state and federal preparations were similarly short-sighted or inadequate (Dyson 2006).

Katrina was the first major hurricane to hit the United States with the accompaniment of continuous coverage by the twenty-four-hour news networks. Initially, the inaccessibility of many affected areas of the Gulf Coast to the news media meant that small pockets of survivors received a disproportionate amount of coverage (Shrum 2007). The immediacy demanded of such coverage during disaster situations tended to contravene the generally time-consuming processes of collecting and reporting facts, which led in this case to a particularly virulent strain of traffic in rumor and innuendo in the storm's immediate aftermath (Rodríguez and Dynes 2006). The news media has received harsh criticism for its depiction of racial minorities in New Orleans as either violent looters or passive victims and its sensational implications that the city had fallen into chaos (Rodríguez and Dynes 2006; Voorhees, Vick, and Perkins 2007). These reports became a sort of self-fulfilling prophecy as law enforcement officers and residents alike began to believe that the city had indeed fallen into lawlessness and responded in ways that exacerbated this lack of civic trust (D. Miller 2006). However, news media were also frequently critical of the inadequate scope and insufficient pace of government rescue and recovery efforts. Without the usual level of access to government sources in the early days of the storm, news reporters broke from the kinds of unifying themes so prominent after September 11 and instead adopted an outraged, populist tone (Durham 2008). In fact, television news frequently portrayed its own reporters, producers, and camera crews as heroes "fighting the evil that was government ineptitude" (Fry 2006, 83).

Thousands of Americans were moved by this media coverage to volunteer their time or money to relief efforts for Hurricane Katrina victims, and Hurricane Rita's victims were eventually added to many relief funds as that storm hit the area a month later. Just eleven weeks after Katrina, private donations totaled $2.7 billion (Frank 2005), and the total amount of donations eventually exceeded $5 billion (Aaron Smith 2011). Although organizations such as the Red Cross, which by one estimate received 60 percent of all Katrina-related donations (Strom 2006), handled the bulk of the immediate relief work, new constituencies came together, especially in the African American community. Black churches and political organizations raised millions, and many African American artists and athletes organized telethons, raised money, and promoted volunteer efforts (Dyson 2006). In fact, celebrities from all walks of life teamed up for a variety of charitable efforts—perhaps the most notable of these was "A Concert for Hurricane Relief," which was broadcast live on NBC and its affiliated networks on September 2, 2005, and in which Kanye West went off script to pronounce that, among other things, "George Bush doesn't care about black people." Americans engaged with the storm through more mundane consumption choices, as well, of everything from commemorative Katrina T-shirts, bumper stickers, and Beanie Babies to a variety of documentary films and even eventually a Hollywood feature film called *Hurricane Season* (2009), starring Forrest Whitaker.

The April 16, 2007, shootings at Virginia Tech, while similarly dominating the news media, had somewhat less staying power in popular culture. However, the demands for immediate coverage, constant updates of news stories, and frequent interviews with victims or survivors that were so apparent during Hurricane Katrina remained part of the news network protocol in this tragedy. Reporters quickly flocked to the campus of Virginia Tech as word spread of a shooting there, and they, or the stations' news anchors, relayed each new tidbit of information as soon as it was released. The reporters pushed for interviews with clearly shaken students who were still trying to cope with the shooting and learn the whereabouts of friends. Television networks set up temporary studios on campus, broadcasting entire programs, such as NBC's *Today*, from inside the school, and backlash against the heavy media presence on campus quickly emerged among students and faculty (Gravois and Hoover 2007).

The most controversial news coverage came two days later, when *NBC Nightly News* with Brian Williams decided to air portions of a package it had received from Seung-Hui Cho himself, likely mailed between his double murder at the West Ambler Johnston residence hall and his mass shooting at the Norris Hall classroom building later that morning. The package contained what Williams referred to on-air as a "multimedia manifesto," consisting of various kinds of electronic images, videos, and text created by Cho to be aired after the shootings. Many criticized NBC's decision to show some of these photos and videos, but it helped make the show the most watched of the evening newscasts that week by a large margin (J. Steinberg 2007). Cho's familiarity with new electronic media was matched by that of Virginia Tech's students, who used social networking sites such as MySpace and Facebook to communicate with one another and memorialize fallen friends in the aftermath of the shootings (Creamer 2007).

Beside their electronic commemorations, students at Virginia Tech set up several makeshift memorials in the physical space of the campus, and consumers across America and the world took it upon themselves to support the university by purchasing Virginia Tech athletic apparel and other Hokies memorabilia. Wholesale sales of such items rose to more than $5.6 million for the period between April 1 and June 30; this represented a jump of between $1 million and $2.6 million over similar quarters in years past. In the weeks after the shootings, the school also received numerous phone calls from vendors seeking licenses to sell Virginia Tech products, but they were all turned down (Bowman 2007). Thousands of other spontaneous donations to the university in the wake of the shootings were eventually culled into the Hokie Spirit Memorial Fund, $8 million of which has now been distributed among the seventeen injured and the families of the thirty-two killed in the shootings. One victim's tragic death was even transformed into an inspirational book entitled *Lifting Our Eyes: Finding God's Grace through the Virginia Tech Tragedy. The Lauren McCain Story*.

Critics used the Virginia Tech shootings as an indictment against popular culture in many respects. As has become routine in the wake of school shootings, commentators suggested that violent media were to blame (Furedi 2007b). Some focused on Cho's "addiction to a ghastly, violent video game called Counter-Strike" (Stephen 2007, 20), while others noticed the similarity between a pose in one of Cho's photos and a scene from the South Korean revenge film *Oldboy* (2003), which then began to receive blame even though no one could confirm that Cho had ever seen it (Scott 2007). Many were troubled by NBC's handling of Cho's words and images, in terms of both their potential effects on already traumatized victims and their families and their potential to inspire other disaffected youth to commit "copycat" killings—a concern made less far-fetched by the fact that Cho specifically referred to the Columbine shooters in his writings (Deppa 2007). The American Psychiatric Association even issued a press release on April 20 urging the news media to stop airing Cho's images. As a result, many questioned the value of news reporting and the propriety of its conventions during a tragedy such as this. One critic pointed out the particularly crass way in which news channels used graphics to brand their coverage of catastrophes, noting, for instance, that "CNN's animated MASSACRE AT VIRGINIA TECH logo throbbed and twirled with all the subtlety of an 'American Idol' bumper" (Dumenco 2007, 34). Others criticized the tone of such news broadcasts: "Shortly after announcing that the shooting had become the largest campus massacre ever, eclipsing the 1966 Texas Tower sniping, television commentators declared, with nearly gleeful enthusiasm, that it had surpassed in carnage all other mass shootings in the United States at any venue. For the remainder of the day, viewers were told repeatedly that the Virginia Tech massacre had been the biggest, the bloodiest, the absolute worst, the most devastating, or whatever other superlatives came to mind" (Fox 2008, para. 3). These critics nonetheless called for a broader examination of the production of news reports and other violent media as a way to avoid future tragedies. Although some find this very line of criticism hypocritical (see Kellner 2008), it remains a recurring theme in the discourse on disaster and mediation and one that some television networks have taken to heart. For instance, Fox News Channel decided to stop showing clips from Cho's manifesto, stating that it saw "no reason to continue assaulting the public with these disturbing and demented images" (quoted in A. Park 2008, 1).

Similar themes appeared in the debate over Hurricane Katrina's media coverage. The frequent reports of looting, sniper fire, rape, and murder in New Orleans in the aftermath of the storm turned out largely to be fabrications, but the absence of significant government intervention in the region during that first week made the reporting of such unconfirmed rumors more problematic than usual, as many government decision makers believed these reports and tailored their relief plans accordingly or echoed them back to other media outlets. Mayor Nagin dramatically demonstrated this process when he appeared on *Oprah* parroting claims about "hooligans killing people, raping people" in the Superdome, which were subsequently proved false (quoted in Dyson 2006, 171). These visions of chaos resonated with the conventional wisdom, roundly debunked by many disaster sociologists (see, e.g., Rodríguez, Trainor, and Quarantelli 2006) but perpetuated by Hollywood disaster movies, that mass catastrophes invariably cause social breakdown and anarchy. They also resonated with a white audience's negative racial stereotypes about the predominantly poor, African American population who remained in the city (Tierney, Bevc, and Kuligowski 2006; Voorhees, Vick, and Perkins 2007). Thus, as with the Virginia Tech shootings, much media criticism of Hurricane Katrina coverage focused on the issue of sensationalism. In New Orleans, at a time when few state or federal officials, and none of the general public, were in a position to know what was really happening on the ground, the news media could not resist putting the most dramatic and sensational spin on these already incredibly dramatic events and did so by appealing in many cases to people's worst opinions of human nature or their vilest racial prejudices.

Nevertheless, millions watched the television coverage of both tragedies. Many donated money directly to relief efforts or memorial funds, while others bought athletic apparel, charity T-shirts, commemorative books, and benefit concert tickets or recordings. Still others consumed in ways that provided no direct economic assistance to the victims at all, as with certain Hurricane Katrina souvenir T-shirts or fictional novels set during the storm. But more than simply enabling charity or expressions of solidarity, consumer culture and mass media were the focus of many of the proposed solutions to the problems that remained in these tragedies' aftermaths. The main set of preventative measures adopted at colleges and universities across the country in the wake of those shootings involved the creation of early warning systems that sent e-mails and text messages to students' computers and cell phones (Fox and Savage 2009). And New Orleans has attempted to quickly rebound from the disaster with the help of tourism, since its French Quarter has always been the most visited area of the city and was least affected by the flooding. Many companies even offered tours of the devastated and still barely rebuilt areas of the city (M. Park 2006).

One can safely say, then, that mass media and consumer culture are fundamental to the American experience of these two disasters. Although criticisms of the inaccuracy and stereotyping in early news coverage of both disasters have certainly proved valid, it remains important to understand the normative construction of pain and suffering in this coverage. After all, the moral and ethical problems posed by the suffering of distant others have been a subject of philosophical discourse for centuries. However, dominant views on the subject have changed over time, as have norms concerning the appropriate behavior of those bearing witness to others' misfortune. Such a change appears to be at work in the contemporary experience of disaster as well, requiring a new effort to understand the emotional style of disaster consumption and its place among older ways of apprehending tragedy and the pain of others.

The Meaning of Empathy

The previous chapter showed how the emergence of mass media and mass consumption in the eighteenth century helped made the expression of feeling for suffering of others into a modern virtue. In the past hundred years, however, and especially the past half century, an alternative to older notions of compassion or sympathy has emerged. "Empathy" was coined in 1909 as a translation from the German *einfühlung*, meaning roughly the ability to project the self into a perceived object. Eventually coming to refer to one's awareness in imagination of the emotions of another person, it has become the word of choice in psychology (Wispé 1986). Psychologists have been encouraged to improve their "empathic accuracy" (Ickes 1997) by adopting a listening stance not just attuned to but oriented from within the patient's emotions and perspective. Empathy, for psychoanalysts, has become a process of "vicarious introspection" (Kohut 1984; quoted in Bouson 1989, 22). Even President Barack Obama has suggested that "when you choose to broaden your ambit of concern and empathize with the plight of others, whether they are close friends or distant strangers—it becomes harder not to act, harder not to help" (quoted in Bloom 2013, para. 2).

Yet many dispute this activist interpretation of empathy. In fact, one crucial distinction between Enlightenment notions of sympathy and the more recent belief in the virtues of empathy is that the latter may actually signal a decreased moral obligation to act. As the psychologist Lauren Wispé (1986, 314) put it, "Sympathy refers to a heightened awareness of another's plight as something to be alleviated. Empathy refers to the attempt of one self-aware self to understand the subjective experiences of another self." Similarly, the sociologist Candace Clark (1997) has argued that empathy is simply the first step in a process that can lead to sympathy but can also lead to indifference or even disgust toward the other. As a purely emotional exercise in identifying with another, empathy blunts the political or activist implications associated with sympathy.

Thus, rather than simply feeling sorry for someone less fortunate, or feeling an emotion that corresponds to another's emotional state, or sympathizing with that other in a way that accepts a moral obligation to help, empathy refers to an intersubjective understanding of the other's plight devoid of the obligation to intervene. Although sympathy proved fundamental to democratic politics and egalitarian societies, as Alexis de Tocqueville (2000) noted when describing the breadth of compassion he saw in America, contemporary American culture has tended to venerate empathy not only in conjunction with the growing popularity of psychoanalysis but also, more generally, as psychoanalytic ideas have penetrated the marketplace. For instance, self-help books on everything from leadership to anger management emphasize the ability to empathize with the needs and perspectives of those in one's family as well as those with whom one works. Such empathic skills are seen as both strategic and moral. But rather than directing those skills toward helping others attain their needs, the act of empathizing is often seen as an end in itself or simply as a way to gain others' trust (Illouz 2008). In this manner, the explicitly political character of sympathy as an *active* concern for another has given way to empathy's more *passive*, vicarious character. This alternative, empathetic stance is embedded in a particular way of looking at disaster-related media, particularly those media texts that demonstrate the kind of authenticity discussed in previous chapters.

Empathy, Authenticity, and the Virginia Tech Shootings

As mentioned, one of the most controversial aspects of media coverage of the Virginia Tech shootings was the decision by *NBC Nightly News* to air portions of the digital package of pictures, videos, and text that Seung-Hui Cho sent to NBC sometime between his initial double homicide and his larger mass shooting later that day. Although many found this decision inexcusable, and half of the respondents in one survey found the coverage of these shootings excessive (Pew Research Center for the People and the Press 2007), a closer examination of this broadcast can illuminate some of the meanings and motivations behind this decision. The more macabre or sensationalist elements of the broadcast do not simply stem from a desire for spectacle. Rather, they appear to emerge out of the producers' attempts to elicit deeper psychological understandings of Cho and the suffering of his victims, coupled with a preoccupation with the authentic quality of the media that Cho created. In this way, the network established itself as having the only truly authentic coverage of Cho, his motivations, his mindset, and the terrible tragedy he had wrought.

In the opening moments of the broadcast on April 18, 2007, the anchor, Brian Williams, provocatively advertised that the program would air Cho's "last recorded words" and described the package that NBC News had received as a "multimedia manifesto." As a way to establish the authenticity of the images and videos being displayed, Williams brought out a color photocopy of the Priority Mail package in which Cho sent them, pointing out Cho's handwriting; explaining the potential significance of "A. Ishmael," the name he signed; identifying the post office's time stamp; and explaining how the incorrect address Cho left had delayed receipt of the package by NBC for a day.

The real envelope, Williams said, had already been handed over to the police, a nod to the fact that this "manifesto" was indeed evidence in a murder investigation.

Williams then began to make a somewhat more substantial acknowledgment of the ethical ramifications of broadcasting portions of Cho's package, stating, "We are sensitive to how all of this will be seen by those affected, and we know we are in effect airing the words of a murderer here tonight." The statement was an oddly unbalanced one, however, seemingly missing a second half that explained what the benefits of broadcasting the manifesto might be and why they outweighed the concerns of "those affected." Such a statement never came. The news value of Cho's manifesto, and the uniqueness of such a piece of media, seemed so self-evidently important that no justification appeared to be required. NBC News apparently felt it was enough for Williams to state matter-of-factly that he and the rest of his news organization "are sensitive" before relaying Cho's words and images to the masses.

One implicit motivation for this, exemplified in one way or another by all of those on the program who commented on the images and videos, was to *understand* Cho. His manifesto was treated as a window into his soul, as an explanation for the seemingly inexplicable horror of his actions. This psychoanalytic approach was on display in an exchange between Williams and the former FBI profiler Clint Van Zandt, both of whom diagnosed Cho on the basis of his manifesto as egotistic and narcissistic and then tried to tie those personality traits to other infamous school shooters. Van Zandt described the point of the exercise this way: "What I hope we're able to gain is not only perhaps motive that we're starting to hear right now, but what was the final catalyst, Brian, what finally broke the camel's back and moved him on. Why Monday instead of last Monday and not a week from now?" Interestingly, neither Williams nor Van Zandt made the rhetorical leap of using that information to identify and stop other potential shooters. Without it, the empathetic ideal took a turn for the macabre, and the airing of Cho's video became mainly about reconstructing his mental state and decision-making process.

This darker form of empathy came into stark focus in the actual display of Cho's photos and images. As a montage of Cho's still photos began, the NBC correspondent Pete Williams narrated in voiceover, "He looks like a normal, smiling college student in only the first two. In the rest, he presents the stern face and strikes the pose that was very likely what his victims saw later on Monday. In eleven of the pictures, he aims handguns at the camera, likely the very ones he bought in the past two months." Williams went to great lengths to ascribe a kind of authenticity to these images, this time in the hope of giving his audience some real sense of what the victims must have experienced. This sort of empathy is tantamount to a vicarious thrill ride for audiences who may be equally concerned for the victims and titillated by access to a perspective on this tragedy that is usually inaccessible. In fact, Williams's mix of solemnity and excitement about Cho's manifesto attested to a kind of aura surrounding it; these were uniquely dangerous images that Cho, in his role as their singular creator, imbued with potentially traumatizing properties. As Van Zandt put it, "This is his lifetime victory, this is the way he's victimizing, further victimizing all of us by reaching out from beyond the grave and grabbing us and getting our attention and making us listen to his last rambling words and pictures."

Of course, rather than recognizing their complicity in Cho's plot to reach out "from beyond the grave," NBC's commentators presented themselves as somewhat powerless in the face of the incredible newsworthiness of Cho's manifesto. During the thirty-minute program, they aired at least ten different images produced by Cho a total of fourteen times, including many in which he pointed weapons at the camera, and broadcast eight different clips of Cho's videos, in which he angrily railed against a series of anonymous targets for more than two minutes. Yet all the while, NBC's commentators counted themselves simply as members of a rhetorical "us" whom Cho had forced to listen. This was in keeping with the empathetic ideal; the media suffered Cho's ranting alongside the audience, neither of whom had any responsibility to do anything other than try to understand. Rather than discrediting *NBC Nightly News* or marking it as less serious or sincere than the other news networks, all of which also probably would have aired Cho's manifesto (Kellner 2008), this should suggest that the cultural injunction to understand works in tandem with a taste for the spectacular or sensational and that one need not rule out the other. There is a pleasure in understanding, in empathizing, and occasionally that pleasure manifests itself in morbid fascination. Or, as Jean-Jacques Rousseau (1997, 228) once put it, "Pity is such a delicious sentiment that it is not surprising one seeks to experience it."

After some other news segments concerning a Supreme Court ruling on "partial birth" abortion, the third section of the half-hour program involved brief interviews with family members of deceased victims. Then, after an update on the Iraq war, the final segment of the program contained more footage from Cho's press kit, which Brian Williams introduced by reminding viewers that "the same warning pertains about the sensitive nature of the following." Then he simply added, "Here is some more of what we received of video of Cho Seung-Hui, sent today to NBC." The program aired more of Cho's videos at that point, which were followed by more discussion from the correspondent Pete Williams. The program ended with Brian Williams promising that NBC would air more of Cho's manifesto the next day, after law enforcement had combed through it, "because we don't want to create any more heroes or martyrs from this." As an explanation of the channel's moral or legal duties, the remarks once again rang hollow, since NBC had already done as Cho wished and broadcast his manifesto. But as a testament to the influence that Williams and NBC believed the manifesto contained to inspire other potential "heroes or martyrs," the remarks showcased an insistent belief in the unique power of this particular media artifact.

Although Benjamin's use of the term "aura," as discussed in Chapter 1, has generally been hostile to processes of reproduction, the digital character of this "manifesto" seemed actually to have enhanced its authenticity and its aura. Were some handwritten copy of a printed manifesto to have shown up in NBC's mailroom with Cho as its purported author, it would likely not have been read on the air that same evening. Determining its authorship and authenticity would have been more difficult, and its less spectacular character—no moving images or sounds, no inflammatory images, none of the intimate details of Cho's monotone voice and brief, angry inflections—might have marked it as less newsworthy once authorship had been confirmed. But Cho's videos and images contained more than just his angry, demented words. They exhibited the self-produced style of webcam videos and images on social networking sites that have now become a familiar popular culture aesthetic. This new aesthetic serves the same function that the hand-held camcorder style did beginning in the 1980s and continues to today: a guarantor of authenticity. These technical and aesthetic considerations about the look or feel of reality create the conditions within which empathy is acceptable or appropriate. In such a context, the ease with which amateurs can create digital media allows even a disturbed, violent young person such as Cho to exercise control over his media representation, creating digital artifacts that the news media will read as authentic and publicize accordingly.

Of course, like the Zapruder film before it, Cho's manifesto demonstrates that stubborn quality of such genuine, mass-mediated disaster artifacts: its ineffability. Although it hints at a much greater, deeper understanding of the tragic, violent events during which it was created, it ultimately conceals as much as it reveals. Such "understanding" is the siren song of authenticity: it lures audiences and consumers close to some dangerous shores, promising clarity but only ever exposing us to its horrific complexity.

When direct audiovisual evidence from such tragic events is unavailable, the empathetic ideal can still work through documentation of intimate, first-person, subjective experience. One program that reflects this emphasis more than most is the Biography channel's *I Survived*. The program normally consists of three or four interviews over an hour of running time with survivors of some type of near-death experiences. These experiences range from assaults and abductions to plane crashes and wild animal attacks, and the stories are told by the survivors themselves, who are always seated in front of a black background, with no attempt to re-create or reenact the events described. Instead, *I Survived* supplements its interviews with only current footage of the locations where these near-death experiences happened: an empty field where a woman was left for dead, the gas station where men and women were held hostage, the river where a family clung to a capsized boat overnight. The stark, unadorned presentation of such narratives speaks to the ways that "raw experiences and subsequent stories of suffering tell us about selves laid bare and open to view" (Charmaz 1999, 364). In *I Survived* the effect is one in which the emotional reactions of the interviewees are brought to the fore, and audience members are left to imagine themselves in the locations pictured, facing the horrible circumstances that the interviewees describe.

For the ninth episode of its first season, which began airing in 2008, *I Survived* chose two highly visible recent American catastrophes as its subjects: the Virginia Tech shootings and the collapse of a bridge on highway I-35 in Minneapolis. Although three interviewees discussed the Minneapolis bridge collapse over about half of the program, the focus of this inquiry is the other half of the show that dealt with the shootings at Virginia Tech. Three survivors of the shootings were interviewed: a student named Derek, who was shot in his classroom and then helped barricade a door with other wounded students to prevent Cho from returning; a student named Colin, who was shot multiple times in the classroom where Cho eventually killed himself; and a professor named Ishwar, who hid with others in his office while the shooting took place.

The entire *I Survived* series is based on an ideal of audience empathy for survivors, and the Virginia Tech shooting segments were certainly no exception. Derek, Colin, and Ishwar all went to great lengths in their interviews to let the audience know what it felt like to be there during the massacre, emotionally and in some cases physically. Derek described the "repetitive sound of gunshots over and over" and how making eye contact with Cho was "one of the scariest moments of [his] life" because of the "emptiness in [Cho's] face." Colin described what it felt like to be shot in the leg and hip. The show alternated between close-ups of the survivors' faces as they told their stories and footage taken in the classrooms where the students were shot. Although this footage could have been of any empty classroom, the show labeled it "Derek's Classroom" and "Colin's Classroom" so that the audience could understand this was the real site where a real tragedy took place. Avoiding staged reenactments, *I Survived* tried to capture the lingering, haunting traces of tragedy by filming the locations as they existed long after tragic events had taken place.

At times during the program, the interviewees added the kind of small details that only those who had truly experienced such a tragedy could provide. Derek described the way gunshot residue hung in the air, and Colin talked about hearing cell phones ringing in the pockets and backpacks of dead and wounded students lying in the classroom after the shooting. At other times, their narration resembled the kinds of terrifying scenes that could have been scripted by Hollywood screenwriters. Derek told of barricading the door with three other wounded but mobile students as Cho returned and tried to reenter the classroom by pushing the door open about six inches and firing into the space. Colin described himself as wounded and defenseless, lying on the ground and trying to play dead as Cho returned to his classroom. As Colin peeked across the classroom, he watched Cho's boots while the killer methodically walked around the room shooting into the limp bodies of wounded students. These narratives allowed audiences to behave morally, by trying to understand even the mundane aspects of surviving such a harrowing ordeal, and yet still access the small vicarious thrill that came from consuming such dramatic tales.

All episodes of *I Survived* end with each interviewee explaining why they believe they survived. These answers generally take either a spiritual approach, in which god or fate is cited, or acknowledge the survivor's preparedness and resilience. In this episode, Colin sidestepped the question, suggesting that he also wondered why he had survived and others had not, and the third interviewee, Ishwar, discussed how hard it is for a group of people to oppose someone with automatic weapons who has "lost rationality." But Derek gave the lengthiest answer, suggesting that he survived because of "quick reactions, not only of myself, but because of my classmates, and the professors on our floor. In our classroom . . . teamwork definitely played a huge role in not only my survival, but maybe in the survival of other students as well." While the show did not make any suggestions about charitable giving with which the audience could have aided these and other survivors, it did offer the audience a lesson about survival in case the audience members ever found themselves in a similar situation. This amounted to a kind of self-help for other potential victims, a way to better oneself through consumption similar to the consumerism of security after September 11. Contrary to the sympathetic ideal in which spectatorship necessitates action to alleviate the *other's* suffering, the focus on empathy in *I Survived* encouraged audiences to learn from the suffering of others, to better *themselves* by simply understanding that suffering's effects.

Of course, this combination of a therapeutic, self-help ideal with an almost voyeuristic level of intimacy is characteristic not only of *I Survived* but also of the entire genre of reality television. Given the powerful influence on popular culture that reality television exudes today, the genre itself requires a more detailed examination. Reality television creates an empathetic way of looking and encourages an empathetic approach to the pain and suffering of others in general, which must be further investigated to understand contemporary norms concerning disaster consumption.

Reality Television and the Empathetic Gaze

As increasingly sophisticated electronic communication technologies have come to expose audiences to the lives of others with increasing clarity and intimacy, many critics have come to worry about the propagation of voyeurism. As Luc Boltanski (1999, 26) has noted, Enlightenment conceptions of sympathy were predicated on the spectator's "ability to see without being seen." This position gave the spectator of suffering tremendous power and created the potential for voyeuristic visual pleasure within the sympathetic relationship:

> Sympathy is implicated as a particularly perverse, panopticon strategy. It is particularly perverse because its spectator is supposed to be a moral authority moved by images; but he is also like the faceless prison guard who reflects bureaucratic violence in the name of "reform." Sympathy is supposed to encourage the movement of "feeling," through vicarious affect and identification with someone else's emotion. Yet the process of vision prevents any true movement associated with "feeling." Hence, sympathy unleashes its own psychical conflict. Sympathy, even more than the figure of the panopticon, conceals the desire for and use of power through identification. Through sympathy, the aggressivity of sentiment is safely, perversely, released. (Hinton 1999, 16)

Hinton argued that modern notions of sympathy were predicated on a sadomasochistic male gaze, as evidenced by Adam Smith's assertion that sympathy was a male-identified practice, and David Hume's notion that sympathetic moral judgments rely on the spectator's experience of pleasure or discomfort.

However, sympathy's inherent injunction to act or speak out was based on precisely the possibility of this accusation: sympathy required the spectator to take some political stance to demonstrate that he was not taking enjoyment in the spectacle of others' suffering (Boltanski 1999). So while this scopophilic, sadomasochistic impulse may indeed be a latent feature of Enlightenment sympathy, it is perhaps more appropriate to discuss the combination of mass-mediated emotion and visual pleasure in conjunction with the contemporary shift toward empathy. Indeed, reality television is the one genre of media that has emerged over the past twenty-five years based precisely on this combination of empathetic emotional appeals and seemingly voyeuristic viewing conditions.

Reality television is, of course, a broad term that encompasses some very different kinds of programming, but certain themes and particular aesthetic techniques tend to recur in everything from competition-based shows such as *Survivor* to programs such as *Rescue 911*, which rely on retellings and reenactments of real events. Some have suggested that at least two strains of reality television exist—one based on confessional, therapeutic experiences and the other based on more sensational representations of, for example, crime or sexuality—and that these should be analyzed separately (see Dovey 2000). However, both types of reality-based programming exhibit salient features of what I have called the empathetic gaze.

Most obviously, reality television relies on a claim to "the real" that sets it apart from other genres of televised entertainment, despite the fact that much of reality programming is produced, scripted, and edited like any other fictional TV show. The documentary genre no longer has a monopoly on this claim to the real, and although many aspects of documentary making have been absorbed within reality television, new elements have been added to the mix within our now "post-documentary" culture of television (Corner 2002, 257). These new elements reflect a shift in what is considered appropriately public and private: contemporary reality TV emphasizes individual, subjective experience, particularly when individuals have experienced some sort of trauma or tragedy "which would once have remained private but which [is] now restaged for public consumption" (Dovey 2000, 21–22).

This emphasis on the reality of subjective experience in the face of misfortune suggests a crisis in the perception of reality itself. If these are the lengths that television needs to go to in order to claim access to the real, by staging and exposing "real life" suffering, then perhaps Guy Debord (2006), Jean Baudrillard (1994), and other scholars of spectacle and simulation are correct in asserting that reality has been lost. But as Mark Andrejevic (2004, 223) has pointed out, "Such programming stages not the *dissolution* of the real but the inescapably *real* inadequacy of the concept of reality upon which it relies." He argues that reality programming tends not to produce dupes who buy into its artifice as much as savvy viewers who recognize that what they are watching is not truly real but then consume, critique, and enjoy the programs nonetheless.

In any case, reality TV's focus on the subjective experiences of the participants who are the objects of the camera's gaze marks the genre as an exercise in empathizing. Media culture is increasingly populated with "ordinary people," and reality television puts the selfhood of those people on display (Turner 2006). When those selves are seen to suffer, it allows us to believe that their reactions are genuine, that they represent authentic responses to interactions in even the most artificially constructed reality game shows. On a wide variety of television shows, from the risqué couples retreat *Temptation Island* to the therapeutic, discussion-based *Oprah Winfrey Show*, suffering is seen as a means to achieve personal growth and a more fully realized selfhood (Andrejevic 2004; Illouz 2003). Typically, film theorists have defined voyeurism as the pleasure in identifying with the camera and its gaze (see Metz 1992; Mulvey 1992). But in reality television, the pleasure of the spectator comes more from identifying with the subject of the camera's gaze. The spectator is involved not in a relationship of voyeurism and exhibitionism as much as engaged in a "transaction of vicarious witness and empathy" (Corner 2002, 256). Participants in reality-based programming put themselves on display, experiencing what appears to be genuine emotion, and audiences exercise a kind of empathy that is at times savvy or skeptical but ultimately taken as proof of the authenticity of both audience and performer.

This new set of viewing conditions, as well as the relationship between spectator and screen associated with them, constitutes the empathetic gaze. Although it emerged within the genre of reality television, as that genre gained popularity and came to have a pervasive influence across much of Western media entertainment, the empathetic gaze has found its way into most of our mediated interactions with the suffering of others. Thus, contemporary disaster consumption has come to exhibit this empathetic gaze, as well. Just as reality shows such as *Extreme Makeover: Home Edition* used the rebuilding of post–Katrina New Orleans as the setting for its specific brand of uplifting personal transformations (see McMurria 2008), cable news stories and documentaries about Hurricane Katrina have employed a focus on individual suffering and its transformative possibilities in ways similar to those employed in reality TV. Television programs about the Virginia Tech shootings have used similar tropes, as has already been demonstrated. The particular notions of authenticity and emotional identification at work in the empathetic gaze appear frequently in all kinds of disaster consumption. But these sorts of authenticity and identification have their limits, as a closer look at two media texts related to Hurricane Katrina demonstrates.

Hurricane Katrina and the Limits of Empathy

While the empathetic gaze at work in disaster-related media has moved away from the standard model of voyeuristic subject and exhibitionist object, current viewing situations do still reflect and amplify certain relations of power. The empathetic gaze is not innocuous, and the ideal of identifying with and understanding the other's suffering is subject to certain limits and biases, especially concerning race and ethnicity. Those with the power to control their positioning in front of the camera are likely to receive a more fully empathetic depiction, as even NBC's handling of Seung-Hui Cho's Virginia Tech manifesto attests. However, as much Hurricane Katrina news coverage attests, the camera can also exaggerate difference and therefore impede empathetic identification. An analysis of one cable news broadcast and one documentary film about Katrina reveals more about the limits of mass-consumed empathy.

On September 1, 2005, Anderson Cooper had been broadcasting from the Gulf Coast area for four days. Although he was unable to get into New Orleans with his crew until later, Cooper had set up live broadcasts of his *AC 360* from the nearby suburb of Waveland, Mississippi. The September 1 broadcast of the program exhibited just how thoroughly the empathetic ideal has permeated the news media, but also how blatantly limited that empathy can be. Of course, it is worth repeating that many Americans contributed their time and money to relief efforts in the wake of the hurricane, and the assertion that empathy is an ascendant emotional reaction to contemporary disasters should not be taken to mean that no one offers direct assistance in the wake of disasters any longer. Rather, emergent norms concerning empathy within popular culture now offer an emotional and ethical alternative to the requirements of sympathetic action.

The tone of the September 1 *AC 360* broadcast oscillated from a deeply emotional response to the storm, evinced by Cooper himself and many of his reporters and their interviewees, to a wildly exaggerated description of its chaotic aftermath. Although the distinction was not completely clear-cut, African American hurricane victims frequently were associated with the "chaotic" portion of this narrative while white victims were more often involved in an empathetic interaction or portrayal. While Cooper frequently blamed federal and state governments for their failure or inability to act, the recurring footage of looting and lawlessness in New Orleans presented a highly problematic image of the city's African American residents.

Cooper was widely praised for his coverage of the hurricane and specifically for two moments in this particular broadcast. In the first, Cooper angrily confronted Louisiana's Senator Mary Landrieu during an interview, as she appeared via remote broadcast from Baton Rouge. Cooper started by asking Landrieu whether the federal government was responsible and should apologize to the people of the Gulf Coast. Landrieu immediately began to sidestep the question, offering thanks to former presidents Bush and Clinton for their words of support, and senators Frist and Reid, before Cooper interrupted, telling Landrieu:

> For the last four days, I've been seeing dead bodies in the streets here in Mississippi. And to listen to politicians thanking each

other and complimenting each other, you know, I've got to tell you, there are a lot of people here who are very upset, and very angry, and very frustrated. And when they hear politicians slap—you know, thanking one another, it just, you know, it kind of cuts them the wrong way right now, because literally there was a body on the streets of this town yesterday being eaten by rats because this woman had been laying in the street for 48 hours. And there's not enough facilities to take her up. Do you get the anger that is out here?

Interestingly, although the interview began with a question about the material inadequacy of the government's response, the substance of Cooper's anger at Landrieu involved the emotional inadequacy of her personal response, which he felt did not reflect the gravity of the situation and was insufficiently sensitive to the suffering of those on the ground—including himself. The visual elements of the exchange reflected this imbalance of empathy. While Landrieu was thanking politicians, CNN cut to aerial shots of flooded swampland and overturned boats, then back to the senator on dry ground in front of a government building with people leisurely talking in groups behind her and SUVs driving in and out of the frame. In contrast to the pristinely made up Landrieu, Cooper was filmed with his sleeves rolled up, in front of a giant pile of debris and wooden planks that used to be houses.

Later in the program, Cooper offered himself as an example of a properly empathetic emotional response to such suffering. The show broadcast footage of a family in a pickup truck parked in front of piles of wooden beams, an overturned boat, and other debris while the white men and girls in the back of the truck held up a torn and muddy American flag for the camera. The camera cut back to Cooper, who began to explain the footage in very emotional, therapeutic terms, stating, "We are seeing things like this, just an outpouring of love and care for, uh, for people in this community, and people in this community are helping one another, and standing by one another. There has been some looting, yeah, but uh, but uh, well . . ." At that point, Cooper appeared to wave to the people in the truck who were off-camera, then tried to resume speaking, with an obvious lump in his throat. His voice cracked as he sputtered out another "um," then he paused and looked away from the camera for three or four seconds of dead air as he tried to compose himself, clearly fighting off tears. Excusing himself to the audience for his emotional outburst with a quick "sorry," he preceded then to the next segment.

This moment of dead air and choked emotion had a big impact on audiences and media critics alike. During this first week of hurricane coverage, viewership of *AC 360* increased by 400 percent (Van Meter 2005). Cooper was hailed for his empathy, for allowing viewers a peak behind the news anchor veneer to his genuine humanity. Even before the hurricane, Cooper had been regarded as a new breed of "emo-anchor," an exemplar of "a reality TV 'authenticity,' with human dimensions, rather than the stentorian, scripted authority of the network era" (Hagan 2005, para. 11). But his reaction to the suffering of Hurricane Katrina's victims cemented that position and seemed to confirm a shift in expectations about the emotional responses of the news media to tragic events. As one commentator put it, "Not long ago, television was a no-cry zone. The top newsmen were celebrated for their emotional control in the face of gut-punching developments. War, death, terrorism, plague—nothing rattled their composure. . . . These days, everywhere you look you see anchors seemingly on the verge of losing their composure" (Gillette 2009, para. 2, 9). Although Walter Cronkite famously choked up when he announced President Kennedy's death, he later expressed regret, explaining that his momentary loss of composure had been inappropriate for a news anchor (Lloyd 2009). Cooper and the new generation of emotional cable news personalities like him are largely unrepentant about their on-air displays of emotion (Gillette 2009; Van Meter 2005).

But there are limitations to this kind of on-air empathy. Cooper's broadcast crew were stationed in the predominantly white suburb of Waveland, and the anchor's personal interactions with others took place there, including his coverage of a husband and wife returning to find that their home was little more than a pile of wreckage. As the wife picked out photos and other possessions from the rubble in the background, Cooper intoned that "reporters are supposed to remain distant observers. There is no distance in Waveland anymore." Such a statement, especially as CNN's cameras focused uncomfortably closely on this sobbing woman kneeling in the littered debris that was her home, served to excuse that kind of intensely intimate coverage of the suffering of others. After all, audiences saw how moved Cooper had been by the devastation in Waveland and the resilience of its residents, and he had expressed their anger to Senator Landrieu. Clearly he had their best interests in mind. But even though emotionally identifying with the people of Waveland offered some justification for publicly broadcasting their suffering in intimate detail, it seemed to forestall identification with slightly more distant others.

Despite Cooper's attempts to extend the reach of his empathy to the predominantly African American residents of New Orleans, many of the segments that focused on the city and its residents were filled with stereotypes about looting and chaos. There were as many examples of "othering" as of empathizing, and this fear of violence and lawlessness loomed large over the entire broadcast. Perhaps because the network lacked enough footage of this sort of behavior to match the frequency with which the topic was discussed, at least four different video clips containing antisocial behavior or violence in New Orleans were broadcast more than once during this hour-long program. The need to replay these same images of inner-city chaos should have clued producers in to the potentially overstated quality of this threat, but it did not. Instead, voiceover narration reframed the reused footage without acknowledging its previous context. For instance, one shot of a man with his back to the camera drawing a gun on an apparent looter was broadcast in black and white at the beginning of the program as the narrator declared "shop owners armed and dangerous." Later, when the same footage was broadcast in color, it became apparent that the gunman was a law enforcement officer, not a shopkeeper, and the footage was part of a segment on lawmen "restoring order." In both cases, the image portrayed an African American, who may or may not have actually been engaged in illegal activity, as a kind of inhuman or stereotypical other, the target of a defensive shopkeeper or a courageous police officer, not a victim himself of the larger circumstances surrounding the hurricane and its aftermath.

Perhaps the most egregious form of racial othering on this broadcast came from a series of images of a black man attempting to break into a store. The footage showed a young, shirtless man with his back to the camera repeatedly swinging a metal baseball bat into the glass door of what appeared to be an upscale store or bank. In many ways this young man epitomized the type of male African American who scares mainstream white America, with his dark skin and muscular frame and his low-hanging, baggy jeans exposing the top of his buttocks. As if the subtext about this stereotypical image needed emphasizing, the voiceover during these images did not describe this particular man's story or even talk about looting in conjunction with the image. Instead, CNN's Chris Lawrence reported that "some women were walking by. The police officers told them—ordered them, in fact—that they could not go down one particular street, told them that there have been groups of young men going around, shooting people, attempting to rape women, and ordered them to continue walking in the other direction." The fact that the image of this man's violent—though ultimately unsuccessful—attempt to break into a store was accompanied by an anecdote about the threat of rape suggests, once again, that the African American population of New Orleans was subject to frequent racial stereotyping almost as a counterweight to the hyper-empathetic coverage of whites in Waveland.

Of course, many moments of pathos were exhibited by black New Orleans residents during the program, and some very humane, empathetic representations of those residents were exhibited during the course of the show. One man, interviewed at the start of the program moments after he had disembarked from a bus in Houston that had picked him up from the Superdome, described in a voice fraught with tension, "I'm just disgusted right now. My head is killing me. I'm just stressed out right now. I'm tired. I need a bed. I need a bath. I'm just overdue, for everything." The man spoke with the camera in a close-up shot of his face the entire time, his palpably fragile emotional state a testament to the toll that the storm had taken on the New Orleans evacuees.

But CNN's Adori Udoji immediately followed that footage up by mentioning lawlessness and looting, using the oft-repeated, if unsubstantiated, claim that "some took only what they needed to survive, others took whatever they could: appliances, clothes, guns." The footage that accompanied this claim involved African Americans walking into and out of a closed Walgreens pharmacy. The first woman caught on camera covered her face as she exited with apparently looted groceries, including a package of Huggies diapers. Real pathos could have been found in that image, as well, and the reporter could have urged the audience to imagine the conditions that would drive this woman, clearly uncomfortable with her decision, to have to steal diapers in the middle of a flooded, dangerous city. But the image was instead presented as little more than a virtual "perp walk"—not a means to elicit fellow feeling but an impediment to audience identification and empathy.

None of this is to say that the program's producers maliciously edited their footage or scripted their stories with explicitly racist intent. Certainly, the logistical difficulties of reporting from New Orleans in the storm's aftermath contributed to a lack of footage and sources through which a more nuanced and factual take could have been constructed. But without even speculating about the producers' intent, the broadcast itself tells a story in which the empathetic ideal does not extend equally to all demographics of storm victims. This was reflected in the imbalance with which blacks and whites were portrayed as empathetic victims; although empathy sometimes extended to black victims, shown waiting desperately at the Superdome or begging the government on-camera for help, it always extended to the white residents of Waveland, even occasionally transforming into acts of sympathetic aid. Twice the program offered a white hurricane survivor the chance to say his name and have his picture on camera to let his family and friends know that he was safe. No similar announcements were made by nonwhite survivors. The show also told the story of Tad and Helena Breaux, a white couple who had been trying to track down their baby, who had been left in an evacuating New Orleans hospital. With the help of media outlets, including CNN, they were able to locate their infant son and were about to go to Fort Worth, Texas, to pick him up when they appeared on *AC 360*. Again, no nonwhite couple appeared to receive a similar level of assistance from the show or network. While this may be due to the logistics of producing a news program outside a major city in which normal lines of communication have been disrupted, the over-reliance on whites for the most in-depth, humane coverage in the broadcast served to magnify the stereotypical representations of African Americans. This disjunction in news media coverage was reflected in large racial differences in attitudes about the storm, with black audiences more likely to feel that race was a factor in the government's treatment of victims (Herring 2006) and more likely to strongly empathize with those victims (Haider-Markel, Delehanty, and Beverlin 2007).

The empathetic ideal requires the spectator to identify emotionally with an unfortunate victim, but the representation of that victim is highly susceptible to racial stereotyping and othering. The same can probably be said for audiences themselves, who bring their own class, racial, and political biases to the viewing situation. Classical expressions of sympathy were, at least in theory, free from such problems in that they required the sympathetic spectator to prove his emotional commitment was based on only rational consideration for the suffering of another. A valid commitment had to "be purely *moral*, that is to say free from any determination by interests and consequently from any prior communal ties" (Boltanski 1999, 31). Such morality had to be established "without recourse to notions of tribal solidarity or emotional community" (Boltanski 1999, 38). The same cannot be said of the contemporary empathetic ideal—the kind of vicarious, intersubjective emotional bond that constitutes this ideal appears vulnerable to a variety of prejudices.

One might wonder, however, what the story of Hurricane Katrina and its poor African American victims would look like when told by one of those victims and whether different processes of emotional expression and audience identification might be at work. Certainly, initial coverage of Katrina in the black press was more critical of both the government and mainstream news sources (Dolan, Sonnett, and Johnson 2009). But one film that further explored these issues was *Trouble the Water* (2008), which told the story of Kimberly Roberts, a twenty-four-year-old aspiring hip-hop artist who rode out the storm in her Lower Ninth Ward house with her husband, Scott, and their neighbors. Although the film was directed by Tia Lessin and Carl Deal, collaborators of Michael Moore's who had come to New Orleans to do a story on the return of the Louisiana National Guard from Iraq to its flooded hometown, much of the film consisted of camcorder footage Roberts shot of her neighborhood and her experiences before, during, and after the storm. Upon meeting up with

Lessin and Deal, in addition to being filmed by their crew, Roberts continued to record her experiences on a camcorder as she and her husband tried to reconnect with family and friends and begin a new life. With a title that references the old spiritual song "Wade in the Water," the film is ultimately a story of redemption for Kim and Scott, though with some pessimistic undertones about the fate of New Orleans as a whole.

At film festivals, during its limited theatrical release, and when it was broadcast on the HBO network, the film received a host of positive reviews, many of which made reference to the film's ability to expand the empathic capacity of its audience. As one reviewer put it, "No human being I can imagine could watch 'Trouble the Water' and not be overwhelmed by grief and joy, and humbled by one's sudden awareness of one's own prejudices about the lives, passions and dreams of poor people. George W. Bush would weep buckets at this movie" (O'Hehir 2008, para. 7). It is not hard to understand why critics found *Trouble the Water* so emotionally resonant. The film contained numerous acts of heroism: Kim offered food and shelter to neighbors in her flooded house's attic; she videotaped her neighbor Larry ferrying stranded people back and forth between houses using a punching bag as a flotation device; and she commandeered an unused truck with her husband and neighbors and drove everyone out of the city after four days stranded there. It also exhibited the harsh and often maddening realities of post–Katrina New Orleans, specifically the bureaucratic indifference with which the local and federal authorities handled the storm's poorest victims. In one scene, Kim, Scott, and a friend named Brian return to Kim's uncle's house in New Orleans and find his corpse there, despite the fact that search-and-rescue teams have already marked the house as having no bodies inside. Later in the film, Kim's brother tells of being abandoned in a New Orleans prison as guards evacuated without explaining to the prisoners what was happening and without providing food or water. The grandmother who raised Kim also died during Katrina in a New Orleans hospital, and the film briefly records the funeral.

Certainly, through all of this there were many moments of emotional expression that seemed likely to inspire empathetic audience responses. The aesthetic features of the footage itself contributed to this authenticity. The low-resolution "rawness" of such amateur video often "conveys both the massive scale and strikingly intimate details of suffering" (McCosker 2013, 383). Some of these are small moments: after Kim and Scott drive their fellow refugees out of the city, one of the elderly neighbors thanks Kim for saving her life, and Kim's sheepish, almost embarrassed grin proves revealing and heartwarming. Others are focal points of the film: when Kim's cousin meets her at her temporary residence in Memphis, while playing the only surviving copy of her music on his car stereo, her unbridled joy is quite powerful. It also leads to perhaps the most iconic moment in the film, in which Kim raps along to a song she wrote and recorded about her life and the obstacles that she had faced and overcome.

But that moment also exposed some of the film's weaknesses and some shortcomings of the empathetic gaze in general. Throughout the film, one could not escape the feeling that one already knew the outcome. Paradoxically, in the case of such a major disaster, the audience understood from the outset that the story would be a tale of overcoming and perseverance, of forging a better self through adversity and suffering. While such narratives perhaps have always had their appeal, the merger of psychotherapeutic ideas with popular entertainment in formats such as television talk shows has made them more commonplace (Illouz 2003). Not only have audiences come to expect this theme; in this case, the film's subject seemed to be hyperaware of the potential public interest in the footage before Hurricane Katrina even hit. Early in the film, when she took her camera into a small grocery store to record people stocking up for the storm, she declared, "This is a little doc I'm doing, just in case it's all gone, I got it all on tape. See, I'm showing the world that we did have a world, before the storm came." Her almost eerily prescient comment there was followed by a later discussion with some neighbors of the more explicitly promotional possibilities of her recording. "If I get some exciting shit," she joked, "I might gonna send it to them white folks, ya heard!" And indeed, at the start of the film the audience is shown footage of Kim and Scott approaching the filmmakers and promoting the footage that she collected. She tells them that "this needs to be worldwide. All the footage I've seen on TV, nobody ain't got what I got. I got right there in the hurricane!"

Of course, this is not to cast aspersions on Kim, her husband, or the documentary filmmakers with whom she created *Trouble the Water*. Her actions during and after Katrina were indeed heroic, and her desire to promote herself and her fledging music career using the footage of those actions was certainly no different from the motives of any of the thousands of reality television contestants, although her story was far more compelling. But that is also part of the problem. In the end, while the film was highly critical of the government's response to the hurricane, its need to graft the standard narrative of overcoming and perseverance onto Kim's life story felt almost unfair to the thousands of other Katrina victims for whom the storm offered no redemptive possibilities. Certainly, the film's narrative did justice to Kim's personal interpretation of suffering as the key to building a better self, which she emphasized throughout. Discussing her impending move to Memphis, she stated that she planned to "go out there, start my music career, find me a church where I can go worship. I'm already at the bottom, I can't go down, I can't do nothing but go up. Hope I can put this hurricane stuff behind me, but if not I'm ready to face them head on, nose to nose, neck to neck too. It don't matter to me, but at least I'm trying to do something different, trying to, you know, trying. When you try, you know, you get results, so I'm trying to better my life."

Scott expressed a similar desire to start his life over, to "see how it is to do it right from the beginning," and Kim explained how she was refusing to let her fear about the move control her. While these were laudable sentiments, they didn't sound that different from the concluding remarks of reality show contestants on even tawdry shows such as *Temptation Island*. One such contestant, whose long-term relationship was almost ruined because of his behavior on that show, put it this way: "Every time I made a choice, I made the difficult choice because I knew that would be the way of growing and that would be my way of learning about myself and becoming who I am and learning about my individuality" (quoted in Andrejevic 2004, 192). In both cases, suffering was seen as an opportunity for personal growth.

However, if such giant catastrophes as Hurricane Katrina end up boiling down simply to opportunities for their victims' self-improvement, then certainly the onus is no longer on spectators to take sympathetic action in the wakes of catastrophes. Rather, the emotional work of empathizing with suffering others as they attempt to better themselves is proof enough of one's moral worth and a chance to improve oneself vicariously in the process. At the end of the film, Kim is shown working on a song in a music studio, and her husband is seen enjoying his new job doing construction work. Both are back in New Orleans, seemingly better for the experience. These are definitely stories to be celebrated, especially given how hard the storm hit so many of the area's other poor African American residents. Yet the viewer's identification with this against-all-odds success story offers a sense of narrative closure that is perhaps anathema to the film's larger political mission. After all, the film's advertising tagline, "It's not about a hurricane. It's about America," suggests that it will offer a systemic critique of inequality and racism in the urban United States, but in Kim and Scott's story, one may instead see a variant of the Horatio Alger myth. By displaying these two disaster victims as actually empowered and improved by the experience, the film establishes the vicarious consumption of others' suffering as the audience member's primary moral requirement: viewers can feel good about themselves simply by feeling for these ultimately fortunate protagonists.

Thus, in stories of tragedy or triumph, the empathetic ideal drains disaster of its political potential. Although anger at the government's inept response to Hurricane Katrina was certainly a big part of the emotional response to *Trouble the Water* and *AC 360*, that anger was steered away from some explicitly political avenues. The process of translating emotional identification with a suffering unfortunate into an active critique of the social, economic, or governmental forces behind that suffering, and of making compensatory demands on the responsible parties, exemplifies classical notions of sympathy within a robust public sphere. Although such a process was at times suggested by these two texts, both ultimately went in other directions that highlight some of empathy's limitations. In this way, the conditions for an active, critical, and sympathetic public sphere are challenged by this alternative, empathetic, consumerist style of apprehending the suffering of others and the potential for racial and class bias in its emotional forms of identification.

Mainstream American culture in the first decade of the twenty-first century was more familiar with individualistic narratives of self-help than collective struggles for civil rights or fair labor practices, a fact that helps explain why individualistic, empathetic ways of looking at disaster resonated so much. Coupled with the almost limitless amount of others' suffering to which contemporary mass media can expose audiences today, one can see why a kind of depoliticization of such suffering may be desirable for audiences. This is especially true when one considers the time frame over which these events develop. News stories in a consumer society, even ones as monumental as Hurricane Katrina, have a shelf life; they get consumed and quickly lose their appeal. Eight months after the hurricane, news coverage of the painstakingly slow reconstruction of New Orleans had dissipated, due supposedly to audiences' and producers' "Katrina fatigue" (Kurtz 2006). Even Anderson Cooper was criticized for CNN's seeming abandonment of the story he himself promised not to give up on in a June 21, 2006, interview on *The Daily Show with Jon Stewart*. The empathetic gaze offers the assurance of personal catharsis as an alternative to the uncertainties of political commitment in our fast-moving, media-saturated world. Thus, the deeply empathetic response to the suffering caused by Katrina could not outlast the speed of contemporary news cycles and, less than a year later, seemed to have made little difference in on-the-ground reconstruction efforts that have continued into the present day to privatize the city's public goods, gentrify its neighborhoods, and leave out its poorest residents (Akers 2012; L. Graham 2012; Green, Kouassi, and Mambo 2013).

Conclusion: Empathy and the Paradoxes of Authenticity

In some ways, Hurricane Katrina and the Virginia Tech shootings were very different kinds of catastrophes. In terms of the loss of life and property, and their immediate political implications, the two events varied greatly. The government's inadequate response to Katrina was regarded by many as a referendum on the Bush presidency and on the persistence of racial inequality in urban America, while the Virginia Tech shootings prompted a brief "advocacy free-for-all" (Furedi 2007b) that resulted in little public consensus and in some ways seemed to rehash familiar media frameworks adopted after the Columbine shooting in 1999. Even the news broadcasts and documentary films discussed in this chapter have vast differences. The anchors of the two news broadcasts, Brian Williams and Anderson Cooper, have very different emotional styles that were reflected in their news coverage. And the purposefully somber narratives delivered by Virginia Tech shooting victims on *I Survived* varied greatly from the eyewitness camcorder footage and occasional exuberance of *Trouble the Water*. Yet the mass consumption of both disasters, as reflected in all four of the media texts examined here, exhibited certain common themes.

Although the empathetic ideal encourages emotional identification with the people on screen, it requires some guarantee of the genuineness or authenticity of what one is watching. In the programs discussed in this chapter, such guarantees were based on a combination of the technical or aesthetic qualities of the media at hand and the personal self-performances of those on-screen. The technical qualities of the slightly shaky and grainy footage of stranded, grief-stricken, or frightened Katrina victims lent added weight to their emotional on-camera testimony. When the broadcast lacked any traces of this aesthetic, as in the footage of Anderson Cooper anchoring the live broadcast from Waveland, Cooper painted himself as a fellow sufferer of the storm by losing his composure on camera. Kim Roberts's camcorder footage from the eye of the storm served a similar function: it cemented her identity as a compassionate, heroic, and authentic storm survivor and propelled that status through the long, post-hurricane portion of the film, where the camera quality improved and outside filmmakers got involved.

When no live disaster footage was available, as in the *I Survived* episode dedicated to the Virginia Tech shootings, an intense focus on the personal experience of the victims sufficed as an assurance of authenticity. That program eschewed the use of recycled news footage and reenactments of dramatic events, and even edited the interviewer completely out of the traumatic narratives relayed by the shooting's survivors, to focus on the interviewees' intimate, personal performances of trauma and grief. By contrast, the episode of *NBC Nightly News* with Brian Williams that contained Cho's multimedia manifesto attested, once again, to the incredible power of first-person disaster footage, although in this case the person in question was actually the cause of the disaster. American consumer culture venerates such footage of the tragic or disastrous precisely because it is thought to be more authentic than the rest of the media landscape, and in this case Cho's authorship of the images imbued them with a powerful aura. This aura attracted Brian Williams and NBC's producers enough for them to ignore the public outrage that airing such controversial documents was bound to, and did, stir up. But the empathetic ideal extended to Cho, too, as Williams and his guests led the audience through his words and images on a search for psychological clues to the killer's mind-set and motivation.

Film theory has long established the potential of cinema's projection technologies and viewing conditions to create audience identification with the camera's objectifying gaze. More recently, scholars of reality television have described the different kinds of audience identification associated with that genre of entertainment. This chapter has suggested that a kind of empathetic gaze, derived in part from the ways of seeing associated with reality television, is embedded in the four media texts analyzed here and the consumption of disaster more generally. This gaze involves a way of looking at and identifying with the subjective experiences of those on whom the camera's gaze is fixed. Rather than the detached, voyeuristic gaze of Hollywood cinema, the empathetic gaze elicits the spectator's vicarious emotional connection to the subject on the screen and is especially prominent when that subject has been shown to have genuinely suffered. In a culture that greatly esteems the ability to empathize with one's lovers, family members, or co-workers, the emotional work of empathizing with on-screen suffering is itself a pleasurable aspect of the viewing experience called forth by the empathetic gaze.

In stark contrast to the ideal of sympathy, which involves acting or, at least, speaking out on behalf of those who suffer, this mediated empathy is more about self-improvement than improving the condition of unfortunates. In that way, the empathetic gaze meshes well with other forms of mass consumption such as the purchasing of T-shirts, athletic apparel, CDs, or souvenirs. While much of the proceeds from these kinds of purchases have gone to relief efforts for victims of Hurricane Katrina and the Virginia Tech shootings, such purchases also serve to mark consumers as emotionally sensitive individuals who care about the fate of others. The positive impact on one's own identity of such seemingly altruistic behavior is a motivating factor even for people who volunteer directly (Hayes 2004; McMurria 2008). Rather than reawakening the long-standing debate over the possibility of truly altruistic behavior (see Piliavin 2008), the consumption of disaster mitigates the tension between egotistic and altruistic actions, suggesting that empathetically motivated consumption is in and of itself a moral action, regardless of its limited effect on the conditions of those who suffer. This ideal works in tandem with contemporary pop-psychological attitudes that suffering and victimhood can always be transformed by victims themselves into opportunities for self-improvement and renewal.

This sort of consumption-oriented empathy for distant others has its limits and lacunae, however. Basing one's fellow feeling for distant others on how identifiable one finds them leaves the entire empathetic process vulnerable to personal prejudices. The philosopher Jesse Prinz (2011, 227) has noted, "Empathy is partial; we feel greater empathy for those who are similar to ourselves." The fact that looped, often out-of-context footage of African American looters co-existed on *AC 360* with a segment in which the news anchor was close to openly weeping at the site of a truckload of white hurricane victims suggests no less. Studies, in fact, have confirmed the existence of empathy's racial biases; one found that whites who strongly identified with their own racial group heavily biased their charitable giving against black hurricane victims (Fong and Luttmer 2007), and another confirmed that even on a sensory level, we experience more empathy for people with the same skin color (Avenanti, Sirigu, and Aglioti 2010). In this sense, Enlightenment notions of sympathy that disqualified communal, familial, or ethnic considerations in favor of a more rational, objective consideration of others' suffering are superior to the empathetic ideal, at least in theory. Of course, in practice the same racial biases, as well as class and gender prejudices, likely rendered many unfortunate sufferers invisible to classical advocates of sympathy such as Smith and Hume.

More than simply racial biases, then, the empathetic gaze is vulnerable to the larger paradoxes of authenticity. If one is to properly identify with the suffering of others, one must first be assured that their suffering is genuine. But unlike the rational consideration of claims to victimhood associated with sympathy, this empathetic ideal rests on the spectator's subjective evaluation of the authenticity of the other's suffering. Although skillfully presented personal narratives such as those on *I Survived* are often enough to guarantee that the subjects' emotions are genuine, first-person footage and live broadcasting from disaster zones are more effective, and the aesthetic and technological cues associated with these scenarios transform the authenticity of unfortunates from a question into a given. The results, however, are a ceaseless quest for increasingly intimate footage of suffering; an increasing number of reporters on the scene as a disaster unfolds and mounting pressure to broadcast traumatic images, regardless of who produced them or what their broadcast might mean for victims or potential imitators.

This is part of the *empathetic hedonism* of catastrophe consumption. Disasters are undeniably real, and empathy for their distant victims marks one as an authentic, moral human being. At the same time, the exhilaration of these emotions and the novelty of the most harrowing disasters are themselves pleasures with a very powerful appeal to consumers. "Indeed, so-called 'negative' emotions often evoke stronger feelings than the others, they actually provide a greater potential for pleasure" (C. Campbell 1987, 70). But, of course, empathy is never fully achieved. We can never be sure how well we really understand another's pain. And coverage of that pain could always be timelier, more intimate, more emotional. Thus, the appetite for empathy cannot be easily sated and must be fed repeatedly, frequently resulting in the kinds of "disaster marathon" (Blondheim and Liebes 2003) coverage for which news organizations are often criticized.

Such coverage is, in its pursuit of deeply authentic emotional experiences, often experienced as highly insensitive and inauthentic. Throwing a camera in the face of a shocked Virginia Tech student moments after the shootings or following a Waveland homeowner as she combs through the rubble of her house may generate a certain kind of intimacy, but it can also appear craven and obvious. What is more, the stubborn distance between spectator and sufferer persists no matter how intimate the coverage. The only thing that is certain in the quest for such a fleeting authenticity is that it will continue to rely on the raw materials of tragedy and disaster, mining the ore of real emotion that such harrowing events contain.

In strict terms, it is inaccurate to call contemporary disaster consumption voyeuristic. The contemporary emphasis on empathy means that spectators of suffering are less likely to objectify the on-screen sufferer and more likely to identify with him or her. It is similarly unfair to call such consumption immoral; instead, one might more accurately suggest that alternative moral and normative codes concerning the suffering of others have emerged that encourage ethically minded consumers to engage in an empathetic form of spectatorship. This approach recasts the consumers of disaster from voyeuristic spectators to ethical bystanders. But the empathetic ideal does serve to neutralize the political potential of disasters. If, in the face of mass destruction, one is asked only to empathize with the victims, then even the most widespread anger, outrage, and sorrow need not motivate any political act more involved than the purchase of a T-shirt whose proceeds go to charity.

This discontinuity between actual aid and emotional connection was perhaps best reflected in a moment on *AC 360* in which Kathleen Koch, a CNN reporter who grew up in Waveland, talked with Cooper about her emotional response to the devastation there. The lack of resources for survivors, Koch said, "[made me] want to throw down my microphone and just take all the water that we have in our vehicle and give it to them and start driving up and down the streets," a sentiment with which Cooper appeared to agree. But, of course, Koch and Cooper did not drop what they were doing and give away all their water; nor had they planned to. It is particularly indicative of the contemporary cultural moment that Koch's failure to follow through on her desire to help was not seen as an indictment, yet her expression of the emotional urge to do so was presented as laudatory in and of itself. In such a context, disaster victims can expect powerful, widespread public support for their recovery, but that will likely mean emotional support and psychological recovery. The empathetic gaze is thus a means to cope with our own powerlessness as we watch tragedies unfold, not a tool to encourage positive social and political change. What is more, as the next chapter shows, this sort of empathy can lead to heightened levels of fear and their manipulation by elite interests.

3

THE AUTHENTICITY OF FEAR

*September 11 and
the Financial Crisis*

On September 15, 2001, after four days of live coverage of the September 11 attacks without commercial breaks, network television began to return to its regularly scheduled programming. This pause in the televisual routine was the longest in American history, surpassing the three days of nonstop coverage triggered by President John F. Kennedy's assassination and funeral in 1963 (Carter and Rutenberg 2001). The nightly news shows and cable news channels continued their coverage of the attacks, however, focusing as they had been on the victims and their families, the recovery efforts at the World Trade Center, and the investigations into who was responsible. And like the rest of the American public, a majority of whom believed that another terrorist attack was likely (Pew Research Center for the People and the Press 2001b), television news began to look ahead. As the CBS reporter John Roberts suggested in one *Evening News* broadcast, "American fears have turned to what might be next." He went on to claim, "This most recent attack was of such an Apocalyptic nature we may have to redefine the very meaning of the word 'terrorism.'"

Roberts's commentary was prescient on multiple levels. In the month and a half that followed, the United States launched its global war on terror with the invasion of Afghanistan and signed into law the Uniting and Strengthening America by Providing Appropriate Tools Required to Intercept and Obstruct Terrorism Act (the USA PATRIOT Act, which is commonly referred to as simply the Patriot Act). With these two moves, the word "terrorism" was indeed redefined; no longer simply describing a particular tactic, it became the justification for foreign wars, the rationale behind an explosion of domestic security procedures and surveillance programs, and a buzzword for a host of new fears and suddenly looming threats. One new threat was biological warfare. Unknown sources started sending anthrax through the mail to seemingly random targets in the government and news media beginning on September 18 and proceeding for several weeks. Although only seventeen people were infected and five died, these anthrax attacks were presented as proof that the threat of terrorism persisted in the United States beyond 9/11 in ways that were not necessarily suggested by 9/11 and that could affect any and all Americans. As one unidentified female bystander said in an October 12, 2001, edition of *CBS Evening News*, "Checking your mail just took on a new meaning."

Roughly six-and-a-half years later, a very different sort of threat exploded into public consciousness. From March to October 2008, Americans came to understand themselves as enmeshed in a global financial crisis, as major banks and venerable investment houses began to admit to insolvency and lawmakers started debating the merits of massive federal intervention in the financial markets. As the months proceeded and new revelations made clear that the entire U.S. financial industry was threatened, officials and experts came on television to repeatedly make the case for government intervention. The resultant federal legislation, the Emergency Economic Stabilization Act, like the Patriot Act before it, was a wide-reaching and controversial act of governance with vast consequences that were only dimly understood at the time.

These two very different catastrophes were nonetheless treated similarly in American media and political culture. Both inspired extensive news coverage, political commentary, advertisements, and a variety of consumer goods and services. Both disasters were described by politicians, financial or military experts, and journalists as worst-case scenarios that were largely unforeseeable, even though warning signs and historical precedents existed for both cases (see Eichenwald 2012; Reinhart and Rogoff 2009). Most important, the news media presented both terrorism and financial crisis as potential threats to all Americans, not just those living in major cities or working in the finance industry. As Diane Swonk, chief economist at Moody's, cautioned the audience of *ABC World News* on March 17, 2008, "What you care about on Main Street is that this crunch on Wall Street doesn't spill over to Main Street."

Yet although both the Patriot Act and the Emergency Economic Stabilization Act were successfully signed into law in response to these two threats, only one of these was the subject of fierce public resistance. The Patriot Act was quickly enacted with almost unanimous support from lawmakers, and opinion polls showed widespread public support for it initially and even two and three years after its passage (Moore 2003; Saad 2004). But the Troubled Asset Relief Program (TARP), the initial name for the federal government's proposed intervention into the markets, faced heavy public opposition, resulting in its rejection in the House of Representatives (Hulse and Herszenhorn 2008). A few days later, TARP was passed in the Senate and then in the House in the form of the Emergency Economic Stabilization Act of 2008, thanks to increased public relations efforts by government spokespeople and financial industry experts and, presumably, much behind-the-scenes arm twisting of hesitant elected officials. Nevertheless, in this case the public had initially reacted much less trustingly to the government's proposed solution to a crisis than it had in the days after September 11.

Understanding the public reaction to these catastrophes necessarily entails understanding how fear is socially distributed and constructed. Although the sociological conception of risk or a "risk society" contains somewhat obvious affective dimensions—as people are likely to have emotional reactions to the notion that their well-being is in jeopardy—social science research often neglects this facet of risk perception and rhetoric (Lupton 2013; Zinn 2006). If one takes both the threat of terrorism after September 11 and the threat of a financial collapse in 2008 as legitimately fearful topics, the divergent public reaction to these two possibilities still begs the question of why. Why do some fears resonate where others do not? Why do some proposed solutions to these fears seem acceptable while others do not? When do widespread social fears lead to acceptance of authority, and when do they lead to resistance?

Examining the ways that television news responded to the threat of terrorism and financial crisis can help us answer these questions. To do so, it is not necessary to argue that the news media imposed an agenda concerning these catastrophes on the public or that the media manipulated public opinion. After all, the news media may simply reflect public concern over newsworthy events rather than creating these concerns, and the causal direction of that relationship can be hard to determine (see Kosicki 1993, 108–110). But it is fairly uncontroversial to suggest that the news media both shapes and reflects social norms as one component of a broader public discourse surrounding fear and risk. An examination of television news broadcasts thus provides access to one important component of mainstream discourses about the appropriate responses to threats such as terrorism and financial crisis.

This chapter analyzes the transcripts of television news programs in the month and a half between the September 11 attacks and the signing into law of the Patriot Act on October 26, 2001, and compares them with television news programs from an early point in the financial crisis until the signing of the Emergency Economic Stabilization Act on October 3, 2008. The analysis focuses on not only what claims were made about fear, risk, and panic but also who was allowed to be part of this public discussion. Despite significant similarities in the discourse at work in both samples, the post–September 11 coverage featured commentary from more average citizens than did the financial crisis coverage. In that coverage, finance industry experts and politicians spoke more frequently than average people. This discrepancy helps us understand the larger public reaction of acquiescence to the Patriot Act and resistance to TARP: in the case of September 11, the public could more easily identify and empathize with those people making risk claims around terrorism since they were often made by people like themselves. The over-representation of government officials in discourse surrounding the financial crisis, by contrast, surely contributed to public distrust of those risk claims.

Furthermore, the shared spectacle of the September 11 attacks and the resulting sense of national unity discouraged critical discourse concerning the Patriot Act in ways that had no analogue during the financial crisis. As such, both cases offer larger lessons about the dangerous ways that publics engage with disasters and come to understand risks.

Risk, Mass Media, and Crisis

Ulrich Beck's *Risk Society* (1992), along with Anthony Giddens's (1990, 1991) work in the early 1990s, first drew attention to a heightened concern with risk in modern Western societies. These scholars claimed that modernity had moved past its classical stage devoted to defeating scarcity and creating wealth and into a new, reflexive stage in which modernity was concerned with its own byproducts and unintended consequences. The risks that modern science produced had themselves become the objects of much modern scientific effort, and the management of such potential hazards had emerged as a critical part of contemporary social life for technical experts and governmental authorities, as well as the general public. Giddens explained, "Many people, as it were, make a 'bargain with modernity' in terms of the trust they vest in symbolic tokens and expert systems. The nature of the bargain is governed by specific admixtures of deference and skepticism, comfort and fear" (Giddens 1990, 90). Individuals in a risk society thus weigh competing expert opinions on risks and assume responsibility for their own assessments of the variety of threats they face. This development works in tandem with the neoliberal project of turning individuals into "entrepreneurial selves," who must increasingly take care of themselves as the social safety net recedes (M. Peters 2012). They then make decisions about where to live, what to eat, where to travel, and how else to protect themselves based on their trust in technical experts and other authorities.

Although risk society theorists initially focused this framework primarily on the threats of toxic pollutants and environmental degradation, it has been applied to terrorism and financial crises, as well. In an essay written shortly after September 11, Beck added terrorism to the list of global risks with which citizens of the modern Western world must now contend (U. Beck 2002), and the widely dispersed effects of high-finance decision making similarly confirmed early on for Giddens (1990) the notion that modernity produced unintended feedback or boomerang effects. For example, the uncertainties surrounding the likelihood of terrorist attacks have spawned new formulas, technologies, and practices of risk assessment and control, but these have often inspired new fears and increased insecurities related to terrorism as well (Aradau and van Munster 2007). Just as with techno-scientific and environmental risks, the threats and uncertainties surrounding terrorism and financial crises persist even in the wake of policies and technologies designed to minimize them. As one discussion of the Asian financial crisis of 1997–1998 concluded, "If the financial realm—dominated by the confident certainties of mathematics and economics—is in fact inherently ambiguous, then what spaces of human existence are free from ambiguity" (Best 2008, 370)?

The recognition of such persistent risks and ambiguities—either despite or because of the efforts of scientists, security experts, and government agencies—has led some to conclude that the power of authorities to influence public perceptions of risks and threats is in decline. Various high-profile examples of scientific mistakes and cover-ups have fueled public skepticism about scientific research in general and about the risk claims of its representatives in business and government. In this way, failures of scientific technology and examples of governmental or corporate negligence, such as the nuclear catastrophe at Chernobyl and the Bhopal chemical disaster, have helped foster a climate of public mistrust concerning subsequent scientific developments such as genetically modified foods and other biotechnologies (see Almås 1999; Brown and Michael 2002; Grove-White 1996). Each time authorities are found to have concealed dangers or, worse yet, dangers materialize that were unforeseen by such authorities, it calls into question "the very idea of expertise" (Giddens 1990, 131).

However, the crisis of legitimacy that supposedly describes modern publics' growing skepticism of authorities (see Habermas 1975) was not reflected in the American public's response to claims made by authorities regarding terrorism in the wake of September 11. Instead, the public largely supported government officials and security experts as those entities quickly assigned responsibility for the attacks and almost immediately made the case for foreign military intervention, and then again as they acquired much greater domestic policing and surveillance powers with passage of the Patriot Act. In the first week after the September 11 attacks, 53 percent of Americans were willing to "sacrifice civil liberties to curb terrorism," although 70 percent were opposed to the idea of allowing the government to monitor their phone calls and e-mail (Pew Research Center for the People and the Press 2001a). In the same survey, President George Bush's approval rating reached 80 percent, up from 51 percent before the attacks, and 85 percent said they approved of how he had handled the terrorist attacks. In the following year, when surveys started measuring attitudes specifically toward the Patriot Act, there was similar public support—just 11 percent in one survey conducted in June 2002 thought the act "went too far" in restricting people's civil liberties, while 60 percent thought it was "about right" (Moore 2003).

Yet public skepticism about elite narratives and federal intervention did return by the time the financial crisis hit in 2008. From mid-September, when the plan was being heavily debated, until mid-November, two weeks after it had been signed into law, support for the government's bailout plan plummeted. The percentage of Americans who thought that the government's plan to secure the nation's financial system was the "right thing to do" dropped from 57 percent in a poll taken on September 22, to 45 percent on September 29, and to 40 percent on November 17 (Pew Research Center for the People and the Press 2008a, 2008b). Many members of the public expressed their anger during the debates over the legislation leading up to the first failed vote on TARP by engaging in grassroots protest, signing petitions, or contacting elected officials in unprecedented numbers (Sirota 2009). So what accounts for the discrepancy between public reactions to the Patriot Act and TARP?

Certainly it is not because the proposed solutions to post-9/11 terrorism were less risky than those proposed for the financial crisis. In hindsight, the claims of antiwar critics that the invasion of Afghanistan would be a quagmire, that there was no connection between Saddam Hussein and al-Qaeda to justify an invasion of Iraq, and that Iraq did not possess weapons of mass destruction have all been proved correct (Associated Press 2005; Englehardt 2012; Strobel 2008; Walt

2012). The concerns of civil libertarians about the domestic dangers of the Patriot Act and the other clandestine elements of the global war on terror have also proved prescient in the wake of the Abu Ghraib photos and the Edward Snowden domestic spying revelations (Roberts and Ackerman 2013; Stanley 2007; Weisbrot 2013). TARP, which ultimately became the Emergency Economic Stabilization Act of 2008, has similarly proved its critics correct. Although it did prevent many major financial institutions from failing, it did little to protect homeowners with underwater mortgages from foreclosure and could not get credit flowing to consumers or get companies hiring again as they had before the crisis. Ultimately, it did not steer the country away from what has come to be known as the Great Recession (Mian and Sufi 2014; see also Barofsky 2011; Glink 2012; Herkenhoff and Ohanian 2011; S. Johnson 2010; Lowrey 2011). All this is to say that the government's responses to both of these catastrophes were flawed and deserving of the public skepticism and resistance that only the latter fully received.

The news media necessarily played a large role in public discourse surrounding both the September 11 attacks and the financial crisis of 2008. "What we now think of as '9/11' is a product of choices made by news workers, political officials, and others regarding what to say about those events and how to describe them" (Monahan 2010, 10). Critics such as Brian Monahan contend that in the case of September 11, "the media's efforts to present these events in the most dramatic and emotional terms" meant that "September 11 became primarily a story about patriotism, loss, and heroes and, for the most part, not a story about U.S. foreign relations, U.S. military policy, poor interagency coordination, government inefficiencies, or other interpretive frames" (Monahan 2010, 10). But such criticisms assume that military policy or government abuses of power are somehow inherently less dramatic or emotional than stories about patriotism and heroism, or that these kinds of frames are mutually exclusive. That may not be the case—after all, the news media is also frequently accused of being "obsessed with scandal" (see, e.g., Underwood 2001, 102), and it is not hard to imagine the pre-9/11 incompetence of a variety of government agencies becoming more central to post-9/11 reporting, if that line of inquiry had been framed appropriately.

This was indeed what happened during the financial crisis. Reporters, financial analysts, and other television news personalities accustomed to lauding the virtues of the free market—especially during a period in which deregulation was the norm—found it very difficult to fall in line behind the government's initial $29 billion contribution to the deal that sold Bear Stearns to JP Morgan. The incredulity of television journalists about this early federal bailout was clear, for instance, in the remarks of Lou Dobbs, who intoned on a March 17, 2008, broadcast of *Anderson Cooper 360 Degrees* (*AC 360*) that he hoped all the viewers would "let their congressmen and their senators know that they're quite aware of the outrage that is being committed . . . given what is happening to millions of Americans in this country who are being denied the same advantage as are the barons of Wall Street." These sorts of comments set the tone for financial crisis coverage that was often critical, or at least ambivalent, about the federal government's possible responses to the escalating crisis.

Coverage of terrorism leading up to the signing of the Patriot Act was much less critical of official responses, at least partly due to widely held journalistic norms about protecting democracy and comforting the citizenry during times of distress (Mogensen 2008). Indeed, news coverage of the disaster constructed a notion of "the American people" that emphasized the communal responsibilities and emotional resilience of a supposedly unified electorate (Hart, Jarvis, and Lim 2002). One content analysis of President Bush's pre- and post-9/11 speeches found a similar shift in rhetoric toward more collective, patriotic, and faith-based themes (Bligh, Kohles, and Meindl 2004). Another study found that nightly television news programs in the run-up to the invasion of Afghanistan were almost twice as likely to employ a war framework as opposed to a crime or law enforcement frame (Edy and Meirick 2007). Yet another study found that, although both American and Canadian news magazines frequently adopted "revenge" or "retaliation" frames around the war on terror, the American publications were more likely to justify such actions by demonizing those on the receiving end as "evil" and showing more emotionally gripping photographs (Deveau and Fouts 2005).

Although only about 20 percent of Americans reported that they or their friends or relatives knew anyone who was missing, hurt, or killed in the 9/11 attacks (Pew Research Center for the People and the Press 2001a), people from all walks of life were shaken enough by the events of September 11 that, in one survey, 53 percent believed that they or a family member were very or somewhat likely to be a victim of terrorism (Pew Research Center for the People and the Press 2001d). The mysterious anthrax mailings of the following month confirmed for Americans that the risks of terrorism were not confined to the attacks of September 11, to the citizens of major cities, or even to those who traveled in commercial airliners. Television news coverage reflected these expanded fears. Indeed, in this way disasters and crises—which are usually the culmination of looming risks and threats—can be constructed as evidence of even greater risks to come and yet unaddressed vulnerabilities. This could have been the case for the financial crisis, which quite clearly had the potential to affect all Americans, not just those who worked in investment banking or those who owned stocks. Yet as one study found, "media exposure was not a significant predictor of opinions of TARP," and "individuals did not perceive TARP as having a direct impact on their own lives or being tied to the issues they were experiencing, including the foreclosure crisis, inflation, unemployment, or the financial crisis" (Sears 2013, 197). This is despite the fact that, as in the lead-up to the Patriot Act, coverage of the financial crisis did heavily emphasize the fearful nature of the crisis and the anxieties it was generating. It thus remains to be determined how the sense of threat posed by both disasters contributed to these two divergent responses.

Discourse Analysis of Television News Coverage

To solve this mystery, this chapter compares television news coverage of terrorism leading up to the signing of the Patriot Act with coverage of the financial crisis leading up to the signing of the Emergency Economic Stabilization Act. I selected four significant dates in each time period on which to focus. For 2001, I examined coverage on September 16, the day after network television began to return to its normal schedule; October 8, the day after President Bush announced the invasion of Afghanistan and the day that the first anthrax letters were revealed to the public; October 12, the day that more anthrax letters were mailed to NBC News; and October 26, the day that the Patriot Act was signed into law. For 2008, I examined coverage on March 17, the day after Bear Stearns was bailed out by the federal government and sold off to JP Morgan for $2 per share; September 15, the day after Lehman Brothers declared bankruptcy; September 19, the day the Treasury Department proposed TARP; and October 3, the day that President Bush signed into law the Emergency Economic Stabilization Act of 2008, which authorized the government to purchase $700 billion in troubled assets and provide other aid to distressed financial institutions.

For each of these dates I read transcripts from three of the most widely watched American network television news programs: *CBS Evening News*, *ABC World News*, and *NBC Nightly News*. I also read transcripts of three widely watched CNN programs from each time period. For both 2001 and 2008 this included CNN's *Larry King Live*.[1] In 2001, the other two shows in the sample were what would become known as *NewsNight with Aaron Brown* and *American Morning with Paula Zahn*, although at the time the names for the programs hosted by those anchors had not yet emerged. In 2008 the two other shows were *AC 360* and *The Situation Room with Wolf Blitzer*. The aim of this sample was to get a sense of the mainstream discourse concerning the risks posed by terrorism and financial crisis and to see how the federal government's responses to these risks were portrayed. I was not interested in comparing the performance of the various shows or in looking for explicit political biases between networks, so I excluded programs from more obviously partisan networks such as MSNBC on the left and Fox News on the right. Although many Americans read newspapers rather than watch television news, and an increasing number of Americans receive their news from websites, television was still the number-one source for news in this country during both time periods (Gammeltoft 2009; Pew Research Center for the People and the Press 2001a), and its rhetorical conceits and semiotic strategies can be expected to inform the discourse around any particular crisis.

---

1. Three of the dates in the financial crisis had to be shifted slightly for *Larry King Live* because many of his shows dealt with a single, predetermined issue and thus did not cover breaking developments in the financial crisis until a day or two after they happened.

The running time of the network evening news shows was a half hour each, while the running times for the CNN shows varied between one and as many as three hours. For all of the CNN programming, only the first hour of each program was analyzed. In the 2001 programs, almost every segment was about September 11, the war in Afghanistan, or the anthrax attacks or else it was filtered through a lens of terrorism—such as how the Columbus Day Parade was affected by fears of terrorism. For that reason, almost all of the stories in the 2001 broadcasts were analyzed and coded, since they all provided examples of how the news depicted the fear of terrorism and the government's war on terror. By contrast, the 2008 programs had segments on many other topics besides the financial crisis. Chief among these was the campaign for the presidency in 2008. When a topic such as the presidential campaign was covered through the lens of the financial crisis—for instance, in a segment about how the candidates were weighing in on economic woes or the proposed bank bailouts—it was coded and analyzed. But when a story had nothing to do with the financial crisis—for example, when election polling and insider campaign strategy were the topics—it was not analyzed. Thus, the 2008 portion of the sample had fewer people speaking overall and contained less total coverage of the unfolding financial crisis, a significant distinction in and of itself.

I analyzed the transcripts that constitute this sample in a manner consistent with the principles of "critical discourse analysis" (Fairclough 1989, 1995), inasmuch as this approach posits that texts themselves, when couched in their larger social milieu, provide the cues for their interpretation. In this chapter, this approach meant that I first coded the transcripts to see how often fears were explicitly discussed. I coded comments as relating to "fear" any time they mentioned that particular word or related words such as "panic," "worry," or "anxiety." Of course, I did not code mentions of these terms that were not germane to the actual threats being discussed, such as an anchor's comment "I fear we are out of time" in the broadcast. To capture the context of these comments, I did make a distinction in my coding between comments that discussed fear or panic as something happening or potentially happening and those that were actually urging the public against fear or panic. Although the argument can be made that even such inducements against panic attest to the presence of some looming threat that may indeed be worth worrying about, it is still an important distinction.

I also coded the transcripts to see who besides the network's journalists were speaking as guests or commentators on these shows. I placed these guests into four categories: average people, government officials, independent experts, or interested stakeholders (in 2001, these were first responders, police, and members of the military; in 2008, these were financial industry employees). In this way, I could examine not only the discourse surrounding fear and crisis in these programs but also who had the largest and smallest roles in propagating this discourse. Of course, any individual viewer brings her own, varied resources to each text's interpretation (Fairclough 1989), and any given text may be decoded by audiences in ways anathema to its explicit, encoded meanings (S. Hall 1980). As such, I also coded for several other common kinds of discourse, including the presence of war, crime, or disaster frames and comparisons to other historical events, but fear was the most frequently occurring topic in both samples. In my analysis I have thus aimed to situate the language about fear in the larger context of not only the rest of each broadcast but also larger debates, ongoing at the time, about the appropriate personal and collective responses to the emerging threats of terrorism and financial crisis.

Fear in Post–September 11 News Coverage

Claims about fear were a regular feature of news coverage after September 11 and leading up to the passage of the Patriot Act. As Table 3.1 indicates, comments about fear were roughly twice as frequent as reassurances not to be afraid through the first three days of the sample, and on the final day the ratio ballooned to 11:1. The most fearful day of coverage in the sample was October 12, the day that an NBC News employee was revealed to have contracted anthrax, which marked the fourth confirmed case at that point.

Even as early as September 16, although the fearful images of the September 11 attacks were still fresh in the public's mind, news coverage had begun imagining the next set of terrorist attacks. In one

TABLE 3.1. MENTIONS OF FEAR IN NEWS COVERAGE LEADING TO PATRIOT ACT

Themes	September 16, 2001	October 8, 2001	October 12, 2001	October 26, 2001
Fear/panic/worry	12	18	35	11
Don't fear/no panic	7	9	15	1

exemplary segment, journalists from the *New York Times* who had recently written a book on biological warfare convened on *Larry King Live* to discuss such threats, and one, William Broad, set the tone by suggesting, "There is [sic] new technologies out there that will let terrorists do things they could never, ever have imagined doing a decade ago." Larry King asked Broad's co-author Judith Miller whether she "fear[ed that] the people that did what they did last Tuesday have these weapons," and Miller confirmed, "We don't think they have them yet, but we do know that they have tried very hard, and they are continuing to try very hard very, very hard to get them." Broad followed up by making the assertion "Today we're vulnerable. We are—people could come in and hit us just as hard, horribly, much harder than we just got hit at the World Trade Center and the Pentagon."

On his October 8 broadcast, King asked Representative Jane Harman, a member of the Select Intelligence Committee of the House of Representatives, a similar question: "How do you balance that fear with trying to live ordinary lives?" Harman began by offering reassurances that "there is no option. . . . [I]f we hide under our beds we become what the terrorists would hope to make use." But she quickly pivoted to more alarmist rhetoric as a way to make the case for new federal legislation. She brought up the possibilities of a new attack: "There could be one tomorrow, there could be something else on Thursday. This may be the beginning of a second wave of attacks, and rather than careen from one attack to the next, I think it is imperative that . . . if we can pass a law tomorrow [or] this week . . . [to] force all of the agencies of the federal government . . . to comply with a national strategy plan."

This balancing act between fear and reassurance was a frequent feature of the post–September 11 television news discourse. Many government officials made sure to sprinkle such reassurances throughout their descriptions of the new threats facing the country. In remarks aired during Aaron Brown's CNN broadcast on October 8, Attorney-General John Ashcroft urged all Americans "to continue to have a heightened sense of awareness of their surroundings" and to "report suspicious activity to our partners in law enforcement" but also reminded the audience that Osama bin Laden "seeks fear . . . and swears to steal our sense of security." For those reasons, he cautioned, "we must not yield to fear."

But on October 12, when the story had broken of the anthrax mailed to NBC News, a growing sense of fear about seemingly unimaginable new threats had become widespread across the sample. Brown began his program on a personal, empathetic note, stating, "I am as confused, as anxious, as angry as anyone. . . . [T]he country has a real anthrax scare on its hands." Similarly, Dan Rather began his *CBS Evening News* broadcast by stating, "In this time of heightened alert and anxiety for America, there is a new source of fear and worry tonight: another case of anthrax." Rather's program that night was filled with claims about fear, from the possibility that there was a "biological Unabomber" on the loose who "gets his jollies scaring the bejesus out of the rest of us," to the idea that these latest anthrax revelations were "enough to send an already jittery nation right to the brink of panic."

By October 26, when the Patriot Act was signed into law, such fear had subsided a bit, though the act was not explicitly mentioned as the reason for this. In fact, the Patriot Act was not heavily covered in these broadcasts; it was mentioned only twelve times in the six broadcasts in the sample on this date, with CNN's Paula Zahn covering it the most extensively. Zahn's program contained one of the only substantive moments of criticism of the Patriot Act in the entire sample, from the columnist Julianne Malveaux. She stated, "It's a horrible piece of legislation . . . because we rushed into it, because there are not enough checks and balances, because all these things that are directed at terrorists can also be directed at ordinary Americans." She went on to assert, "I think the terrorists have won, if we end up deciding our normal way of life is going to be changed because of our fears, that we are going to take away the civil liberties of ordinary people because of fears."

The other shows in the sample made passing nods to the legislation and its critics but often gave the last word to government sources who insisted that no one's rights would be violated or that "we will preserve the rule of law," as Attorney-General Ashcroft put it on ABC's *World News Tonight*. On programs such as Brown's, however, another group of experts was convened to discuss "worst-case scenarios and solutions" to problems such as "cyberterror." Guests such as the so-called infrastructure warfare expert Peter Black advocated for "unconventional thinking, built around the premise of coming up with fast, agile and unexpected responses to these kinds of attacks." Even the security adviser Richard Clarke, who worked for three presidents—George H. W. Bush, Bill Clinton, and George W. Bush—claimed that terrorists could take down the Internet, as they could "reroute traffic . . . disrupt content flows. In the financial industry, they could disrupt the markets."

Frank Furedi (2007a) has connected such post-9/11 rhetoric to a broader cultural trend in which "fear entrepreneurs" on topics ranging from crime to child safety to terrorism focus on "possibilistic," not probabilistic, thinking about threats that are not statistically likely but simply imaginable as the worst possible outcome: "Worst-case thinking encourages society to adopt fear as one of the dominant principles around which the public, its government and institutions should organize their lives. Through popularizing the belief that worst cases are normal, it incites people to feel defenceless and vulnerable to a wide range of future threats" (Furedi 2007a, 73). Such fear is "one of the few perspectives that citizens share today" (Altheide 2002, 3). According to critics such as David Altheide, the mass media shoulders the blame for this persistent fear-mongering: "News and popular culture are laced with fear. Both play significant roles in shaping audience members' expectations and their criteria for self-preservation" (Altheide 2002, 9). Others, such as Peter Stearns, blame larger changes in social norms, of which the media is but one reflection, such that "it has become more acceptable . . . to talk about fears, and therefore . . . to acknowledge them to oneself" (Stearns 2006, 13). But whether or not the news media, the government, or the public at large is responsible for pushing this increase in public fearfulness, one certainly saw it reflected in the coverage of terrorism leading up to the Patriot Act.

Fear in Financial Crisis News Coverage

Even higher amounts of fear discourse were contained in the 2008 financial crisis coverage, however. In comparison with the 2001 sample, there were slightly more mentions of fear overall (101 in 2008 to 76 in 2001; if comments urging audiences not to fear are included, the comparison is 120 in 2008 to 108 in 2001). But the raw numbers hide the fact that almost half the segments in the 2008 sample were not about the financial crisis at all and so were not coded. That was not the case in the 2001 sample, which was almost always covering something related to the war on terrorism or the September 11 attacks. So in the 2008 sample there are more total mentions of fear in what amounted to about half the actual number of news stories. Moreover, the ratio of fear to admonishments not to be afraid is much more pronounced in 2008, never even approaching the roughly 2:1 balance of the 2001 sample. Instead, the ratio of fear-to-"don't fear" is a little under 3:1 in the first day of the sample and 29:1 by the fourth day, when the Emergency Economic Stabilization Act was passed (see Table 3.2).

Indeed, television journalists immediately labeled the collapse of Bear Stearns cause for serious concern. As Wolf Blitzer put it in his March 17 CNN broadcast, "Economic nightmares are coming true for many Americans right now, and the political leadership knows they can't ignore the growing sense of fear that is out there." With allusions to the Great Depression, Brian Williams intoned on *NBC Nightly News*, "You can't help people for being worried when they see this coverage. They hear expressions like 'a run on the bank,' and that conjures up bad memories, depending on your age." On *CBS Evening News* that night, the anchor Russ Mitchell succinctly labeled it "a bear of a scare."

At the same time, these early programs took pains to explain that this was not cause for panic. They urged investors not to pull their money out of the markets and reassured them that deposits in traditional banks were safely insured by the federal government. They also hopefully speculated that the government's unprecedented actions would calm the markets and help prevent further financial problems. For instance, on the March 17 edition of *World News*, ABC's Dan

TABLE 3.2. MENTIONS OF FEAR IN NEWS COVERAGE LEADING TO EMERGENCY ECONOMIC STABILIZATION ACT

Themes	March 17, 2008	September 15, 2008	September 19, 2008	October 3, 2008
Fear/panic/worry	22	21	29	29
Don't fear/no panic	8	3	7	1

Harris posed the question "The sky is not falling. Why not?" and later answered himself by claiming, "What may really have prevented the market from going into full panic mode today was the Fed's historic move to set up a loan program to help investment banks get the money they need to stay in business." On *Larry King Live*, the author Jean Chatzky cautioned investors that "what we need to do about it is not panic. If you try to guess the market, you're going to get out and get in at precisely the wrong time."

But while these broadcasts all contained agreement on the fearful possibilities brought up by the failure of one of America's major financial institutions, there was less consensus on the appropriateness of the federal government's intervention and its long-term effects on the country's financial security. By spending $25 billion to bail out Bear Stearns and broker its sale to JP Morgan, the federal government had violated norms that many guests appeared to hold dear, and had opened itself up to much scrutiny and criticism. On that same *Larry King* broadcast, the author Robert Kiyosaki criticized Ben Bernanke, chairman of the Federal Reserve, by arguing, "I think he saved the rich. What Bernanke did is called welfare for the super-rich. The investment bankers made a huge mistake on betting on those subprime and CDO mortgages, and now we're going to bail them out." On *AC 360*, the CNN correspondent Tom Foreman highlighted the issue of executive compensation in these terms: "Who's afraid of the big, bad mortgage crisis? Financial analysts say Bear Stearns executives should not be. They could well walk away with millions, even as their company collapses." Correspondent Ali Velshi agreed that "even when these guys get kicked out . . . they earn more than most Americans will ever see in their entire lives."

On September 15, when Lehman Brothers collapsed, television news broadcasts once again recognized the dire scope and searched for precedents or analogies. On *CBS Evening News*, Katie Couric accurately called Lehman's "the biggest bankruptcy in U.S. history." The CBS reporter Jeff Glor similarly spoke of "the worst housing crisis since the Great Depression" and reminded viewers that "a lot of people are scared right now." Still, on that same program, *Smart Money* magazine's editor Russell Pearlman appeared to caution investors, "Don't panic. As bad as things look today, they're just going to be a blip on the market radar 10, 20 years from now." Even Glor ended his report on a hopeful note, saying, "There's a growing consensus on Wall Street today that this past weekend may have been the worst of it," although he admitted that "it will likely still be well into next year before the economy's fully back on track."

Other journalists and guests were less sanguine. Wolf Blitzer described the nation's "financial anxiety" concerning Lehman Brothers and the sale of Merrill Lynch very personally: "It's one punch in the gut after another for all of us who have money in the stock market or in some of the nation's biggest investment banks, our retirement funds, all of this at risk right now." On the September 15 edition of *Larry King Live*, a panel began to discuss who was to blame for this cascading crisis, with *Fortune* magazine's editor Andy Serwer pointing to "greed and fear going on on Wall Street." Later, he claimed that "regulators clearly did not do enough here. And the CEOs of some of these firms believed their own voodoo." On the same program, the *Wall Street Journal*'s Stephen Moore and the Princeton economist and *New York Times* columnist Paul Krugman put the blame on Alan Greenspan, who, according to Krugman, was repeatedly "standing in the way of any oversight on sub prime" and offering "repeated assurances that . . . it was impossible to have a housing bubble." The program followed those remarks with comments from presidential candidate Barack Obama attesting to the impact of policies that "loosened oversight and regulation and encouraged outsized bonuses to CEOs while ignoring middle class Americans." Meanwhile, on *NBC Nightly News*, the reporter Carlos Quintanilla spelled out the consequences even for those without investments because of "a new era of tight credit, where banks are nervous about giving loans for appliances, cars, homes. Making Wall Street's troubles a Main Street issue."

This rhetorical connection between Main Street and Wall Street was a recurring theme throughout the financial crisis coverage, occurring thirty times in the twenty-four broadcasts. For example, in her September 19 *CBS Evening News* broadcast, Katie Couric spoke of "jitters on Wall Street and questions from Main Street." Reporting shortly thereafter, CBS's Ben Tracy confirmed that "Wall Street's woes are weighing heavily on the minds of Main Street." The repetition of these two terms in connection with one another seemed a subtle rejoinder to criticisms of the federal bailouts for favoring the rich—indeed, such framing established the fortunes of average citizens and Wall Street tycoons as inherently bound together. Sometimes these programs went further, implicating those same average citizens in the overall economic woes of the large financial institutions. Dylan Ratigan explained the situation this way on a September 19 broadcast of *NBC Nightly News*: "So who's to blame? In a sense, we all are, from the small mom and pop that took advantage of the low minimum payment on their credit cards to grow their business to trillion dollar institutions. If you thought you could reap the rewards of easy credit without the consequences, this is the proof that you can't." Leaving aside the somewhat obvious point that the banks are the ones tasked with determining who should be able to secure how much credit at what rates, this framing was part of a subtle shift that began around September 19, the day that the TARP proposal was made public.

Much of the coverage of TARP was about the behind-the-scenes decision-making process. "Fear" became a term that not only described investors or bankers or even the general public but was also applied to politicians. On ABC's *World News*, Charles Gibson described how the Federal Reserve "put the fear of God into congressional leaders" at a briefing that day. The reporter and former Clinton staff member George Stephanopoulos agreed, adding that "Fed Chairman Ben Bernanke was especially frightening" to members of Congress, as he declared that the country was "days away from a financial collapse." An appearance by Senator Chris Dodd on the September 19 edition of *The Situation Room* was particularly noteworthy in this respect. Asked to describe the same briefing, Dodd said:

> Well, I'm going to be reluctant to repeat exactly the words, not because I can't remember them, but, because, if you were to repeat them exactly, I'm fearful it might cause even more concern. I can't begin to tell you. I have been here for twenty-eight years, Wolf [Blitzer], been in a lot of very critical meetings involving a lot of important events over the last quarter of a century. I can't recall another occasion when I was in a room where statements were made about the conditions of not only our economy, but the global economy, that caused every member in that room, the leadership of the House, the Senate, Republicans, Democrats, leaders of committees, that, when Chairman Bernanke finished his appraisal, a brief appraisal, along with Hank Paulson, there was dead silence in the room for maybe five to ten seconds. The oxygen went out of the room. People were stunned by what they heard.

When Blitzer asked Dodd whether he thought the American people had a right to know what members of Congress were told about the consequences of doing nothing, Dodd responded, "Well, again, I'm telling you how dire it was without, without getting into specific wording."

Dodd's response was perhaps the best example of a new way of explaining risk that appeared in coverage of the financial crisis as well as in the aftermath of September 11. In both cases, although authorities asked the public to trust that they would be taken care of, they also sought to reaffirm the frightening possibilities of the risks of future terrorism or further financial collapse. Traditionally, official communications about risk have sought to reassure publics that the risks in question are manageable and that authorities are in control. Essentially, the message of this sort of risk communication has been "trust us and be reassured." But post-9/11 risk communication has evinced a shift in rhetoric that emphasizes the continued dangers of certain risks, despite the limited threat that they pose to most citizens, using rhetoric that states, in effect, "Trust us and be scared" (Handmer and

James 2007). In this form of risk communication, "the first priority of some governments is to spread fear and implement a range of expensive measures in the name of dealing with a threat that may make little difference locally" (Handmer and James 2007, 129). Although the problems posed by the collapse of many large financial institutions would likely have transcended particular localities and affected many millions of Americans, the fact that unemployment and home foreclosures rose tremendously in the wake of this crisis, consumer credit dried up, and Americans saw huge losses in their 401(k)s and other retirement savings, suggests that the government's bailout has indeed made less difference for average Americans than its supporters claimed it would (see Mian and Sufi 2014). In any case, Dodd's insistence on the dire consequences of inaction coupled with his reluctance to actually explain these consequences contributed to a hazy sense of looming dread on that program.

Still, although politicians from Dodd to Mitch McConnell to John McCain to Barack Obama all affirmed their support for TARP in the news programs analyzed here, the simple act of laying bare the machinations behind the scenes of this giant form of "disaster capitalism" (Klein 2007) offered space for critique and skepticism. This was especially true after the TARP proposal was voted down on September 29, thanks to a flood of calls and e-mails to legislators by angry constituents. By the time it was passed on October 3, in an only slightly modified form but with many reluctant legislators having been persuaded to shift their votes, the populist anger had not subsided from television coverage.

On his October 3 program, Charles Gibson described the "week of high anxiety" leading up to the successful vote and the "dire predictions about what would happen if the measure failed again." Later in the same broadcast, Jake Tapper called President Bush's initial explanation of TARP a "poor sales job." Others on the program, such as House Republican Roy Blunt, agreed: "Using words like 'Wall Street,' 'bailout,' 'illiquid assets' was a formula for the kinds of concern that developed around the country." Katie Couric attributed the reversal on TARP to "pressure from skittish markets and voters worried about dwindling nest eggs." And on the October 3 edition of *The Situation Room*, the correspondent Jessica Yellin laid bare the framing strategy of TARP supporters: "Some of the leaders are saying the biggest mistake they ever made with this bill was saying that it's a bailout for Wall Street. They say this is about Main Street, and they needed to communicate that message all along. That's what they failed to do effectively."

But the House Democrats Brad Sherman and Peter DeFazio had another explanation for the bill's passage on the October 3 edition of *AC 360*. Sherman explained, "Wall Street wants the $700 billion so bad, they can taste it. To get it, they need two things. First, you create panic. Then you block alternatives. And then you heard the stampeding cattle toward passing a bad bill." DeFazio concurred that "Henry Paulson set this up . . . saying the world is going to collapse and then going out to the public and saying if Congress doesn't pass this in three days, the world economy crashes." Comments such as these highlight a crucial distinction between the 2001 coverage of terrorism and the 2008 coverage of the financial crisis. Throughout the entire debate about and passage of the Emergency Economic Stabilization Act, there was a high level of criticism of the government's response to this crisis that had no analogue in the coverage of the invasion of Afghanistan and the Patriot Act, despite their similarities. In one particularly broad critique of the bailouts, on the September 19, 2008, edition of *AC 360*, the author Peter Schiff voiced his opposition to TARP in these terms: "Government loves crises, because they get more power. . . . The problem is, the government never cedes this power." Although equally applicable to, for example, the Patriot Act, whose provisions were supposed to expire in four years but have been consistently renewed and even expanded thereafter, criticisms such as this were either not considered at all by television journalists and their guests in the run-up to the Patriot Act or were not considered appropriate for mainstream television audiences at that time.

Who Speaks in Crisis Coverage?

The affiliation or identification of speakers is another important factor in the tone of the discourse surrounding these two catastrophes. In both the 2001 and 2008 samples, experts and analysts made up a little under a quarter of the guests (24 percent in 2001; 22 percent

TABLE 3.3. WHO SPEAKS IN CRISIS COVERAGE?

Speaker type	2001 Terrorism news	2008 Financial crisis news
Average citizens	39%	18%
Government	28%	48%
Experts/independent analysts	24%	22%
Stakeholders: Military/police (2001) or Banking/finance (2008)	9%	12%

in 2008). Similarly, a small amount of both samples were made up of what I have called "stakeholders"—in 2001, these were defined as members of the police and other first responders or members of the military, since the government's responses to terrorism covered in this sample directly involved rescue efforts around the World Trade Center, criminal investigations into the September 11 attacks and the anthrax mailings, and, of course, the war in Afghanistan. In 2008, these stakeholders were defined as bankers or other members of the financial industry, who had a more immediate stake in the bailout of failing financial institutions than did the rest of the American public. But somewhat curiously, as shown in Table 3.3, these stakeholders were the least represented group in both samples (9 percent in 2001; 12 percent in 2008).

The main distinction between these two samples, however, came from the number of government sources and the number of average citizens who appeared on these broadcasts. Average citizens, defined as members of the general public who did not fit into any of the other categories in the sample, made up the largest percentage of speakers in the post-9/11 coverage, at 39 percent. And yet these accounted for only 18 percent of the financial crisis news. This ratio was reversed with government officials, who made up a little over a quarter of the post-9/11 sample (at 28 percent) but who accounted for almost half of the financial crisis guests, at 48 percent. What accounts for this discrepancy?

The "mood of the nation," as Peter Jennings called it in a segment on his October 8, 2001, *World News Tonight* broadcast, became an important story after 9/11. Much coverage in this sample was devoted to the way ordinary Americans coped with the emotional aftermath of the attacks. Although Jennings's segment featured one unidentified man asserting, "We can't live in fear," other average citizens on the broadcast expressed fears such as "I don't think that the terrorist attacks are over" or attested to anxiety such that they "just keep looking over [their] shoulder." Still others in that same segment voiced support for the invasion of Afghanistan, as when one man intoned, "It's going to be a hard, maybe long fight. But we got to do it." Another segment on a September 16 broadcast of *CBS Evening News* focused on how "a congregation looked for hope after a week of horror." On that broadcast, even the minister of a church in Ridgewood, New Jersey, said, "It does sound that in some way we are going to go to some variety of war." In these ways, the discourse of post-9/11 national unity (see Hucheson et al. 2004; Spigel 2005) was reflected and amplified in these programs by this inclusion of average citizens voicing the same sorts of fears and concerns, and supporting the same sorts of policies, as government officials.

Interestingly, other content analyses have argued that post–September 11 news coverage leaned too heavily on government sources. Immediately after the attacks, on September 11 and 12, newspapers and television news programs relied mainly on government officials as sources (Li and Izard 2003), though this may have been a result of the demands of breaking news coverage, since government sources are likely to be more readily available in the beginning stages of this sort of crisis than those with opposing or minority viewpoints. Similarly, Altheide (2006, 417) compared newspaper coverage from eighteen months before and after the 9/11 attacks and found that "reliance on government officials as news sources promoted reports that joined fear to terrorism and victimization." This finding might be true for my sample, as well, if one were to count the total number of words uttered by each variety of speaker, since government officials often had more to say and more time to say it than average people. But it is still important to note that in comparison with the financial crisis, the post-9/11 coverage of terrorism actually looks more balanced.

After all, the many average citizens quoted in the post-9/11 coverage largely disappeared in the 2008 sample. Despite the fact that the financial problems of "Main Street" were a frequent concern voiced by journalists, government officials, and financial experts in these samples, actual voices from Main Street were few and far between. Instead, it was more common for the program's elite guests to speculate about the effects of the crisis and the bailouts on average people. For instance, on September 15, Larry King asked his guests, Andy Serwer and Paul Krugman, about what would be "the effect on a bus driver in Hialeah" of the bailouts. Sensibly enough, Krugman reminded King that "if he's got a 401(k), he has to worry . . . and also, he's got to worry about his job," but, of course, an average person could have been asked about her worries for her job or her 401(k). A week later, this trend of elites speaking for average people reached perhaps its most absurd moment when King asked Donald Trump to "try to put yourself in their shoes, the average American family," to which Trump replied, "It's both a very tough time and a great opportunity" before urging average Americans to "go out and make a deal."

On aggregate, then, the financial crisis coverage featured much discourse concerning the fate of average Americans, either explicitly or through framing that implicitly connected Main Street and Wall Street as rhetorical equals in the crisis and equal beneficiaries of the resultant bailouts. But few average Americans were actually allowed to participate in that discourse. In this way, the crisis coverage both reflected and likely amplified the public's initial distaste toward the bailouts and distrust of the TARP proposal—a distrust that led directly to TARP's initial defeat in the House of Representatives.

Conclusion: Empathy, Authenticity, and Fear in Public Discourse

Television news is, of course, only part of the public discourse surrounding these two catastrophes. Mass media and consumer culture offered almost innumerable responses to the 9/11 attacks. From American flags, 116,000 of which were sold at Walmart stores on September 11 alone (Scanlon 2005), to September 11–themed comic books (Foster 2005), country music songs (Hart 2005), FDNY and NYPD teddy bears (Sturken 2007), and other 9/11-themed collectibles (Broderick and Gibson 2005), Americans were encouraged to express their grief and patriotism through mass consumption. Consumption in general took on an explicitly patriotic and politicized meaning when Vice President Dick Cheney told Americans to "stick their thumb in the eye of the terrorists and . . . not let what happened here in any way throw off their normal level of economic activity" (quoted in Reich 2001, B1). Americans were even able to make themselves and their families feel safer and more secure through the purchase of products such as terrorism survival guides (Lockard 2005) and executive parachutes (ABC News n.d.).

Mass culture responded to the financial crisis with a similar array of products and messages. Television after the crisis produced more "down market sitcoms" focusing on the plight of poor or laid-off protagonists (Gay 2009) and an explosion of home remodeling shows in which houses are renovated to take in renters or in which people compete for mortgage payments (Patterson 2009). Reality television also picked up on the post-crisis concerns of the emerging Great Recession by producing shows about pawn shops, salvagers, and hoarders (Mrozowski 2013). Kirk Boyle and Daniel Mrozowski label this "bust culture" in their research on "post-crash mass cultural artifacts inflected by diminishment, influenced by scarcity, and infused with anxiety" (Boyle and Mrozowski 2013, xi). Perhaps the best example of such consumer anxiety was the rush to purchase gold amid inflated fears about the U.S. dollar's impending collapse (Mencimer 2010).

Returning to television news broadcasts with this larger cultural context in mind allows one to hone in on ways that disasters generate either support for or resistance to elite policies. Clearly, identification with the people who are visibly engaged in public discourse concerning disasters and disaster response is key in this regard. When those people are "average citizens" with whom the viewer might sense a similarity, or who at least seem to have the same sort of stake in the outcome of these debates, then the discourse is likely to be greeted with empathy and trust. This is true even if that discourse itself is quite fearful and not reassuring. This, at least, was a central difference between those who spoke in the 2001 terrorism coverage and the 2008 financial crisis coverage, and it helps us understand the divergent public reactions to those two catastrophes.

Such a divergence is partly explainable by the "identifiable victim effect," in which bystanders or distant spectators are more inclined to want to help a known victim than an unidentified victim or one identified only as part of a statistic (see Jenni and Loewenstein 1997). But it is also a question of empathy, since merely identifying an individual victim does not necessarily increase one's trust in that person or, as one study has shown, does not increase one's desire to help if that person is seen as having been responsible for his own plight (Kogut 2011). Clearly, the investment bankers and finance industry chief executives who stood to benefit most directly from government bailouts were often framed on television news as having caused their own problems and thus unworthy of taxpayer assistance. Yet they also did not appear frequently on these programs and instead let experts and government officials make the case for them.

The distinction between empathy and identification is one that psychologists and therapists have struggled to delineate (see Greenson 1960; Marwell 1964). Nonetheless, it is safe to say that television audiences may identify with people they see on-screen (see J. Cohen 2001; Hoffner and Cantor 1991). If these are presumed to be real people, not fictional characters, as we saw in the previous chapter's discussion of the documentary *Trouble the Water* and the reality television show *I Survived*, then audiences may especially empathize with the plight of those they see on-screen. But as with those media, such identification and empathy is not necessarily an accurate or just way to assess the experiences and claims of others. As discussed in Chapter 2, studies have shown that audiences tend to experience more empathy for people who are similar to them (see Avenanti, Sirigu, and Aglioti 2010; Fong and Luttmer 2007). So it certainly makes sense that public discourse in which average citizens play a leading role is likely to appear more authentic, and generate more empathy, than discourse in which elites take center stage.

The lack of average citizens on the news during the financial crisis thus rendered the fearful language around that disaster less authentic. Instead, the preponderance of government officials making claims about the risks of inaction in the run-up to the passage of the Emergency Economic Stabilization Act set off alarm bells for the general public, who could not identify with these elite claims makers or the most immediate victims in need of assistance: the members of the financial industry. Somewhat clumsy attempts to rhetorically connect Wall Street and Main Street aside, the public debate around the financial crisis and its federal resolution was initially resisted by a public that did not see itself authentically included in the discussion.

Of course, another important element of these programs is certainly the fact that those average people and financial experts who did speak about the financial crisis and the bailouts were much more critical of the government than those who spoke about terrorism and the Patriot Act. It suggests that the spectacular nature of a crisis—its visual novelty, its brevity and shock value—plays a substantial role in determining social fears and public acceptance of official risk claims. September 11 was such a spectacle, at least as it was initially received on television by so many Americans. As Lilie Chouliaraki (2004, 191) put it, "The main features of the Manhattan visuals are random shots, erratic camera movements, imperfect focus and framing, and camera lenses covered in white dust. This is clearly a projection of unstaged reality." In that initial moment of horror, "the repercussions of the event were so strong that, while watching the news, viewers found themselves mirroring the feelings they viewed" (Gonçalves 2012, 233). The images from September 11 of planes striking the towers, people fleeing a giant cloud of dust and debris, and firefighters combing the smoking wreckage thus quickly attained a serious emotional weight and iconic status. The same cannot be said for any single image or set of images from the financial crisis. Without this aura of authenticity, without the powerful collective trauma of 9/11 creating "a certain uncritical sense of sacredness" (Smelser 2004, 34), television journalists and their guests were emboldened to criticize the government's actions during the financial crisis in ways they were not in the aftermath of September 11.

Given the lack of any defining image or discrete, encapsulating moment of shared national spectatorship related to the financial crisis, and given the fact that average people were shut out of the public discourse surrounding the financial crisis in favor of government officials and experts, it makes sense that the public failed to find the financial crisis as authentic a threat as terrorism and failed to accept official assessments of risks or proposed policy solutions as readily as they had after September 11, despite the very similar deployment of fear discourse in the media coverage of the two catastrophes. The solution to this public intransigence would seem to be simple, however, at least for elites looking to steer a fearful public toward support for their preferred policies in the wake of some future disaster. The discourse surrounding September 11 and terrorism is a model for that. It simply requires finding enough average people who support your preferred policy, feel the level of fear you believe is appropriate, fear the types of others you want them to fear, and trust authorities in ways that are helpful to you, and getting those people out in front of the television cameras as much as possible.

Thus, the connection described here between empathy and risk is cause for concern. If our assessment of risks and our trust in official responses to those risks stem from these highly subjective and malleable forms of affect, then our ability to protect ourselves is truly in peril. After all, it is doubtful that the threats most likely to adversely affect us will match up so easily with those catastrophes that produce the largest spectacles or the most widely shared experiences, or that generate the most emotion and discussion among average citizens with whom we might identify. Some threats, such as the financial crisis, are slow, take time to accumulate, and produce little in the way of mass-mediated spectacle. Discourse about such ambiguous threats and their potential solutions is likely to be greeted with incredulity, as it deservedly was in the case of the financial crisis and TARP. But such suspicion will not always be the right response. In fact, one of the greatest risks to our entire civilization, climate change, is an even more slowly moving threat that lately is being met with increasing public skepticism (Leiserowitz et al. 2014), thanks to the efforts of increasingly well-funded political advocacy organizations that are skilled at simulating or inciting a sense of distrust around climate science among average citizens (see Brulle 2014). This alone should be enough to cast doubt on the larger cultural patterns in which fear and empathy currently intertwine. At the very least, it points to the need for new cultural norms around the consumption of catastrophe and the assessment of risk, and perhaps new media technologies that can help us envision them. It is to such new media technologies, and the ways they allow us to commemorate disasters, that I turn in the next chapter.

4

MEMORY AS THERAPY

*September 11, Hurricane Katrina,
and Online Commemoration*

A recent CNN.com article told the story of Judson Box, a man whose firefighter son, Gary, had died in the attacks of September 11. Buoyed by their daughter's visit to the National 9/11 Museum's Tribute Center in 2009, Mr. Box and his wife, Helen, spent hours scouring images available at the museum and those directly uploaded by users on the museum's website. They hoped to find an image of Gary and learn more about what he had done that day and how he had died. The Boxes eventually did find a photo online, taken by a Danish businessman who had been stranded in traffic in the Brooklyn Battery Tunnel. It showed their son rushing on foot through the tunnel from Brooklyn to Manhattan, since his company's fire truck could not get through the traffic. Mr. Box described his reaction to the photo as "out of control, emotionally . . . [t]hanking God, being so happy that [we] had something to see" (quoted in Solomon 2010, para. 10). Since finding the photo and eventually meeting the photographer during a fundraiser, Judson Box has helped promote the National 9/11 Museum because, in his words, "too many people forget" (quoted in Solomon 2010, para. 21).

Thanks to this relatively new form of online commemoration and archiving, the Box family was provided with the comfort of a new image of their son, and a new understanding of his last day on Earth, nine years after his passing. As this story illustrates, the Internet is changing the way that society stores information and relates to the past. Of course, collective memory has always been constituted through the development of "mnemonic technologies" used to extend social capacities for storage and recollection beyond those of the individual human brain (Olick 1999, 342). From the "arts of memory" associated with medieval storytellers to the nineteenth-century creation of museums and archives in Europe and more recent developments in broadcast media, technologies of information collection and communication have helped shape the ways in which societies remember (Olick 1999). Yet there are distinctive features of new online forms of commemoration that require further investigation, especially given the critiques of mass culture in the preceding chapters. Many scholars have highlighted the revolutionary potential of the Internet's public accessibility. "Just as the printing press gave everyone access to readership," Douglas Rushkoff has proffered, "the computer and internet give everyone access to authorship. The first Renaissance took us from the position of passive recipient to active interpreter. Our current renaissance brings us from a position of active interpretation to one of authorship" (Rushkoff 2002, para. 13). Similarly, Clay Shirky has suggested that new online forms of communication offer "long-term tools that can strengthen civil society and the public sphere" (Shirky 2011, para. 17). But when disaster strikes, does it matter? Do spaces of digital commemoration offer a distinct alternative to television news and documentary media? Are the forms of emotional expression in online spaces and the uses to which they are put noticeably different?

One way to investigate these questions is to explore the growing variety of websites that are devoted to the exercise of collective memory and the creation of memorials devoted to tragic or catastrophic events. In addition to the online component of the National 9/11 Museum, the September 11 attacks have been commemorated and memorialized online in a number of other websites, as has another recent disaster, Hurricane Katrina. This chapter focuses on two digital memory banks devoted to these disasters, the September 11 Digital Archive (http://911digitalarchive.org/) and the Hurricane Digital Memory Bank (http://hurricanearchive.org/), to examine the kinds of meaning created for, and by, contributors to these new online sites of commemoration.

Digital archives and memory banks are online databases that allow users to upload images, music files, links, news items, and personal messages or stories to an archive that other users may then browse or search. Although the roots of such databases predate the September 11 attacks, a software platform developed by the Center for History and New Media (CHNM) at George Mason University has been used since 2001 to create digital memory banks for many historical events, not only the attacks of September 11 but also hurricanes Katrina and Rita and the Virginia Tech shootings, among others. The architecture of these memory banks seeks to "embody the relationships of participatory cultures and communal memories that are being constructed through next-generation Internet technologies such as Second Life, blogs, wikis, and social networking sites such as Facebook and MySpace" (Jesiek and Hunsinger 2008, 193). Although the objects in these memorials are not rewritable in the same vein as Wikipedia entries, some memory banks allow users to add tags to existing items, and memory bank developers are currently exploring new possibilities for added interactivity in future iterations (Jesiek and Hunsinger 2008, 193).

This chapter examines the September 11 Digital Archive and the Hurricane Digital Memory Bank as forms of *prosumption*, because the users who produce and upload content to these sites are also the consumers of the sites. By analyzing the stories and messages uploaded to these two digital archives, this chapter attempts to better understand the uses and rhetoric of online commemoration. It argues that the messages and stories left at these sites frequently featured claims about emotions, trauma, and healing that reflected a therapeutic ideal, in which the restoration of one's mental health after a tragic or difficult event is of paramount importance. Although this therapeutic ideal has been a salient feature of American culture for a century, by some accounts (see Moskowitz 2001), it has emerged as a goal of commemoration and collective memory only in the past thirty years (Savage 2006). The contemporary convergence of therapeutic principles with new forms of online collective memory accounts for the power of digital archives today, as exemplified by the Box family's experience. However, their story is also in many ways exceptional, and the everyday uses of online memory banks rarely feature such dramatic ends. Instead, the sort of therapeutic experience on offer at the digital memory banks studied here was primarily about individual catharsis, not helping others. Thus, what one views at digital archives and memory banks is the convergence of the practice of therapeutic self-help with new forms of user-generated online media. This chapter seeks to discover whether these new spaces of online collective memory might still offer challenges to the memorial strategies of traditional media, and how they may either confront or reinforce many of the inequities embedded in mainstream responses to September 11 and Hurricane Katrina.

Prosumption as Self-Help

Visitors who submit messages to digital memory banks can be described as *prosumers*. Like other forms of online activity associated with the phenomenon commonly described as Web 2.0, in which websites offer users a platform or framework that they can add to or modify, contributing to a digital memory bank is simultaneously a form of production and consumption. The consumption of these online archives and memory banks constitutes a form of production, as well, because users frequently add their own stories, submit files, add links, tag existing content, or even simply search through the database as a means of customizing their experiences. Today, an ever growing number and variety of websites are devoted to various forms of user participation and information exchange (Beer and Burrows 2010).

The ramifications of these interactive, participatory forms of online prosumption remain hotly debated. Their advantages over older models of web portals, which simply presented visitors with a one-way flow of information, are in some ways obvious. Today, social networking sites, blogs, and wikis can create new communities scattered over wide geographical areas (Feenberg 2009), supplement face-to-face interaction and increase participation in voluntary organizations (Wellman et al. 2001), and provide a more reflexive, open, and democratic alternative to older forms of journalism (Goode 2009), to name but a few benefits. However, many view this incorporation of consumers into the production process as simply an advanced form of exploitation. The popularity of open-source software, online product reviews, and so-called citizen journalism does not change the fact that today "consumers do these formerly paid tasks for no recompense" (Ritzer and Jurgenson 2010, 26). Contemporary capitalism has sought to increase the rate of innovation and invention by drawing consumers more fully into the process (Thrift 2006), and these consumers generally receive little economic reward for their work beyond the simple pleasures of co-creation itself or the benefits when products and services are improved as a result.

But the blurring of consumption and production far predates the computer or the Internet. Alvin Toffler, who coined the term "prosumption" (Toffler 1980), has pointed out that the ascendance of market economies during the Industrial Revolution cleaved productive work from consumption, and before then most economic activity consisted of a kind of "production for self-use" (Toffler 1980, 295) similar to contemporary forms of prosumption. One of Toffler's earliest examples of modern prosumption involved the growth of self-care and self-help in the 1970s. With the appearance on the market of home pregnancy tests and blood pressure kits, and then the increasing popularity of bereavement groups and twelve-step programs, millions of people began to perform services for themselves that previously would have been performed for them by a doctor—in other words, they began actively prosuming their own physical and mental health care.

As Toffler explained, such self-help groups especially "rely entirely on what might be termed 'cross-counseling'—people swapping advice based on their own life experience, as distinct from receiving traditional counseling from the professionals" (Toffler 1980, 285). This is similar in some ways to what happens today at digital memory banks, in which one user's message of hope or consolation might be read by a victim's family member and perhaps responded to in kind. These kinds of therapeutic dialogues between non-experts are exceedingly common in a media culture filled with self-help chat rooms and television talk shows focused on the public disclosure of one's psychic pain (Illouz 2003; Moskowitz 2001).

In fact, although self-help ideals were initially seen as incompatible with the less optimistic Freudian notion of the psyche, the convergence of Freudian psychology and the self-help ethos in American culture today was made possible precisely "because the language of psychotherapy left the realm of experts and moved to the realm of popular culture" (Illouz 2008, 155). This new language converted large numbers of Americans to what Eva Moskowitz (2001) has called "the therapeutic gospel," in which personal happiness and self-fulfillment are primary goals, and unhappiness is a condition that can and should be treated. While the therapeutic assertion that one must make or remake oneself into a happier, more fulfilled person certainly reinforces the power and prestige of professional counselors and psychotherapists, it also serves as a powerful motivator for many forms of prosumption. By taking one's physical, mental, or spiritual health into one's own hands, one has already adopted the active stance of the prosumer. In this sense, digital memory banks showcase a further intertwining of the ideals of therapeutic self-help with newer forms of digital prosumption.

Spontaneous Commemoration and Therapeutic Monuments

The Internet is not the only place where prosumption and collective memory intertwine, however. Some of these same cultural trends toward consumption for self-use and the active participation of non-experts have been at work in commemorative efforts in the physical landscape for at least thirty years. As such, the growing preponderance of "spontaneous shrines" (Santino 1992) and the contemporary mandate for therapeutic commemoration shed more light on the ramifications of prosumption for collective memory in the physical landscape and for other forms of prosumption, as well.

Traditionally, memorials have been constructed at the behest of elites to enshrine dominant points of view and to celebrate the lives and deaths of heroic individuals. The physical construction of a memorial frequently marks a spot in the geographical landscape as meaningful and sacred, due either to the lives lost there—as at the site of a famous battle—or simply to the ability of memorial architecture to convey a sense of sanctity and solemnity. Such memorials have the power to sustain a particular interpretation of events within collective memory at least partly because of the physical durability of the landscape to which they are attached (Foote 1997).

Despite their hallowed status, however, memorials do contain the potential for alternative readings and interpretations outside the intentions of their originators, and they are always evolving as new visitors and viewers bring new interpretations (Santino 2006; Young 1993). In fact, the creation of memorials, monuments, archives, and museums is necessarily a contested process in which the adherents of competing views of history jockey for control over its representation. The decisions undertaken by the archivists, architects, historians, and politicians involved in such efforts to include or exclude certain documents, images, or perspectives from institutions of collective memory show that such memory is not merely guarded or acquired but actively shaped through the very processes of its collection (Brown and Davis-Brown 1998). While not the norm, these processes do occasionally result in official forms of commemoration that challenge hegemonic ideologies and elite histories, as has been the case with memorials and monuments dedicated to the American Civil Rights Movement, for instance (O. Dwyer 2000).

Moreover, rituals of mourning and commemoration are not undertaken only by, or at the direction of, government officials and other elites; vernacular forms of commemoration have long been a part of the memorial landscape (Bodnar 1992), and spontaneous public memorialization appears to be a growing trend (Santino 2006). Whether on the site of a deadly traffic accident or at the spot where a political figure was murdered, or even scattered around a city that has just been subjected to a terrorist attack, spontaneous shrines composed of some combination of messages to the dead, pictures, flowers, poems, teddy bears, and other kitsch commodities are an increasingly common feature of mourning practices (Santino 2006; Sturken 2007).

These assemblages reflect a breakdown of boundaries between elite and popular culture (Thomas 2006) and between production and consumption. The spontaneous displays of commemorative artwork, sculpture, banners, and other mementos that spring up quickly at the sites of tragedies and disasters serve to personalize these events for their creators. Some commentators have also argued that spontaneous commemoration is an inherently political act. As Jack Santino (2006, 13) put it, "We who build shrines and construct public altars or parade with photographs of the deceased will not allow you to write off victims as mere regrettable statistics." In any case, this prosumption of memorialization speaks to the growing influence of increasingly diverse constituencies who feel ownership over the commemoration of wars, disasters, and other tragedies, as well as an increasing number of "reputational entrepreneurs" (Fine 2001) who are emotionally and politically invested in these processes. The designing of memorials and monuments has increasingly become a hotly disputed affair in which elites, victims' families, survivors, and ordinary citizens struggle to establish guiding frameworks (Linenthal 2001; Sturken 1997, 2007).

But despite the frequency and vigor of political debate over memorial designs today, an increasingly common aspect of both official and spontaneous commemoration is the requirement of a therapeutic component. The design and construction of the Vietnam Veterans Memorial in the 1980s inaugurated the ideal of the "therapeutic monument" (Savage 2006), which aimed to help individuals and the nation as a whole heal the psychic wounds inflicted by the Vietnam conflict rather than simply honor soldiers or make a political statement. That ethos, with its emphasis on survivors and ordinary citizens, has been applied to the creation of many subsequent monuments and memorials, such as the U.S. Holocaust Museum and the Oklahoma City National Memorial (Sturken 2007).

Of course, the healing function of memorial planning, dedication, and construction has always been at least a latent feature of the process, given that such activities have the power to reunite communities that have been fragmented by wars and other disasters (Foote 1997). But beginning with the Vietnam Veterans Memorial, monuments and memorials have been designed as more open-ended and reflective experiences, which allow visitors opportunities to empathize with victims, survivors, and their families or to reflect on the personal and national meaning of the commemorated event without being pushed toward a particular conclusion or overarching narrative. This represents a form of prosumption in and of itself, since the consumer of the memorial or monument is now expected to produce a therapeutic experience for himself or herself rather than have the terms of such experience explicitly dictated by the text, architecture, or imagery of the memorial. Digital archives and memory banks flourish today within this context of spontaneous, therapeutic, and prosumer-oriented commemoration.

The September 11 Digital Archive and the Hurricane Digital Memory Bank

Although printed magazines and newspapers have long provided forums for national mourning in the wake of tragedies (Kitch 2003), the speed and interactivity of online networks often allows them to supplement or contradict traditional mass-media coverage. In the immediate aftermath of September 11, online communities such as Slashdot.org put up mirror sites of news organizations' websites that had been jammed by the increased traffic, and they added commentary on their forums. Mental health organizations immediately focused their websites and online newsletters on the potential posttraumatic stress that Americans might be experiencing, and blogging sites reported a significant increase in postings (Fisher and Porter 2001). Many message boards across the web provided a quick source of comfort for the countless users who posted prayers for and messages to the victims and, in some cases, spread anti-Muslim rage and racist vitriol (J. Brown 2001; see also Martin and Phelan 2002). Similarly, during Hurricane Katrina, online contributors to the message boards of major news networks and writers on Katrina-themed blogs challenged the narratives presented by mainstream journalists and asserted the rights of citizens to tell their stories (Robinson 2009).

Online information gathering during a crisis can quickly transform into spontaneous electronic shrines and digital memorials, as was the case with the social networking profiles of the deceased from the Virginia Tech shootings (Creamer 2007). Similarly, a site called MyDeathSpace.com archives the social networking pages of people who have died and allows visitors to leave comments. Social networking sites also enable users to join groups devoted to various social causes, including the commemoration of disasters. In 2010, MySpace had more than thirty-six groups with 6,561 members devoted to remembering Hurricane Katrina, although many of those members may have belonged to two or more groups, and most of those groups were small—only two had more than one thousand members, and only fourteen had more than one hundred members. It should be noted that by the time Katrina struck, however, MySpace's popularity was already waning, potentially pushing some of the memorial traffic to competing sites such as Facebook. It makes sense, then, that MySpace hosted a larger number of September 11–themed groups. There were 165 groups with at least ten members devoted to "9/11" in some form or another, making up a total of 66,316 members, although again some of those may have belonged to multiple groups. Even with that high number, only four groups had more than one thousand members, and only thirty groups had more than one hundred. Many of the smaller groups were local chapters of the 9/11 Truth Movement or advocates of related September 11 conspiracy theories, but the larger groups used less controversial or conspiratorial rhetoric and favored more traditional and patriotic themes.

Such websites produce digital archives as a byproduct. Threaded posts, profiles, photos, and avatars create a history of online exchanges and allow for the past to be reconstructed on blogs, social networking sites, and wikis, among other platforms (Chayko 2008). In this way, the interactive and participatory aspects of the Internet generate a kind of "writable collective memory" (Ulmer 2005, xii) that captures contemporary norms and mores about a whole host of social issues. Rather than crafting a coherent story about disaster, as mainstream media outlets tend to do, the sum total of online disaster commemoration is much more descriptive and fragmentary; its model is the database rather than the narrative (Manovich 2001; see also Walker 2007).

The digital archive or digital memory bank format makes this database ideal explicit. The September 11 Digital Archive, created by the CHNM and the American Social History Project at the Graduate Center of the City University of New York, currently holds more than 150,000 digital items, including more than forty thousand e-mails and electronic communications, forty thousand firsthand stories, and fifteen thousand digital images. Although the archive stopped posting new submissions in 2004, it remains publicly available online and through the Library of Congress, which made the collection its first major digital acquisition in September 2003. The Hurricane Digital Memory Bank, which was created by the CHNM, the University of New Orleans, and the Smithsonian's National Museum of American History, holds more than twenty-five thousand digital items related to hurricanes Katrina and Rita.

The two websites have described their missions in similar terms. The September 11 Digital Archive sought to use September 11 "as a way of assessing how history is being recorded and preserved in the twenty-first century" while also hoping "to foster some positive legacies of those terrible events by allowing people to tell their stories, making those stories available to a wide audience, providing historical context for understanding those events and their consequences, and helping historians and archivists improve their practices based on the lessons we learn from this project" (http://911digitalarchive.org/about). The staff of the Hurricane Digital Memory Bank also hoped to cultivate "positive legacies by allowing the people affected by these storms to tell their stories in their own words, which as part of the historical record will remain accessible to a wide audience for generations to come" (http://hurricanearchive.org/about).

Each site emphasized its utility as a form of historical documentation, and both described their objectives as simply "collecting and preserving" the memories associated with these events. But by emphasizing the promotion of "positive legacies," their creators seem to see the sites' functions not only in terms of historical documentation but also as a form of therapy, akin to the recent move toward therapeutic memorialization in the physical landscape. As the creators of the similarly designed April 16 Archive (devoted to the Virginia Tech shootings) put it, "If the items we have archived provide some measure of healing and recovery for those touched by the violence of that fateful day . . . then this project will have been a success" (Jesiek and Hunsinger 2008, 203). Thus, these sites make explicit the connections among digital prosumption, self-help, and commemoration.

Common Themes

To better understand the deployment of therapeutic and commemorative rhetoric in digital memory banks, I analyzed the stories submit-

TABLE 4.1. COMMON THEMES

Themes	Hurricane Digital Memory Bank	September 11 Digital Archive
Pro-social behavior	14%	6%
Antisocial behavior	10%	< 1%
Rebuilding/resilience	11%	< 1%
Charity	4%	2%
Trauma/memory	5%	8%
Heroes	3%	7%
National identity	3%	35%
Community/local identity	5%	2%
Anger at government	14%	1%
Praise for government	1%	4%
Anger at media	4%	< 1%
Religious themes	12%	33%

ted by users at the September 11 Digital Archive and the Hurricane Digital Memory Bank (see Table 4.1).[1]

The diversity of subjects described in the messages left at these two sites means that very few themes appeared in a high percentage

---

1. At the time of my research, the Hurricane Digital Memory Bank had 1,209 user-submitted stories. For this study, I read all of them, but I omitted several types of entries, including any that were written in languages other than English, any that were not actually submitted by their authors (some people posted news articles or other content that they had not written), and any that were classified incorrectly (e.g., that described a picture and thus should have been in the Images section); I also omitted poetry, on the grounds that having to interpret poetry would stretch the reliability of my analysis. This left me with a sample of 963 stories or messages. I used the same criteria for the September 11 Digital Archive, but because its section of Stories from Site Visitors contained 7,126 entries, I randomly sampled 41 pages of entries, for a total of 369 stories or messages, which decreased to 345 entries after entries that met the exclusion criteria given above were omitted. All quotations from user stories are transcribed verbatim and without interpolation.

of the entries at both archives. Nevertheless, some important ideas emerge from this analysis. For instance, both archives made reference to the psychological after-effects of these disasters, such as depression, stress, or compulsively reliving the events in one's head. Five percent of the entries in the Hurricane Digital Memory Bank made these sorts of references to trauma, as did 8 percent of those at the September 11 archive. A Hurricane Katrina survivor explained:

> Hurricane Katrina has been a tremendous strain on my life and I continue to try to put it behind me. It has been such a struggle for almost 3 years. When I went back home after Katrina that I was so traumatized that I chose to not remember much of those 6 months there. I would always go to my house just so I could get disgusted and angry. . . . Katrina didn't just take my house. She took my home, my childhood, and my mental state. The person I used to be was lost along with everything else.

Other authors told similar tales of disaster's lingering psychological effects, although they had only watched the September 11 attacks on television. One user explained, "A year later, I finally came out of my state of shock. It turned to depression. My fiancé and I broke up. I left to return to Chicago. I am receiving treatment and am trying to piece my life back together again. I will, but there will be a few pieces missing. . . . I wasn't in the World Trade Center, so I can't tell you what they lost, I only know how adversely it affected my life." Another described the symptoms of this vicarious trauma: "For weeks after September 11 I had terrible nightmares involving hijacked planes and buildings. . . . I would hear a jet go over head and do what I think many did in the immediate aftermath, look to see where it was and what it was doing. . . . For weeks afterward the sight of low flying aircraft would send a shiver down my spine."

Such messages speak to the ways in which mass-mediated national tragedies can be personalized by individual viewers and intertwined with other painful aspects of one's past. One commenter recalled:

> On September 11, 2001, I had taken the day off to be at home in my own grief. My oldest son was killed on September 11,

1996. I never watch television, but on this sad day for me, I found myself pouring another cup of coffee and bringing it into the bedroom and turning on the TV. Not five minutes later, I watched in horror as the events began to unfold. I cannot explain what this did to me, but I was shaking uncontrollably, crying . . . not only for my own loss, but to know that now so many others will mourn the loss of their own children and loved ones. It is a pain that no one should have to know. The anniversary of my son's death is now shared by so many in our country. As was my son's death, the deaths on 9/11/01 were senseless and at the hands of others. My heart goes out to each and every person who has lost a loved one. It never gets any easier, the pain never goes away. It just gets "different."

Stories such as these make explicit the psychological damage that disasters may inflict on those directly affected and distant spectators alike. In their telling, they seek to enact a therapeutic transformation for themselves and others. Implicit in many of the comments on both sites was the hope that one's own story would help others to heal or at least understand the grief that they feel, as the commenter's remark that "the pain never goes away. It just gets 'different'" seemed to suggest. But users also hoped to provide themselves with a psychic salve by writing out their thoughts and feelings. One user acknowledged that people may have "heard enough stories of Hurricane Katrina" but stated, "The rest of this story is my psychological outlet for what has built up for a year." Later in the entry, the user wondered, "How do I condense the rest and make it meaningful?" but decided to continue with his lengthy story "because this is my therapy, finally." Similarly, one September 11 survivor put this hopeful spin on the disaster's painful aftermath: "The images and memories are haunting me, and the scars are very deep at this moment. I'm not always able to keep it together emotionally. But despite the horror of it all, there is a great feeling of hope inside me. I must be around for some reason, and I certainly intend to find out."

Thus, many of the messages left by survivors, victims' family members, and distant spectators appropriated rhetoric from the language of therapeutic self-help. Occasionally this came in the form of a "cross-counseling" dialogue that offered palliative advice to other imagined readers who shared in one's suffering over a disaster. At other times, the act of contributing to these memorials was explicitly framed as self-help, as a way to work through one's own trauma by the simple act of telling one's story.

Although the comments quoted above explicitly addressed the therapeutic quality of such online commemoration, many other messages focused on healing of a more traditional, spiritual nature. Some of the most frequently expressed sentiments in the messages left at both the September 11 Digital Archive and the Hurricane Digital Memory Bank were explicitly religious. Thirty-three percent of messages in the September 11 archive contained religious references (although some were simply phrases such as "God Bless America"), while 12 percent of the Hurricane Digital Memory Bank postings contained religious content. Many authors, such as the following who posted to the September 11 collection, were steadfast in their religious beliefs:

> Watching the news the entire evening with our children was a difficult but memorable experience. We had an opportunity to explain why evil exist in light of what the Bible teaches. More importantly, it provided a reference point for giving them an eternal perspective to the fallen nature of this world and the hope we have when Jesus Christ returns. . . . In many respects, although I would never wish the atrocity on any other human being, I'm glad that my children were exposed to the tragedy.

Some users also found these tragedies to be cause for religiously motivated introspection. A post in the 9/11 archive mused, "To say God has a plan is all well and good I suppose, but the hijackers also believed they were carrying out God's plan didn't they?" And a Hurricane memory bank user admitted:

> I'm still trying to work through why my life and the lives of my children were spared. Why was I at the right place at the right time when so many clearly were not? Do I have an obligation to the people who suffered so directly and profoundly? If so,

what is it? If not, why not? Is life that random? And if life is that random then why do we spend so much time in churches, synagogues, and mosques?

Such musings combined questions about luck and theodicy with concerns over the moral obligation to help others in need. These same sorts of questions have become commonplace in other parts of American popular culture, as well, especially on daytime talk shows (Illouz 2003).

Many entries at these sites reflected a basic desire to express or vent one's emotions, especially one's fear, sadness, anger, or frustration. Some expressed anger at the media for inaccurate or overly sensational coverage. One submission to the September 11 Digital Archive asked, "The next time there is a major attack or tradegy in America, . . . the media, please DO NOT constantly bombard us over and over and over with the same images. Think of what this is doing to the minds and hearts of the victims families, children, etc." A Hurricane Digital Memory Bank contributor critiqued the unsettlingly quick and ultimately inaccurate way in which television news media came to consensus about the initial effects of the storm: "All these reporters were reading from the same script. There was no healthy disagreement, as if the source of all the information was one guy." Still others focused their ire on the longer period of post-Katrina coverage, as did one author who wished "that the media would try to focus on the rebuilding efforts as they did with the destruction."

Similarly, anger was directed toward federal, state, and local government in 14 percent of the entries at the Hurricane Digital Memory Bank. However, such messages of anger were far less common in the September 11 Digital Archive. Instead, entries in that archive were much more likely to praise the federal government, as well as local police and firemen. When anger was expressed, it was usually directed at terrorists. One user summed up these post-9/11 sentiments this way:

> As the day continued into days and weeks and months, I became very proud to be an American as we were watching the heroics of all the police & fireman and construction crews

working around the clock to save people and recover the bodies of the victims. Regardless of the costs, we must continue the war on terrorism until it is wiped from this planet.

Other messages referred to the fear and sadness associated with these disasters. A typical user described September 11 as "such a sad day for America." Another stated, "I now felt that I was living in fear and that 'they' could attack from anywhere. Not only in the air, not only on land, but by chemical warfare. They could put things in our water; they could put things in our food, or even make us inhale things that were unsafe to humans. The question that still remains is why? And when will this end?" By providing an outlet for raw emotional expression, the September 11 Digital Archive captured the grief and paranoia of post-9/11 America; both websites offered the chance for users to undergo a kind of catharsis through such emotional sharing.

Another common trope in the messages on both sites—albeit one that appeared to span several of the categories I have tallied—was the notion that these disasters might ultimately have served a beneficial purpose by inspiring acts of kindness toward others, calling renewed attention to the preciousness of human life, or offering a chance to rebuild in an improved fashion. For instance, one user commented, "On that day, I saw the true New York that everyone knows lies beneath the usual reputation. NYC became one big village that day." Another commenter asserted, "In some ways, I hope we don't return to the days before September 11. We were, I'm sorry, but such greedy, selfish, self-absorbed, spoiled brats. Dear God, please don't ever let me lose my perspective again." And a Hurricane Katrina survivor ended her comments by writing that her "Katrina story now merges with that of all my co-workers, neighbors and friends who have returned to 'Rebuild a Greater New Orleans.' We are now part of a bigger story that will be written in the history books. The same faith that sustained us all through our travails will sustain us through the months and years ahead. Our individual stories will serve as prelude to that story, not as epitaph."

One contributor to the 9/11 digital archive said simply, "Remembering that horrible day helps to bring some closure for me." Indeed, this notion of "closure" is another way in which the experience of posting a message or story on a digital archive is a form of self-help. Such sentiments provided a measure of relief by describing a world in which one's nation, one's family, and even one's self had suffered but had nonetheless transformed that suffering into something positive. Of course, such closure is itself a construct of a culture in which "the focus on people's grief is common but mostly constrained by limited patience and expectations that the person will solve the problem within a brief amount of time" (Berns 2011, 11). Even in a context where disaster victims and their families may be wary of being exploited by the mass media, the assumption that "closure [is] real and something people need" (Berns 2011, 9) is shared by many. In this sense, contributing to a digital archive in the hopes of enacting some kind of healing is still part of the larger cultural turn in which the market offers solutions for grief and loss.

National Identity and the Limits of Empathy

It is safe to assume that most of those who went online and uploaded a message at either of these two digital archives did so, at least in part, due to some emotional connection to these disasters or those who suffered through them. But this emotional connection varied between the two disasters and caused two groups of people to submit to these sites in very different proportions. User-submitted stories and messages at both the September 11 Digital Archive and the Hurricane Digital Memory Bank tended to make reference to the author's experience with the disaster. Thus, it was generally easy to determine whether a respondent had been directly affected (i.e., had been in lower Manhattan or Washington, DC, on September 11 or in the geographical area hit by hurricanes Katrina and Rita), whether she had a friend or loved one who was affected (in the Hurricane Digital Memory Bank sample this occasionally referred to those who volunteered after the storm and forged close relationships with those who had been affected), or whether the respondent was not directly affected at all (as with the contributors who described watching the events on television, although many of these users would likely have described themselves as directly affected *because* they watched the events on television). (See Table 4.2.)

TABLE 4.2. USERS' CONNECTIONS TO DISASTERS

User status	Hurricane Digital Memory Bank	September 11 Digital Archive
Directly affected	73%	8%
Loved ones affected	10%	11%
Unaffected/distant spectators	10%	80%
Can't determine	7%	1%

Some of the stories and messages posted by those with affected friends or loved ones fulfilled a very basic function of memorials: commemorating the dead. Like spontaneous shrines in the physical landscape, these entries in the digital archives commemorated the life of a particular victim; in these cases, the entries' authors were usually friends or family members of the deceased. Some messages described what it was like to experience the loss of a loved one or commemorated aspects of a particular victim's personality. One user whose brother worked on the one-hundredth floor of Tower One wrote, "I could not believe what was going on and then when the towers collapsed my heart stopped. I sat there helplessly and watch as my brother die right before my eyes and I could not do a thing to help him, it was the worst felling in the world. . . . I will miss my brother very much."

Another described the loss of her close friend who was a passenger on American Airlines Flight 11: "My friend perished in the blaze aboard flight 11. She was a fighter and I am sure she did what she could to prevent those men from trying to get into the cockpit. . . . She is a hero as all who were on that plane and the other planes are. As the plane crashed through the tower with what I can imagine as terrified faces of those aboard, I envision her smiling face. Her lively personality, her generous spirit, her laughter is what I think of." Stories at the Hurricane Digital Memory Bank described such losses in similar ways:

> As the sun was going down on August 29, 2005, my 95-year-old, invalid mother died in my arms as we tried to escape the rising flood waters coming into our house by climbing the fold-down stairs into the attic of our house. . . . Without going

into exhaustive detail, I will simply say that my past life died that day with Mother and my dogs. I now wish to devote my life to living my life to be a blessing to others.

Yet messages written by those with affected loved ones were a relatively small percentage of the overall number of messages on both sites. In my sample of the September 11 Digital Archive, the large majority of stories (80 percent) were submitted by those not directly affected by the attacks, while 11 percent of the stories were submitted by those with an affected loved one and 8 percent by those who were directly affected. (In 1 percent of submitted stories, it was impossible to discern the author's relationship to the 9/11 attacks.) By contrast, the large majority of stories (73 percent) in the Hurricane Digital Memory Bank were submitted by those who were directly affected by one of the storms, while 10 percent were submitted by those with affected loved ones; 10 percent, by unaffected authors; and 7 percent, by those whose relationship to the storms was impossible to determine. Part of this discrepancy is surely due to the very different geographical reach of these two catastrophes. Hurricanes Katrina and Rita destroyed countless homes and properties across a huge swath of the country, and even those whose properties and homes remained unharmed may have had to evacuate for several days—a scenario that was described many times in the sample by those directly affected. By contrast, only those in or near the World Trade Center complex, the Pentagon, or the Shanksville, Pennsylvania, crash site of United Airlines Flight 93 on September 11 were directly affected in this same sense.

But another explanation for the fact that many unaffected people submitted stories to the September 11 archive while far fewer did so in the Hurricane Memory Bank has to do with the role September 11 played in constructions of American nationalism overall. Five percent of Hurricane Digital Memory Bank users framed their stories in terms of the local community—either as a crisis in their towns or cities, such as Waveland or New Orleans, or as a tragedy for the entire Gulf Coast—while only 3 percent described the storms as affecting the entire nation or as having repercussions for the United States as a whole. One user who applied a regional framework to Hurricane Katrina said:

> I love New Orleans, its people and culture. There truly is no other place like it in the United States. During my evacuation travels, people said ugly things like let it go, why go back, the sins of the city caused this, etc. I explained the life style here. They all marveled at it and understood. Do we tell the midwest to evacuate and leave forever because of tornadoes; or California people to leave forever because of fire storms and so on? Of course not. We will rebuild I said.

Entries such as this reflected the sense that, as coverage of Hurricane Katrina dragged on, Americans in other parts of the country began to blame the citizens of New Orleans and the rest of the Gulf region for the terrible aftermath. For instance, many messages sought to correct the national news media's portrayal of survivors as "looters," as did one contributor who argued, "The so-called looters are simply grabbing water, food, diapers and medicines, because the federal and state officials have refused to provide these basic necessities."

By contrast, the commemorative messages at the September 11 Digital Archive reflected an understanding of that disaster as a national event that largely transcended the regional boundaries of affected areas. Thirty-five percent of the September 11 archive sample framed the 9/11 attacks as part of American national identity, while only 2 percent described them solely in terms of the local community. One author commented, "Terrorists tried to bomb the life out of New York City, but ordinary people saved each other," yet such a New York–centered framework was rare. Instead, many authors of submissions to the September 11 archive ended their messages with some variation of the phrase "God Bless America." Similar national frameworks did not appear nearly as frequently in the hurricane archive, although one memory bank contributor did remark that "when Katrina hit, I saw a change in the way Americans view 'attacks' on the United States even if it was a national disaster compared to a terrorist attack."

The nationalistic response in the digital archive mirrors the overall reaction to the September 11 terrorist attacks in the mainstream media and in public life in general, all of which were flooded by an immediate surge of patriotism and support for the government. This was somewhat reflected in the September 11 archive sample, as well:

4 percent of messages expressed pro-government sentiments, while just 1 percent expressed anger at the government. One digital archive contributor used the site to describe her post-9/11 renewal of nationalism: "I've come to realize how much I love my country. I appreciate the people in the armed services, the firemen and the policemen more than I ever thought I would. I love the American flag." Another contributor expressed very similar sentiments on the one-year anniversary of the attacks, but with a slightly ominous, militaristic tone: "Today, a year later, our nation still stands proud, strong, and united, as promised by President Bush. As we keep those lost in this act of terrorism in our thoughts and prayers, the fight against terrorism continues. And trust me, the battle has JUST begun." This idea that the September 11 attacks were an act of war and that the subsequent war on terror was a just one was perpetuated by frequent historical comparisons to Pearl Harbor, which happened in 4 percent of the sample, making it by far the most frequent historical comparison, much as it was in the print and televised media discussed in Chapter 3.

In contrast, 14 percent of submissions to the Hurricane Digital Memory Bank expressed antigovernment sentiment directed at federal, state, or local authorities, while just 1 percent of those submissions praised government authorities. As one fairly representative comment from the memory bank stated, "In the immediate aftermath of Hurricane Katrina, the federal government did a terrible job. No doubt about that. Americans stranded on roofs. Americans without food and water. People in war-ravaged, dysfunctional nations looking at us on television saw that our country could be just as dysfunctional as their own." Another user lamented the lack of disaster preparedness on the part of the Army Corps of Engineers:

> Of all the things that happened that week, the one I cannot get over is that the city and the Army Corp of Engineers did not have an emergency plan to patch a levee breach. Certainly they would have a few helicopters or barges and a few hundred tons of sandbags sitting around waiting to be rushed to a breach. It was inconceivable that if a levee started to break the emergency plan was to watch it on television. But that, in fact, was the plan.

These sentiments were also in keeping with public opinion as a whole on Hurricane Katrina, which was largely seen as a failure on the part of numerous state and federal agencies (Pew Research Center for the People and the Press 2005).

The fact that most Hurricane Digital Memory Bank users were themselves directly affected by the storm, while most September 11 Digital Archive users were not directly affected by the terrorist attacks, reflects the ways that national identity has been constructed around September 11 by political and media elites in the past decade. September 11 was experienced as a national turning point in which unspeakable tragedy had called forth many acts of heroism and kindness and a renewed sense of American resolve. By contrast, Hurricane Katrina and the government's inept response to it became a mark of national shame. As such, although both of these disasters were witnessed by millions of Americans on live television, and although both monopolized popular culture for many weeks, people from all over America felt moved to commemorate September 11 online, while the majority of Americans who posted online reflections of Hurricane Katrina were those from the affected region. Despite its mission to collect and preserve memories of hurricanes Katrina and Rita, the Hurricane Digital Memory Bank abetted national forgetting as well as remembering, since few who were not from the immediately affected regions contributed.

Of course, all forms of commemoration and archiving necessarily involve the exclusion of certain perspectives, thereby enabling a gradual forgetting of details not included in official collections or representations. But in this case, the lack of a nationwide contingent of contributors to the memory bank speaks to the perception of those in the region that their plight was too quickly forgotten by the rest of the United States. One user described this as a waning of national sympathy:

> When Hurricane Katrina hit, our nation offered us sympathy. Millions of Americans accepted us into their cities. They sent 18-wheelers heavy with goodwill and provisions. Others came here, donned hazard suits and helped us. But I fear this compassion is wearing thin. It has been nearly 18 months. By now, the thinking goes, real Americans, self-reliant Americans,

would have picked themselves up by their stiff upper lips and gotten on with life.

This drying up of compassion—"Katrina fatigue," as some have called it—speaks to the limits of contemporary mass-mediated empathy. Inasmuch as it is possible to experience the pain and suffering of others vicariously, this experience is still refracted through one's own preexisting biases based on age, race, class, gender, or even geographical region. In addition, one may be more likely to engage empathetically with the kinds of suffering that reaffirm one's existing belief system rather than suffering that calls one's core beliefs into question. The pain of 9/11, with its grieving widows, heroic firefighters and police, and calls for national unity, confirmed the belief in American exceptionalism that many already held. Thus, many felt encouraged to post their reflections in a digital archive even though they did not know anyone who was directly affected by the attacks, a sign that September 11 was the whole nation's disaster and that vicarious, mass-mediated empathy in a national crisis was an appropriate response for distant spectators. Indeed, the promise of such communion and catharsis is part of the appeal of empathetic hedonism

Yet despite similar levels of media coverage and an initially similar outpouring of national emotion, Hurricane Katrina's victims were beset by various forms of victim blame and racial stereotyping (see Garfield 2007), which aided a national distancing and ultimately marked the disaster as a regional one, even though federal agencies such as the Federal Emergency Management Agency, the Army Corps of Engineers, and the National Guard had played such a large role. In that sense, the fact that so few unaffected individuals posted online remembrances at the Hurricane Digital Memory Bank shows that digital archives can also reflect the processes of forgetting that have occurred throughout American culture regarding Hurricane Katrina, and thus reaffirm the limits of our mediated empathy.

The Politics of Online Commemoration

The stories and messages submitted to the September 11 Digital Archive and Hurricane Digital Memory Bank exhibit several forms of therapeutic rhetoric and commemorative strategies that are also associated with sites of collective memory in the physical landscape. One very traditional type of rhetoric employed in these messages involved the use of religious language and references to God. Such rhetoric sought to provide comfort to an imagined audience of suffering readers—and, perhaps, to the authors themselves—through tried-and-true references to the wisdom of a higher power. However, some of these religious reflections also turned inward, adopting a more personal, diary-like style to ponder age-old philosophical questions about the role of God in times of great pain and loss.

Another seemingly traditional function of the messages at these sites was the commemoration of the dead. However, it is worth remembering that monuments and memorials to everyday people and victims of tragedies are, with some exceptions, a rather recent phenomenon. A number of entries coped with this commemorative tradition by labeling the victims of these disasters "heroes," since heroes have always been popular subjects for commemoration. But interestingly, some authors simply used their entries to describe personality quirks and other mundane details about the deceased. This reflects a more populist, less didactic style of commemoration, in which users themselves determine the significance of the words and images that are to be collected and made part of a memorial and in which mundane aspects of daily life may be deemed worthy of collection and memorialization.

In this way, digital memory banks and online archives sidestep some of the political questions about the representation of disasters within collective memory. Traditionally, archives and other repositories of collective memory in physical space have had to decide which documents and artifacts were worth storing and which ones they did not have room for, as well as how to display the artifacts they did collect. These decisions were necessarily political and frequently elicited objections "voiced by conservatives who abhor efforts of archives and museums to educate (and not only to edify) their publics" (Brown and Davis-Brown 1998, 20). While the memory banks described here did not have to deal with physical space limitations and thus were able to include any and all submissions from survivors, victims' family members, and distant spectators in an equal fashion, such inclusiveness meant that no larger narrative about the disaster existed on these sites. This may ultimately be a more equitable way to collect and store the past, but it does suggest a shift away from older pedagogical forms of commemoration that inspired political debate over what to collect and how to present it.

This movement away from explicit efforts at meaning making is a phenomenon associated with recent memorials in the physical landscape, as well, one that Kirk Savage has discussed in relation to the plans for a World Trade Center memorial:

> Some might decide that the best way to create a memorial that "evolves" is to avoid the question of meaning altogether, to create a "neutral" memorial that asks visitors to generate their own "personal and private" interpretations of the event. But another response to these requirements would be to confront the question of meaning, not to fix it or impose it in the traditional didactic manner but to frame questions rather than answers, still leaving room for understanding to evolve. (Savage 2006, 115)

In online memorials where users supply all or most of the content, the sites' creators have little ability to guide visitors or frame questions. Instead, the more haphazard navigation of online archives and memory banks allows for a panoply of potential experiences for users that, to paraphrase Savage (2006, 115), are just as likely to "inspire hate and a desire for revenge," as to create some sort of psychic healing or deeper understanding, depending on the particular entries one searches for or stumbles on. Moreover, one wonders whether the sheer number of submissions to these sites will make it hard for visitors in the future to find any particularly insightful or moving messages amid this cacophony of commemoration.

This remains a potentially problematic aspect of this new and democratic form of collective memory. Recollection of the past has always been an "active, constructive process, not a simple matter of retrieving information" (Schwartz 1982, 374). The "fundamentally interactive, dialogical quality of every memorial space" (Young 1993, xiv) means that we are all, to some extent, prosumers of history each time we visit even the most rigid of official monument sites. Digital archives provide a more literal version of the kinds of interactivity or co-construction associated with memorials in the physical landscape, by inviting anyone and everyone to contribute, and by refusing to rank those contributions. But the resultant hodgepodge of memorial messages is likely to forestall certain kinds of user actions and interactions even as it encourages others.

Most importantly, the difficulty of navigating as a reader through the multitude of submissions on these sites reinforces the fact that they are designed primarily as outlets for contributors rather than simply to be consumed by other readers. While the experience of the Box family described at the start of this article was certainly one in which a similar archive was successfully "consumed," these archives appear to be used more often for a therapeutic form of self-help in which prosumers can leave their messages and stories behind to enact their own psychological fulfillment. In that sense, these archives provide ample opportunities to work through the trauma associated with surviving a disaster or simply watching it on television and can simulate a kind of cross-counseling dialogue with an imagined readership of suffering others. Although emotional self-expression often generates new and somewhat unpredictable emotions (Reddy 2001), it seems fairly uncontroversial to believe that the public talking- or writing-through of one's pain or suffering surrounding a disaster can indeed elicit a positive emotional transformation and at least help ease a tiny bit of that suffering. In that sense, these digital archives and memory banks presumably fulfill their missions of fostering "positive legacies."

However, if one takes these digital memory banks seriously as therapeutic experiences, then the memory banks also warrant scrutiny on those grounds. Critics have taken America's popular faith in therapy to task for offering fast and simple solutions to complex problems and because "our emphasis on the individual psyche has blinded us to underlying social realities" (Moskowitz 2001, 283). Something similar may have been at work in the therapeutic messages within these digital archives, which largely presented disasters as obstacles that had caused pain and suffering for individual authors but that could and would be overcome by those individuals. Even messages that addressed the nation as a whole frequently transposed this narrative of individual self-improvement to a national context. As Eva Illouz (2003, 234) has pointed out, "Recycling narratives of suffering into narratives of self-improvement . . . erases the scandal of suffering." Thus, when a user explained that September 11 offered a profound lesson on good and evil for her young children and another hoped that America would never return to the "spoiled" days before 9/11, and even when a Katrina survivor spoke passionately about rebuilding a greater New Orleans, they risked minimizing the real horror and scandalous injustice of both these disasters, no matter how measured their language might have been or how understandable the impulse was to positively reframe these tragedies.

Critics of therapeutic culture have long suggested that such individual comfort may come at the expense of the larger, more conventional purposes of community (see Reiff 1966). The past several decades in the United States have seen "lifestyle enclaves" geared toward private forms of leisure and consumption supplant more traditional forms of communal organization (Bellah et al. 1985). Inasmuch as online sites of commemoration reflect this trend, then the simple act of reaffirming one's identity and having one's framework of meaning reinforced by others online is likely a therapeutic experience.

"However," writes Felicia Wu Song (2004, 144), "where communities had once functioned as a source of these identities and moral frameworks, there is now a tendency to emphasize how individuals can choose and construct communities that share and affirm their pre-established, self-derived identities. As a result, there is little to keep online communities from being reduced to communities of therapeutic function alone, again at the expense of external communal ends." Thus, one wonders about the aggregate effects of this largely individualistic, therapeutic approach to commemoration.

If there is a politics behind vernacular forms of commemoration such as digital archives and spontaneous shrines, then it is an individualistic one, in which the commemoration of individual victims serves as protest against the urge to forget or the depersonalization that is somewhat inherent toward victims of mass tragedies (Santino 2006). As John Torpey (2006) has argued regarding reparations politics, however, such a perspective is in many ways a poor substitute for the progressive visions of the future associated with older political movements. He asserts that "a legalistic, therapeutic, and theological attitude towards the past has tended to supplant the quest of active citizens and mobilized constituencies for an alternative future" (Torpey 2006, 15). This backward-looking, individualistic politics is essentially a form of nostalgia. As Maurice Halbwachs recognized long ago, "That faraway world where we remember that we suffered nevertheless exercises an incomprehensible attraction on the person who has survived it and who seems to think he has left there the best part of himself, which he tries to recapture" (Halbwachs 1992, 49). Such nostalgia was often evident in the messages at both archives, a fact that speaks to some of the more conventional or conservative qualities of these new forms of online prosumption. It also suggests that these archives have missed an opportunity to encourage a more explicitly collective experience, as thousands of users have been motivated to contribute to this new form of commemoration, but have done so in a largely atomized, inward-looking manner.

In this sense, therapeutic online commemoration may be at odds with progressive collective political mobilization around disasters, since it teaches that the mass suffering brought about by catastrophes such as September 11 and Hurricane Katrina is something to be overcome through many disparate acts of individual healing rather transformations in the social structure. Given the many problematic aspects of the government's response to both these disasters and the general hostility to collective action in the current neoliberal moment, it makes sense that digital memory banks and archives reflect the predominantly individualistic, therapeutic attitude toward many social problems in American society today. With no strong, progressive political movements emerging from these two disasters, at least individuals may find comfort for themselves at these digital archives, either by reading the messages of others or by contributing their own stories and reflections. Still, if the construction of "positive legacies" means more than simply making individuals feel better—if it means contributing to the creation of a more just society in which such tragedies are less likely to be repeated—then these archives may not be living up to their admittedly enormous missions.

Conclusion: Commemoration and Inequality

Recollection of the past has always been a subjective process in which meaning is made and re-made over the years (see Schwartz 1982). In this sense, the collective construction of historical memory has exhibited aspects of what may be called prosumption since long before various forms of online collaboration between producers and consumers made the term fashionable. War heroes, politicians, workers, teachers, screenwriters, television viewers, museum architects, archivists, and memorial visitors all participate in the co-construction, and frequent revision, of collective memory. We are all, to some extent, prosumers of history.

Yet collective memory is more than an aggregation of idiosyncratic individual recollections. As Jeffrey Olick (1999, 342) reminds us, "There are clearly demonstrable long-term structures to what societies remember or commemorate that are stubbornly impervious to the efforts of individuals to escape them. Powerful institutions clearly value some histories more than others, provide narrative patterns and exemplars of how individuals can and should remember, and stimulate memory in ways and for reasons that have nothing to do with the individual or aggregate neurological records." As bottom-up, largely non-hierarchical spaces open to any and all contributors, digital archives have the potential to challenge institutionalized forms of collective memory and top-down interpretations of historical events. But did these two particular archives realize that potential?

In some ways, yes, particularly as a challenge to the mainstream news media. Although they accounted for less than 5 percent of the overall submissions to the Hurricane Digital Memory Bank, there were nonetheless entries in that archive that exposed the flaws, inadequacies, or ethical lapses of the mainstream news organizations' Katrina coverage. As has already been discussed, some contributors sought to correct the frequent mischaracterization of storm victims, especially African Americans, as looters. In fact, pro-social behavior was one of the two most frequently occurring themes in the stories posted to the memory bank, appearing in 14 percent of entries and offering a much needed corrective to the notion that Katrina loosed mere anarchy on the world.

Some users of the memory bank even struggled with the ethics of media representation itself. One contributor described his media-induced disregard for the suffering of others and his eventual change of heart when he met an actual survivor of Hurricane Katrina. He wrote, "I'd seen the flashes of shredded houses and frantic victims of Hurricane Katrina on television. Sure, I'd felt pity for them and their families, but honestly, after the media stopped posting headliners of the disaster on newspapers, I'd let the event slip out of my mind. . . . It was horrifying what Katrina did, but it didn't really affect me." Another contributor described the events behind the creation of what eventually became an iconic photo:

> They told us we had to lay him at the side of the road. At my insistence he was brought to the entrance of City Park. I covered him with a green cloth and a properly folded American flag. When we saw him a couple days later the green shroud had been replaced by the unfolded flag. Someone told me that *Newsweek* had published the picture. It bothered me to think that someone may have changed the tableau (i.e., put the opened flag and lay it over the body) just to "get the shot." I think I'm OK with it now that I understand the picture might have had enough emotional impact to jar those with the ability to help out of complacency.

Such nuanced criticism shows that the Hurricane Digital Memory Bank offered thoughtful, alternative perspectives on the media's coverage of the storm and its aftermath and a venue in which those who harbored such perspectives could express themselves. Furthermore, unlike so many of the examples of disaster consumption described throughout the book, these archives have remained nonprofit ventures with no advertisements and no access fees. It should be noted, however, that less than 1 percent of the messages in the September 11 sample contained similar media criticism.

Besides critiquing mainstream media, both of these digital archives essentially circumvented the political and cultural gatekeepers who normally decide on the content of permanent, official memorials in the physical landscape. Spontaneous commemorators of tragedy online and in the physical landscape were able to have a say in the content of the memorials they helped create, even if they had no training in architecture or design and even if neither they nor any of their family members had been victimized. Furthermore, these contributors got to decide for themselves what images, messages, and stories were worth collecting and archiving, thus evading the power of archivists and museum curators to make such determinations.

Like other forms of vernacular memorial expression, this online commemoration also sped up the time frame of memorial creation. Rather than waiting to visit an official memorial that might have taken more than a decade to complete, spontaneous commemorators began to contribute to the construction of memorials on the Internet and on street corners and in city squares even while these disastrous events were still under way. This emerging norm of near-immediate commemoration has actually begun to change the pace with which official memorials are designed and constructed—for example, the 1966 shooting at the University of Texas was not commemorated with a memorial on that campus until 1999, but Virginia Tech had begun planning a temporary memorial on campus within weeks of its shooting in 2007 (Stearns 2008). New York City's Union Square was a similar site of spontaneous commemoration in the immediate aftermath of the September 11 attacks (Zukin 2002). Yet one advantage of vernacular spaces of online commemoration over spontaneous physical memorials is that online memorials have actually tended to last longer: although some physical locations of tragedy and death have become permanent shrines, the initial, vernacular contributions to these spaces are usually eventually moved away and either destroyed or housed elsewhere, especially if such sites are in everyday use or have been slated to be rebuilt.

That said, the bulk of what has been collected at both the September 11 Digital Archive and the Hurricane Digital Memory Bank has tended to reflect, rather than challenge, mass-mediated public opinion and conventional wisdom about these two disasters. The most frequently occurring themes in the messages of the September 11 archive, by a wide margin, were national patriotism and religion, thus mimicking much mainstream discourse in popular culture around that disaster. Along with the theme of pro-social behavior, anger at the government was one of the two most frequently occurring topics in the Hurricane Digital Memory Bank, followed very closely by stories of antisocial behavior, religious topics, and rebuilding or resilience. In both archives, such themes were entirely appropriate and understandable, but they nonetheless echoed the sorts of ideas commonly expressed in mass media and consumer culture, as well as those enshrined in official memorials and archives. Even the therapeutic potential of reading and contributing messages at these digital archives was very much in keeping with prevailing norms surrounding mass-mediated emotion and the empathetic consumption of others' suffering.

This is in some ways not surprising. The digital and the physical are not separate realms of existence but increasingly constitute each other (see Jurgenson 2011). They are subject to the same social structures and inequalities. But the fact that these digital archives reproduced the mainstream rhetoric and ideology surrounding these two disasters at least puts a damper on any kind of cyber-utopian longing for distinct alternatives to disaster consumerism. The problems of disaster consumerism in the print and televisual media follow it online, as well.

If the messages and stories of thousands of archive contributors are to be believed, these sites facilitated genuine emotional reactions, thoughtful responses, and descriptions of disaster in all of their messy, quotidian reality. There is certainly value in collecting such responses for posterity, even if they fail to contest prevailing belief systems or resist existing normative structures. Indeed, the mundane and conventional character of these messages are part of their seeming authenticity. As Pierre Nora put it in his discussion of an explosion of pre-digital archiving, "The less extraordinary the testimony, the more aptly it is taken to illustrate the average mentality" (Nora 1996, 9). An archive filled primarily with comments that were politically challenging, aesthetically sophisticated, or wildly idiosyncratic would likely be perceived as inauthentic and would appear as if it had been created by a specialized audience or group. Sites such as the September 11 Digital Archive and the Hurricane Digital Memory Bank, in which challenging or oppositional entries were tempered by many others consisting of ordinary details and conventional wisdom, are much more likely to radiate the appropriately authentic aura, which serves as an assurance to visitors that other regular people created these entries. If nothing else, such an aura helps establish the kind of trust in strangers on which therapeutic online encounters typically rely (see Song 2004).

Beyond its therapeutic purposes, the constitution of an aura at digital archives calls into question the larger role of authenticity in disaster consumption. As a set of subjective, aesthetic criteria, authenticity ultimately has to do more with form than with substance. In these online archives, authenticity was derived from open access to the process of record keeping and from one's ability to co-create a small portion of the records being kept. In other examples discussed throughout this book, it has emanated from shaky camera work, intimate close-ups of traumatized interviewees, frightened voices of normally calm news anchors, the home-made digital "manifesto" of a deranged killer, or artifacts and souvenirs taken from physical locations marked by tragedy. These cues to the authenticity of products or media have little to do with the substance of what is said or meant by disaster-related texts and commodities. In this way, the authenticity of disaster allows individuals with a wide variety of viewpoints and backgrounds to forge vicarious emotional connections, but in ways that are unlikely to challenge an individualistic understanding of disasters and their consequences. Such an understanding often reinforces the existing inequalities responsible for disasters in the first place.

To drive home this point, it is worth comparing these digital forms of commemoration with the official, physical memorials devoted to September 11 and Hurricane Katrina. The idea of a 9/11 memorial became a national priority almost immediately after the attacks, and the money devoted to that tragedy's three memorial sites reflects this. The cost of the Flight 93 National Memorial in Shanksville, Pennsylvania, has been estimated at $56 million and that of the Pentagon 9/11 Memorial, at $32 million. The budget for the World Trade Center memorial and museum is more than $500 million, which was drastically decreased after the initial plans topped the $1 billion mark (BBC News 2006; T. Dwyer 2006; Frangos 2006; Pitz 2009). By contrast, like much of the effort to rebuild New Orleans and the rest of the Gulf Coast, plans for an official memorial to

Hurricane Katrina have been modest and have received little national attention. The blueprint for rebuilding New Orleans initially called for a $3.5 million memorial (Bohrer 2007), but the actual design conceived and stewarded by the New Orleans coroner Frank Minyard is projected to cost just $1.5 million, plus $500,000 for perpetual care (MacCash 2007). It is telling, then, that the digital memorials studied here largely mimicked this unequal division of national interest and resources: the September 11 Digital Archive had many times the number of contributors as the Hurricane Digital Memory Bank, and those who did contribute to the latter were usually residents of the affected geographical area, in contrast to the national and even global reach of the September 11 Digital Archive. Thus, despite their potential to elicit powerful emotional responses and occasional critical inquiry, these two online archives constituted an authentic reflection of existing inequities rather than an authentic challenge to them.

"The commandment of the hour is thus 'Thou shalt remember,'" wrote Nora. "It is the self that remembers, and what it remembers is itself, hence the historical transformation of memory has led to a preoccupation with individual psychology" (Nora 1996, 10–11). The same preoccupation with individual psychology that Nora identified decades ago continues today at these two digital archives, in which so many came together to commemorate these two mass tragedies but did so in a series of largely atomized, inward-looking bits of autobiography and therapeutic memory work. These messages and their authors are ultimately a part of a collection but not of anything that might be labeled a community. Perhaps in the future, forms of online collective memory might emerge that are more explicitly concerned with social, rather than individual, change. Until then, let us hope, as one Hurricane Katrina survivor did, that "our individual stories will serve as prelude to that story, not as an epitaph."

CONCLUSION

THE DEEPWATER HORIZON OIL SPILL AND DISASTERS STILL TO COME

On April 20, 2010, the Deepwater Horizon oil rig owned by British Petroleum (BP) exploded and sank in the Gulf of Mexico, killing eleven workers and breaking open a well one mile beneath the surface of the Gulf that began pouring 1.5 million–2.5 million gallons of oil a day into the sea (CNN Wire Staff 2010). For the next eighty-seven days, BP crews, the U.S. Coast Guard, and scores of volunteers cleaned beaches, deployed oil containment booms, and worked to prevent more oil-related damage as BP sought first to cap the damaged well and then to plug the leak. The depth of the leak made the process of repairing the well and halting the flow of oil a painstakingly slow and frequently unsuccessful one, however, as various options failed or were halted due to bad luck, bad weather, or faulty technology. But after a summer mixed with both failure and incremental progress, the well was sealed on July 15. By August 4, the Obama administration had held a press conference to announce that the "static kill" procedure of pumping mud and then cement into the now capped well had worked to stop the flow of oil. The administration also announced that three-quarters of the leaked oil had already been captured on the surface, dissipated, or otherwise dispersed (Achenbach and Mufson 2010; Gillis 2010). When all was said and done, the broken well and its rapidly leaking oil had dominated the news media and the national consciousness during the otherwise slow summer news season and stirred widespread fears of ecological devastation.

Despite the positive pronouncements of relieved White House officials, the public still had reason to worry about the spill's long-term effects. White House officials had already admitted that the spill was likely the worst environmental disaster in U.S. history (Associated Press 2010), so many Gulf coast residents refused to take BP's and the White House's word on the amount of oil remaining in the water and about the degree of risk posed by the oil that did remain (Bluestein and Weber 2010). Subsequent scientific tests seemed to prove these residents right; they suggested that as much as 80 percent of the oil remained in the Gulf and confirmed that the sea floor was covered in oil for many miles around the spill site (Gutman and Blackburn 2010; Gutman and Dolak 2010). Even if the initial assessments had been correct, the amount of oil remaining in the Gulf would have been much greater than the amount in Alaska's Prince William Sound during the *Exxon Valdez* spill of 1989, and many Alaskan fisheries have yet to recover from that disaster (Klein 2010). Thousands of birds and other animals died or were hurt in the weeks immediately after the BP spill, and the damage from oil and oil dispersants to the larvae and eggs of crab, shrimp, and fish are expected to be severe, although exactly how severe is still unclear (Biello 2011; Dute 2014). Taking into account the Gulf of Mexico's incredible diversity and already fragile ecosystem, it is likely that many more animals will ultimately be hurt by the effects of this oil. Of the 1,728 species of plants and animals in the spill zone, 135 are unique to the area and 74 are already endangered; in the worst-case scenario, the spill will permanently alter the marine chemistry of the Gulf to the point that many of these species will simply not survive (Hotz 2010).

Thus, as with the disasters that preceded it, the deleterious effects of the BP spill were likely to persist longer than the attention of most of the national news media. One *Washington Post* story perhaps unwittingly revealed this dynamic: "Analysts compared the spill's tarnishing of Barack Obama's reputation to the damage Hurricane Katrina did to President George W. Bush's image. Both disasters tested presidential responsiveness and sensitivity. Unlike Katrina, however, the spill had staying power. Katrina came and went, leaving devastation behind, but the spill 'is this ogre that keeps coming at us,' one administration official said a few weeks into the disaster" (Achenbach and Mufson 2010, para. 14–15). Although the residents of New Orleans and other communities that have yet to be fully rebuilt would certainly quarrel with the notion that Hurricane Katrina "came and went," this quote unwittingly reminds us that all disasters eventually lack "staying power" in contemporary media culture. As Susan Moeller (2006, 186) put it, "Once the complications of reconstruction begin . . . the media cover 'simple' and 'complex' emergencies in much the same way, which is to say that they do not cover either of them."

Like most modern disasters, this one produced a variety of striking images. Photographs of the massive Deepwater Horizon rig burning and sinking into the ocean garnered early media attention, but the most iconic images came on June 3 when an Associated Press photographer took pictures of brown pelicans and other seabirds covered in, and presumably dying from, a thick, brown coat of oil at Louisiana's East Grand Terre Island. Video footage of the birds soon followed on most major news networks. At a time when the potential environmental impact of the vast and uncontrolled leak was really just beginning to dawn on the American public, these images provided the first concrete proof of the toll that the oil was surely taking on a wide range of wildlife throughout the Gulf.

Although the American public did not initially watch this tragedy unfold in real time as it had on September 11, and despite the fact that BP tried to restrict and control images of the disaster, members of Congress eventually received access to internal video feeds from BP's underwater rovers, which some of those representatives then displayed to news networks without BP's permission (J. W. Peters 2010). BP soon announced it would turn off this live video feed during its first attempt at a "top-kill" procedure on May 26 but relented under pressure from the White House (Werner 2010). The resulting broadcast of what turned out to be a failed attempt to plug the leak was, in the words of one journalist, "an Internet smash" (Jonsson 2010). More than one million people viewed the video embedded in PBS's website, and more than three thousand websites used the feed, which many television news channels also displayed. Although this video feed lacked the visual spectacle of other disasters, its large audience nevertheless speaks to the continued public appetite for live footage of disasters, as well as the perceived authenticity of such footage. Although it was frequently difficult to tell what was happening, and almost absurdly abstract at times, audiences trusted these images of oil ceaselessly billowing into the deep sea to reveal the truth of the matter—or, at least, to keep BP and the White House honest in their public pronouncements.

BP's initial attempt to withhold its own underwater footage of the spill was matched by attempts to block the access of journalists to sites where the oil had surfaced and reached land (J. W. Peters 2010). When coupled with the numerous gaffes of BP's chief executive Tony Hayward, which were heavily covered by a news media attuned to stories on political missteps, the company took a public relations hit that resulted in lowered stock prices and a nationalist American backlash against the suddenly foreign *British* Petroleum company (Gross 2010; Weber and McClam 2010). Many forms of spill-related consumer culture reflected the company's poor public image, as well. The company CafePress, which prints logos and designs uploaded by web users onto T-shirts, mugs, bags, and other products, had more than two thousand spill-related designs for sale on more than seventy thousand possible products, most of which contained slogans such as "give bp the bird" around a drawing of an oil-covered pelican, or bumper stickers that read simply "FUBP."

Much of the spill-related merchandise for sale at CafePress advocated boycotting BP, a sentiment with a strong presence in other online venues, as well. The Facebook account Boycott BP had more than 800,000 fans; the site BoycottBP.org boasted twenty-nine thousand unique visitors; and Public Citizen's boycott petition (http://www.citizen.org/boycott-bp) contained more than twenty-two thousand signatures. But the efficacy of such boycotts has also been called into question. As *Newsweek*'s Sharon Begley put it, "Just as buying green products is better for our eco-esteem than it is an effective way to save the planet, so consumer boycotts of the latest oil company to run afoul of public opinion are emotionally satisfying but ultimately futile" (Begley 2010, para. 9). Indeed, competing oil companies that would likely benefit from a consumer boycott of BP gas have similarly poor records on environmental and human rights issues. Unlike other famous consumer boycotts, such as the Montgomery, Alabama, bus boycott that jumpstarted the Civil Rights Movement, or the 1980s boycott of canned tuna that led to the adoption of dolphin-safe fishing techniques, few real alternatives exist for consumers who are concerned about the environmental effects of deep sea oil exploration and our general dependence on fossil fuels, since electric cars are not an affordable option for the bulk of consumers at this time (Begley 2010).

Perhaps as a result, public protests of BP and the oil industry in general took more symbolic, emotional approaches. For example, one organization called Hands across the Sand (http://www.hands acrossthesand.com) held an event on June 26, 2010, in which people gathered at beaches all across the country to join hands for fifteen minutes as a show of support for "protection of our coastal economies, oceans, marine wildlife, and fishing industry." Like the BP boycott, such events seemed geared more toward their participants' emotional well-being than toward addressing any concrete changes or policies. Indeed, one wonders whether the goals of protecting coastal economies and the fishing industry are at all compatible with the goals of protecting oceans and marine wildlife in any sense other than the symbolic. But, as with other forms of disaster consumerism, the personal demonstration of empathy in the face of others' suffering is an increasingly important cultural norm and participation in these sorts of symbolic protests is an effective marker of both empathy and sincerity. Tony Hayward faced heavy criticism precisely for his perceived lack of empathy, especially after he infamously told the *Times of London*, "I want my life back" (quoted in Guarino 2010) in the wake of a disaster in which eleven people literally lost their lives. President Obama was also criticized early on in the crisis for failing to exhibit an appropriate level of emotional connection. One Associated Press reporter regarded that as a motive for the president's later public appearances: "Eager to demonstrate not just command but compassion, Obama invited relatives of the 11 oil workers killed in the disaster to meet him at the White House, where he cuddled the newborn baby of one of those lost" (Benac 2010, para. 18).

The White House did take some concrete measures early on, including banning the drilling of new wells and all deep water drilling off American coasts. And two months after the spill began, BP started paying out claims to those people and businesses who had been harmed financially by this disaster. But by October 12, roughly three months after the leak was stopped, the Obama administration lifted its moratorium on offshore drilling (Baker and Broder 2010). Two years after that, BP pleaded guilty to fourteen federal criminal charges, including manslaughter and lying to Congress, and agreed to pay $4.5 billion as a settlement. "The terms were generally considered favorable for BP, which made $25.8 billion in profit the previous year" (S. Beck 2014, para. 27). That same year, BP agreed to an uncapped class action settlement that could cost it billions more. Since then, however, after paying almost $4 billion in claims, "BP has declared war against plaintiffs [and] their lawyers" by quite abruptly challenging the terms and conditions of the settlement (S. Beck 2014, para. 5). But whether or not these legal maneuvers are successful, the long-term effects of the spill on the health of the company are clearly less dire than its effects on the health of the Gulf. As one *Forbes* writer put it:

> Realistically, the answer to the question of whether or not BP's public image has recovered is simply "it really doesn't matter." As long as BP sells oil in colossal quantities, it will continue to attract investment. Their share price may not have returned to pre-spill levels, but the company remains an economic behemoth and a major player in a commodity the world hopelessly depends on. The shape of the company's image among the general populace is largely irrelevant, because investors know mental images of Deepwater Horizon will not cause the end consumer in need of fuel to drive past a BP station on principle. And BP knows it too. (Olenski 2014, para. 11)

In these ways, the case of the 2010 Gulf of Mexico oil spill was a fitting end to this decade of American disaster. Like the September 11 attacks, Hurricane Katrina, the Virginia Tech shootings, and the financial crisis, it became a kind of "public drama" (Monahan 2010) or "disaster marathon" (Blondheim and Liebes 2002) to which high numbers of media viewers remained attuned. Although the initial sinking of the oil rig was not viewed in real time as September 11 or Hurricane Katrina had been, the obsession with the underwater footage and the ability to follow live as BP attempted to cap the well does speak to the same desire for authentic and intimate ways to experience disasters. The variety of souvenirs and forms of charitable giving that the spill generated also speak to a trickling down of public concern into more mundane consumer behaviors. Perhaps most importantly, the fact that the broader causes of the disaster have not been systematically addressed—as our dependence on fossil fuels extracted by intractable and poorly regulated oil companies has continued unabated—means that like those disasters earlier in the decade, the Deepwater Horizon spill has also not made the country more secure in the long term.

It is not surprising, then, that Americans throughout the decade have appeared both transfixed by and uneasy with their mass-mediated experiences of these disasters. The September 11 attacks and Hurricane Katrina were the two most closely watched stories of the decade, with 78 percent and 73 percent of Americans, respectively, having watched these stories very closely. The condition of the U.S. economy in September 2008 was the fourth most watched story, while the Gulf oil spill was twelfth (Pew Research Center for the People and the Press 2010c). And yet a month after 9/11, 32 percent of the public thought there was too much coverage of the attacks (Pew Research Center for the People and the Press 2001b). Similarly, 21 percent of Americans thought there was too much coverage of Hurricane Katrina (Pew Research Center for the People and the Press 2005). For some disasters, such as the Virginia Tech shootings, the number of Americans objecting to the amount of news coverage has reached as high as 50 percent (Pew Research Center for the People and the Press 2007).

Many academics have used this public discomfort about the amount of disaster news coverage as a jumping-off point to critique the presumed effects of such an abundance of disaster news and imagery. On the one hand, there is a sense that such media inflame the public's taste for "disaster pornography" such that "viewers . . . do not need to comprehend the causes and implications of disaster because they become addicted to a perverted form of reality television" (Bates and Ahmed 2007, 197–198). At the same time, scholars argue that this intense attachment creates a waning of affect, an "empty empathy" that occurs when news organizations present their audience "with a daily barrage of images that are merely fragments of a large, complex situation" (Kaplan 2005, 93). As Susan Moeller (1999, 9) confusingly put it, "How they typically cover crises helps us to feel overstimulated and bored all at once."

Such claims invite scrutiny. Disasters almost by definition generate a surfeit of highly emotional stories and powerful images. How else would news organizations cover such stories if not emotionally and with striking imagery? Should they ignore these central features of many catastrophes? Critics such as Joan and Arthur Kleinman admit that "the absent image is also a form of political appropriation; public silence is perhaps more terrifying than being overwhelmed by public images of atrocity" (Kleinman and Kleinman 1996, 17). Yet they go on to advocate the simultaneously vague and grandiose position that "we must first make sure that the biases of commercial emphasis on profit-making, the partisan agendas of political ideologies, and the narrow technical interests that serve primarily professional groups are understood and their influence controlled" (Kleinman and Kleinman 1996, 18). But what would such media look like? How would it attend to the public's concern for the suffering of others? How would it "creat[e] public memory that could motivate efforts towards social justice" (Bates and Ahmed 2007, 197)? How would it actually help the victims of disaster in ways that our current media do not? Critics are typically ambiguous on these matters, and history offers few examples to guide us.

Of course, this supposed media-induced waning of concern for the suffering of others has not been born out when measured by the amount of disaster-related charitable giving. Americans donated more than $2.8 billion after the September 11 attacks and increased that to $5.3 billion after Hurricane Katrina. This generosity was not focused only domestically—in 2004, Americans gave $1.93 billion to relief efforts for the Southeast Asian tsunami, and by the decade's end, even in the midst of a crushing recession, Americans still gave $1.45 billion in response to the Haiti earthquake (Aaron Smith 2011). The Ethiopia famine of 1984–1985 is often regarded as the moment in which "instead of charitable giving being seen as worthy and a little dull, it became hip and cool" (Franks 2013, para. 6). But according to the American Red Cross, charitable giving for the disasters of this past decade far outstrips American donations for crises in the 1980s such as the Ethiopian famine or the Mexico City earthquake (Kasindorf 2005). Although such donations are not the only way one might measure Americans' concern for the suffering of others, in the face of such charitable outpourings it seems hard to argue that our increased attention to disasters results in mere boredom or empty sentiment. In the aftermath of catastrophe, Americans clearly want to help. What other avenues are open to us?

True, in the age of the Internet it has never been easier to make a donation or buy a T-shirt whose proceeds go to charity—such gestures do not require much commitment. But for most of us, this sort of consumption remains the most readily available way to publicly express our feelings about tragedies, disasters, and the suffering of others. Seen in that light, the consumption of disaster is really an expression of powerlessness. Following a disaster through the maelstrom of cable television news cycles, buying a souvenir, attending a concert, texting a donation, watching a documentary, or visiting a disaster site: all of these behaviors simulate a kind of control over catastrophes that in reality eludes us. In this way, the empathic ideal behind many forms of disaster consumption reveals itself as an illusion of agency: it makes us feel better about our actual helplessness in the face of mass tragedy, at least until the next disaster comes along to throw that sense of agency once again into doubt. This marks the authenticity of disasters as particularly paradoxical. Certainly disasters are deeply real, with terrible consequences that can be felt by victims, seen by spectators, and measured by reporters, scientists, and government officials. But disasters are also captured, packaged, and sold to their distant spectators in ways that encourage *empathetic hedonism* first and foremost. Imagining another's pain is a powerful form of engagement but, as an act of imagination, it is still ultimately an illusory one.

One of the particular illusions encouraged by disaster consumption is the notion that individual consumption choices can effectively ensure one's safety from future risks and threats. The "consumerism of security" (Sturken 2007) that became so visible after the attacks of September 11 allowed consumers to attempt to take their protection into their own hands. Such security-minded consumption often proves wrong-headed, however, and may actually exacerbate risks. Moreover, by its very nature this sort of retrospective consumption of security is doomed to fail, since it is geared toward disaster scenarios that have already happened and are therefore very unlikely to be repeated. That is the case with the various types of executive parachutes that appeared on the market after 9/11, which are not proven to work and may deter people trapped in skyscrapers from using fireproof staircases or other, more realistic escape methods (ABC News n.d.). In a different context, fear of environmental pollution and unsafe tap water have spurred spectacular growth in the sale of bottled water over the past quarter century, which ultimately has produced massive amounts of plastic waste that is highly detrimental to the environment (Szasz 2007). Americans also frequently keep guns in their homes as a form of protection, despite the fact that those with firearms in the home are at much greater risk of homicide or other violent death (Cummings et al. 1997; Kellerman et al. 1993). Similarly, the ease with which Americans can purchase firearms in the name of self-defense makes mass shootings such as the massacre at Virginia Tech more likely (Kellner 2008). And if we think of the wars in Iraq and Afghanistan as a kind of product that was marketed and ultimately sold to the American public after 9/11 on the grounds that it would make us safer (see T. Miller 2007), it seems clear that this consumption of security has also backfired, as these conflicts have spurred anti-American rage across the globe, inspired more recent acts of terrorism, and generally destabilized the entire Middle East. Thus, attempting to consume one's way to safety and security can have a variety of disastrous consequences.

At the same time, American society continues to showcase a profound lack of risk aversion among its elite decision makers, at least in part because ignorance of risks is so profitable for those in positions of power. As former New York Governor Eliot Spitzer put it:

> It's a depressingly familiar story: A company hides enormous risk in its effort to get outsize returns, hoping that if and when

the risk metastasizes, somebody else will have to pick up the tab. The name of the company may change, the sector of the economy may differ, but the basic narrative is as predictable as a Hollywood sequel. Our two recent cataclysms—the financial meltdown of the past several years, and the more recent eco-disaster in the Gulf of Mexico—follow this pattern. (Spitzer 2010, para. 1–2)

Like the giant financial companies whose "too big to fail" status assured them of government bailouts when the wild profits from their riskiest trading schemes dried up and their debt quickly turned toxic, BP's status as the largest oil producer in the United States (N. Graham 2010) has guaranteed that it will continue to thrive after the spill, which may not be the case for the Gulf's ecosystem or its coastal economy (Elliott 2015).

Nonetheless, understanding the individualistic cultural and political context in which disaster consumption takes place today makes denunciations of those who engage in it seem patently unfair. As consumers, we are tasked with purchasing our own safety and security from risk, despite the aforementioned ways in which consumer society often generates or exacerbates those same risks. This is necessarily an antisocial proposition, because securing only oneself necessarily means shifting the threat to others. Since consuming one's own security has emerged as the norm, it has become an increasingly large gamble to throw in one's lot with that of one's neighbors and community. Zygmunt Bauman has explained the results of this individualistic ideology: "Whatever happens to an individual can be retrospectively interpreted as further confirmation of their sole and inalienable responsibility for their individual plight—and for adversities as much as successes" (Bauman 2008, 22). This individualism often intersects with older forms of discrimination based on class and race but provides a new way to blame the victims of inequality and structural racism. Such was certainly the case during Hurricane Katrina, when the city's evacuation plan, based on access to private transportation, predictably failed the many low-income residents who did not own automobiles (Bartling 2006). Although decades of uneven development and terrible urban planning left many poor, minority residents stuck in the city as the hurricane approached, those residents were demonized in the storm's aftermath for not driving out of the city and then for "looting" much needed supplies from flooded or abandoned stores.

Individuals are also urged today to perform and maintain an attractive, authentic, and even saleable form of selfhood in the face of increasingly unstable family situations and labor markets (Bauman 2007). Self-help books, management guides, and psychotherapists frequently emphasize multi-perspectivalism and empathy (Illouz 2008). Mass culture ultimately translates America's "grand meritocratic promise" into a matter of "self-invention via commodities" (T. Miller 2008, 2). These trends converge during catastrophes, when news media and popular culture make the suffering of others a common public topic of discussion that requires our attention and our demonstrations of empathy, lest we appear insensitive to families, friends, employers, or potential love interests. As the empathetic gaze becomes embedded in more forms of media and the norms associated with empathic hedonism ascend, the lack of a strong, personal, emotional response to any mass-mediated American tragedy is increasingly likely to reflect poorly on individual consumers, just as it does for corporate spokespeople and government officials.

When all is said and done, then, the atomistic properties of consumerism make it a poor answer to disaster. Empathy may reflect well on us as individuals, but can it inspire sustained social and political changes or just disparate acts of charitable giving? While empathetically motivated donations of money or time certainly help, they still suffer from a reactive, backward-looking perspective that ensures the next disaster is as likely as ever. Of course, consumption choices do not always crowd out other forms of activism (see Willis and Schor 2012), but it may nonetheless be the case that progressive, grassroots activism operates in a slower time frame than can accommodate the immediacy of disasters. For instance, although Virginia Tech was the center of a national outpouring of emotional and monetary support after the massacre there, the lack of support for new federal gun regulation afterward set the stage for subsequent shootings in places such as Aurora, Colorado, and Newtown, Connecticut. The National Rifle Association (NRA) has even used these more recent shootings to successfully advocate for the relaxation of existing gun restrictions, including in some instances those that keep firearms out of schools (Beauchamp 2013; Childress 2013). Of course, a complicated politics with a multitude of interest groups is at work here, but at the very least, the failure of gun control advocates and the success of the ever-powerful NRA in the wake of high-profile school shootings have shocked many observers (see Lucas 2014; O'Keefe and Rucker 2013).

This should remind us that governments, corporations, and lobbyists can respond to disasters much more effectively than individuals, though often in only their own, elite interests. As individual consumers concerned with making our world better and safer, we have limited options. Green consumerism will be a niche market, or an empty marketing ploy, unless new laws require many more products to become green and unless regulatory agencies stringently enforce such laws. Even as mainstream consumers increasingly seek out ethically produced commodities, those commodities are subject to corporate "greenwashing" efforts that may merely simulate some sort of social good (K. Brown 2013; see also King 2006). Similarly, tourism-based redevelopment strategies in New Orleans that accentuate the city's authenticity and distinctiveness have often been "silent about issues of social justice, equity, and inclusion" (Gotham 2007). Indeed, cities such as New Orleans will likely be rebuilt only in the interest of developers who plan to gentrify the most desirable areas and shut out the poorest residents unless the federal government takes a more proactive role in the process and does so in ways that take into account the needs of its poor and working-class citizens (see Green, Kouassi, and Mambo 2013). This is, of course, in direct contrast to the way the American government actually operates in the current political moment, dominated by neoliberalism and its related privatization schemes. Yet until these conditions change, the consumerism of security will resemble a kind of "political anesthesia" (Szasz 2007, 195) that diminishes one's sense of risk and reduces the sense of urgency to make political demands about the alleviation of potential hazards. And until those conditions change, the benefits of empathetic spectatorship will manifest primarily for the individual viewer, not for those suffering others to whom that empathy is directed.

Disasters are a kind of commodity, and the ones we value most are often the most immediate and sensational. This does not bode well for their progressive political potential. As we have seen, disasters such as September 11 that are spectacular and novel are easily steered toward disastrous policy outcomes such as the Patriot Act and the wars in Afghanistan and Iraq. Disasters that take longer to develop or that lack a sense of novelty and spectacle may provide a greater opportunity for public debate, as was the case in the financial crisis and, to an extent, in the Deepwater Horizon spill. The oil spill did manage to generate some public debate about the disastrous nature of that particularly cherished American commodity. But even with the huge opportunity that the spill provided for environmental groups to highlight the problem of global warming and the high economic and ecological costs of fossil fuels, public opinion polls taken after the spill found little change in the percentage of people worried about climate change (Fahrenthold and Eilperin 2010). One poll about American energy policy taken three months after the spill showed slightly more support for "keeping energy prices low" than for "protecting the environment from the effects of energy development and use," though both options were heavily supported (Pew Research Center for the People and the Press 2010a). These results seem to suggest that grassroots progressive activists cannot always capitalize on disasters the way that governments, entrepreneurs, and corporations can.

History has shown, going back at least as far as the Lisbon earthquake of 1755, that elites frequently use disasters to consolidate power and eliminate dissent. But fifty years of disaster sociology have also highlighted the innumerable ways in which residents of disaster-stricken communities act with kindness and compassion toward one another, even under the most harrowing of conditions. As Rebecca Solnit (2009, 306) put it, "The joy in disaster comes, when it comes, from that purposefulness, the immersion in service and survival, and from an affection that is not private and personal but civic: the love of strangers for each other, of a citizen for his or her city, of belonging to a greater whole, of doing the work that matters. These loves remain largely dormant and unacknowledged in contemporary postindustrial society: this is the way in which everyday life is a disaster."

Perhaps, then, what distant consumers express when they sit glued to the television watching a disaster replayed over and over, when they buy T-shirts or souvenirs, when they mail teddy bears to a memorial, or when they tour a disaster site is a deep, maybe subconscious, longing for those age-old forms of community and real human compassion that emerge in a place when disaster has struck. It is a longing in some ways so alien to the world we currently live in that it requires catastrophe to call it forth, even in our imaginations. Nevertheless, the actions of unadulterated goodwill that become commonplace in harrowing conditions represent the truly authentic form of humanity that all of us, to one degree or another, chase after in contemporary mass culture every day. And while it is certainly a bit foolhardy to seek authentic humanity through disaster-related media and culture, the sheer strength of that desire was evident in the public's response to all the disasters, crises, and catastrophes to hit the United States in the first decade of the twenty-first century. The millions of television viewers who cried on September 11, or during Hurricane Katrina and the Virginia Tech shootings, and the thousands upon thousands who volunteered their time, labor, money, and even their blood, as well as the countless others who created art, contributed to memorials, or adorned their cars or bodies with disaster-related paraphernalia—despite the fact that many knew no one who had been personally affected by any of these disasters—all attest to a desire for real human community and compassion that is woefully unfulfilled by American life under normal conditions today. Perhaps that is the true aura of disaster.

In the end, the consumption of disaster does not make us unable or unwilling to engage with disasters on a communal level or toward progressive political ends. It makes us feel as if we already have, simply by consuming. It is ultimately less a form of political anesthesia than a simulation of politics, a Potemkin village of communal sentiment that fills our longing for a more just and humane world with disparate acts of cathartic consumption. Still, the positive political potential underlying our spectatorship of others' suffering—the desire for real forms of connection and community—remains the most redeeming feature of contemporary mass culture. Although that desire is frequently warped when various media lenses refract it, diffuse it, or reframe it to fit a political agenda, its overwhelming strength should nonetheless serve notice that people want a different world from the one in which we currently live, with a different way to understand and respond to disasters. They want a world where risk is not leveraged for profit or political gain but sensibly planned for with the needs of all socioeconomic groups in mind. They want a world where preemptive strategies are used to anticipate the real threats posed by global climate change and global inequality rather than to invent fears of ethnic others and justify unnecessary wars. They want a world where people can come together not simply as a market, but as a public, to exert real agency over the policies made in the name of their safety and security. And when disaster does strike, they want a world where the goodwill and compassion shown by their neighbors, by strangers in their communities, and even by distant spectators and consumers will be matched by their own government. Although this vision of the world is utopian, it is not unreasonable, and if contemporary American culture is ever to give us more than just an illusion of safety, or authenticity, or empathy, then it is this vision that we must advocate each day, not just when disaster strikes.

We must, then, abandon the notion that any particular practice of spectatorship is the right way to view the suffering of others. A world where we are less vulnerable to disasters will not suddenly appear if the media become more sensitive and humane. A world where risks are more evenly distributed and more equitably minimized for all people will not emerge because of disaster tourism or because of some popular backlash *against* disaster tourism. Others will not suffer less in the future because we turned our televisions, computers, or mobile devices either off or on or because we viewed some kinds of images and not others. The disasters of the past decade favored elites in almost every policy outcome in ways that have not necessarily made us safer, and all despite so much genuine fear, empathy, and concern from so many diverse viewers and consumers. New strategies of consumption and new media technologies are unlikely to change this. We must conclude, instead, that disasters do not favor progressive activists and populist politics. Social justice is, after all, a long, slow struggle. It is not typically spectacular. It does not often keep television viewers rapt with attention for weeks on end. But unlike many of the highly emotional yet largely symbolic forms of post-disaster spectatorship described in this book, it might just work. After all, much social science research attests to the greater mental health and physical security that accrue in more egalitarian societies (see Ward and Shively 2011; Wilkinson 1996; Wilkinson and Pickett 2009). The creation of a more just and equal society is, then, a way to make us safer and more secure in the face of a whole host of threats—from terrorism and natural disasters to gun violence, financial crises, and climate change. So it is to the everyday quest for a more egalitarian society that those of us who lived through this decade of disaster, and anyone else who wants to forestall such catastrophes in the future, ought to devote our energy, attention, and emotion.

REFERENCES

ABC News. N.d. "Parachutes for High-Rise Safety?" *Good Morning America*. Available at http://abcnews.go.com/GMA/story?id=126613&page=1.
Achenbach, Joel, and Steven Mufson. 2010. "'Static Kill' of Oil Well Deemed a Success." *Washington Post*, August 5. Available at http://www.washingtonpost.com/wp-dyn/content/article/2010/08/04/AR2010080403588.html?sid=ST2010080406374&sub=AR.
Akers, Joshua M. 2012. "Separate and Unequal: The Consumption of Public Education in Post-Katrina New Orleans." *International Journal of Urban and Regional Research* 36 (1): 29–48.
Almås, Reidar. 1999. "Food Trust, Ethics and Safety in Risk Society." *Sociological Research Online* 4 (3). Available at http://www.socresonline.org.uk/4/3/almas.html.
Altheide, David L. 1996. *Qualitative Media Analysis*. Thousand Oaks, CA: Sage.
———. 2002. *Creating Fear: News and the Construction of Crisis*. New York: Aldine de Gruyter.
———. 2006. "Terrorism and the Politics of Fear." *Cultural Studies, Critical Methodologies* 6 (4): 415–439.
Andrejevic, Mark. 2004. *Reality TV: The Work of Being Watched*. Lanham, MD: Rowman and Littlefield.
Aradau, Claudia, and Rens Van Munster. 2007. "Governing Terrorism through Risk: Taking Precautions, (Un)Knowing the Future." *European Journal of International Relations* 13 (1): 89–115.
Araújo, Ana Cristina. 2006. "The Lisbon Earthquake of 1755: Public Distress and Political Propaganda." *E-Journal of Portuguese History* 4 (1): 1–11.

Ariès, Philippe. 1974. *Western Attitudes toward Death: From the Middle Ages to the Present*. Trans. Patricia M. Ranum. Baltimore: Johns Hopkins University Press.

Associated Press. 2005. "CIA's Final Report: No WMD Found in Iraq." April 25. Available at http://www.nbcnews.com/id/7634313/ns/world_news-mideast_n_africa/t/cias-final-report-no-wmd-found-iraq.

———. 2010. "Gulf Oil Spill Is Biggest Environmental Disaster, EPA Official Says." NOLA.com, May 30. Available at http://www.nola.com/news/gulf-oil-spill/index.ssf/2010/05/gulf_oil_spill_is_biggest_envi.html.

Avenanti, Alessio, Angela Sirigu, and Salvatore M. Aglioti. 2010. "Racial Bias Reduces Empathic Sensorimotor Resonance with Other-Race Pain." *Current Biology* 20 (11): 1018–1022.

Baker, Peter, and John M. Broder. 2010. "White House Lifts Ban on Deepwater Drilling." *New York Times*, October 12. Available at http://www.nytimes.com/2010/10/13/us/13drill.html?pagewanted=all&_r=0.

Banet-Weiser, Sarah. 2012. *Authentic(TM): The Politics of Ambivalence in a Brand Culture*. New York: New York University Press.

Barnouw, Eric. 1966. *A Tower in Babel: A History of Broadcasting in the United States, Volume I: To 1933*. New York: Oxford University Press.

Barofsky, Neil M. 2011. "Where the Bailout Went Wrong." *New York Times*, March 29. Available at http://www.nytimes.com/2011/03/30/opinion/30barofsky.html.

Bartling, Hugh. 2006. "Suburbia, Mobility, and Urban Calamities." *Space and Culture* 9 (1): 60–62.

Bates, Benjamin R., and Rukhsana Ahmed. 2007. "Disaster Pornography: Hurricane Katrina, Voyeurism, and the Television Viewer." In *Through the Eye of Katrina: Social Justice in the United States*, ed. Richelle S. Swan and Kristin A. Bates, 187–202. Durham, NC: Carolina Academic Press.

Baudrillard, Jean. 1994. *Simulation and Simulacra*. Ann Arbor: University of Michigan Press.

Bauman, Zygmunt. 2007. *Consuming Life*. Malden, MA: Polity.

———. 2008. "Happiness in a Society of Individuals." *Soundings* 38:19–28.

BBC News. 2006. "9/11 Memorial Plans Scaled Down." June 21. Available at http://newsvote.bbc.co.uk/2/hi/americas/5101048.stm.

Bealer, Paula. 2007. "Short Stories: Empathy." Helium, October 26. Available at http://www.helium.com/items/666434-short-stories-empathy.

Beauchamp, Zack. 2013. "The First Federal Gun Laws to Pass since Newtown Are All NRA-Approved." ThinkProgress, March 22. Available at http://thinkprogress.org/justice/2013/03/22/1760131/the-first-federal-gun-laws-to-pass-since-newtown-are-all-nra-approved.

Beck, Susan. 2014. "How BP Decided to Fight the Deepwater Settlement." *American Lawyer*, March 5. Available at http://www.americanlawyer.com/id=1202643826256/How-BP-Decided-to-Fight-the-Deepwater-Settlement.

Beck, Ulrich. 1992. *Risk Society: Towards a New Modernity*. Trans. Mark Ritter. Thousand Oaks, CA: Sage.

———. 2002. "The Silence of Words and Political Dynamics in the World Risk Society." *Logos* 1 (4): 1–18.
Becker, Ernest. 1973. *The Denial of Death*. New York: Free Press.
Beer, David, and Roger Burrows. 2010. "Consumption, Prosumption and Participatory Web Cultures: An Introduction." *Journal of Consumer Culture* 10 (3): 3–12.
Begley, Sharon. 2010. "Boycott BP? Don't Bother." *Newsweek*, June 7. Available at http://www.newsweek.com/2010/06/07/boycott-bp.html.
Bellah, Robert N., Richard Madsen, William M. Sullivan, Ann Swidler, and Steven M. Tipton. 1985. *Habits of the Heart: Individualism and Commitment in American Life*. New York: Perennial Library.
Benac, Nancy. 2010. "Oil Spill Frustrates President Obama's Effort to Put Focus on Other Issues: Analysis." Associated Press, June 20.
Benjamin, Walter. 1969. *Illuminations: Essays and Reflections*. Trans. Harry Zohn. New York: Schocken.
———. 1999. *Selected Writings, Volume 2: 1927–1934*. Trans. Rodney Livingstone. Cambridge, MA: Harvard University Press.
Bennett, W. Lance, and Murray Edelman. 1985. "Toward a New Political Narrative." *Journal of Communication* 35 (4): 156–171.
Berger, John. 1991. *About Looking*. New York: Vintage International.
Berns, Nancy. 2011. *Closure: The Rush to End Grief and What It Costs Us*. Philadelphia: Temple University Press.
Best, Jacqueline. 2008. "Ambiguity, Uncertainty, and Risk: Rethinking Indeterminacy." *International Political Sociology* 2 (4): 355–374.
Bickford, Susan. 2011. "Emotion Talk and Political Judgment." *Journal of Politics* 37 (4): 1025–1037.
Biello, David. 2011. "How Did the BP Oil Spill Affect Gulf Coast Wildlife?" *Scientific American*, April 20. Available at http://www.scientificamerican.com/article/how-did-bp-oil-spill-affect-gulf-of-mexico-wildlife-and-ecosystems.
Bligh, M. C., J. C. Kohles, and J. R. Meindl. 2004. "Charting the Language of Leadership: A Methodological Investigation of President Bush and the Crisis of 9/11." *Journal of Applied Psychology* 89 (3): 562–574.
Blondheim, Menahem, and Tamar Liebes. 2002. "Live Television's Disaster Marathon of September 11 and Its Subversive Potential." *Prometheus* 20 (3): 271–276.
———. 2003. "From Disaster Marathon to Media Event: Live Television's Performance on September 11, 2001, and September 11, 2002." *Crisis Communications: Lessons from September 11*, ed. A. Michael Noll, 185–197. Lanham, MD: Rowman and Littlefield.
Bloom, Paul. 2013. "The Baby in the Well: The Case against Empathy." *New Yorker*, May 20. Available at http://www.newyorker.com/magazine/2013/05/20/the-baby-in-the-well.
Bluestein, Greg, and Harry R. Weber. 2010. "Static Kill Plugs Gulf Oil Spill Leak, but Much Work Remains." *Christian Science Monitor*, August 4. Available at

http://www.csmonitor.com/From-the-news-wires/2010/0804/Static-kill-plugs-Gulf-oil-spill-leak-but-much-work-remains.

Bodnar, John. 1992. *Remaking America: Public Memory, Commemoration, and Patriotism in the Twentieth Century.* Princeton, NJ: Princeton University Press.

Bohrer, Becky. 2007. "New Orleans Recovery Plan Calls for a Katrina Memorial on a 'Homeric' Scale." *USA Today*, May 28. Available at http://www.usatoday.com/weather/news/2007-05-25-katrina-memorial_N.htm.

Boltanski, Luc. 1999. *Distant Suffering: Morality, Media and Politics.* New York: Cambridge University Press.

Boorstin, Daniel J. 1987. *The Image: A Guide to Pseudo-Events in America.* New York: Macmillan.

Botterill, Jacqueline. 2007. "Cowboys, Outlaws and Artists: The Rhetoric of Authenticity and Contemporary Jeans and Sneaker Advertisements." *Journal of Consumer Culture* 7 (1): 105–125.

Bouson, J. Brooks. 1989. *The Empathetic Reader: A Study of the Narcissistic Character and the Drama of the Self.* Amherst: University of Massachusetts Press.

Bowman, Rex. 2007. "Sales of Tech Goods Hit Record." *Virginia Tech: Reflection and Renewal*, October 13. Available at http://media.mgnetwork.com/imd/VTShooting/article159.htm.

Boyle, Kirk, and Daniel Mrozowski. 2013. "Introduction: Creative Documentation of Creative Destruction." In *The Great Recession in Fiction, Film, and Television: Twenty-First-Century Bust Culture*, ed. Kirk Boyle and Daniel Mrozowski, ix–xxvi. New York: Lexington.

Broderick, Mick, and Mark Gibson. 2005. "Mourning, Monomyth, and Memorabilia: Consumer Logics of Collecting 9/11." In *The Selling of 9/11: How a National Tragedy Became a Commodity*, ed. Dana Heller, 200–220. New York: Palgrave Macmillan.

Brown, Janelle. 2001. "Across the Boards." *Yahoo! Internet Life*, November. Available at https://www.craigslist.org/about/press/across?lang=en&cc=us.

Brown, Keith R. 2013. *Buying into Fair Trade: Culture, Morality, and Consumption.* New York: New York University Press.

Brown, Nik, and Mike Michael. 2002. "From Authority to Authenticity: The Changing Governance of Biotechnology." *Health, Risk, and Society* 4 (3): 259–272.

Brown, Richard Harvey, and Beth Davis-Brown. 1998. "The Making of Memory: The Politics of Archives, Libraries and Museums in the Construction of National Consciousness." *History of the Human Sciences* 11 (4): 17–32.

Brulle, Robert J. 2014. "Institutionalizing Delay: Foundation Funding and the Creation of U.S. Climate Change Counter-Organizations." *Climatic Change* 122:681–694.

Campbell, Colin. 1987. *The Romantic Ethic and the Spirit of Modern Consumerism.* Oxford: Basil Blackwell.

Campbell, W. Joseph. 2001. *Yellow Journalism: Puncturing the Myths, Defining the Legacies.* Westport, CT: Praeger.

Cantril, Hadley. 1940. *The Invasion from Mars: A Study in the Psychology of Panic.* Princeton, NJ: Princeton University Press.
Carter, Bill, and Jim Rutenberg. 2001. "After the Attacks: Television; Viewers again Return to Traditional Networks." *New York Times*, September 15. Available at http://www.nytimes.com/2001/09/15/us/after-the-attacks-television-viewers-again-return-to-traditional-networks.html.
Charmaz, Kathy. 1999. "Stories of Suffering: Subjective Tales and Research Narratives." *Qualitative Health Research* 9 (3): 362–382.
Chayko, Mary. 2008. *Portable Communities: The Social Dynamics of Online and Mobile Connectedness.* Albany: State University of New York Press.
Chermak, Steven, Frankie Y. Bailey, and Michelle Brown, eds. 2003. *Media Representations of September 11.* Westport, CT: Praeger.
Childress, Sarah. 2013. "How the Gun-Rights Lobby Won after Newtown." *PBS Frontline*, December 10. Available at http://www.pbs.org/wgbh/pages/frontline/social-issues/newtown-divided/how-the-gun-rights-lobby-won-after-newtown.
Chouliaraki, Lilie. 2004. "Watching 11 September: The Politics of Pity." *Discourse and Society* 15 (2–3): 185–198.
Clark, Candace. 1997. *Misery and Company: Sympathy in Everyday Life.* Chicago: University of Chicago Press.
CNN Wire Staff. 2010. "Oil Estimate Raised to 35,000–60,000 Barrels a Day." CNN.com, June 15. Available at http://www.cnn.com/2010/US/06/15/oil.spill.disaster/index.html.
Cohen, Jonathan. 2001. "Defining Identification: A Theoretical Look at the Identification of Audiences with Media Characters." *Mass Communication and Society* 4 (3): 245–264.
Cohen, Lizabeth. 2003. *A Consumers' Republic: The Politics of Mass Consumption in Postwar America.* New York: Vintage.
Cohen, Stanley. 1980. *Folk Devils and Moral Panics: The Creation of the Mods and the Rockers.* New York: St. Martin's Press.
Collins, Coleman. 2010. "Coleman Collins Remembers Virginia Tech Tragedy." True Hoop, April 16. Available at http://espn.go.com/blog/truehoop/post/_/id/14975/coleman-collins-remembers-the-tragedy-of-virginia-tech.
"Congress Honors 9/11 First Capitalizers: Recognizes Those Who Rushed to Cash In on Tragedy." 2011. *The Onion*, January 18, 1, 7.
Corner, John. 2002. "Performing the Real: Documentary Diversions." *Television and New Media* 3 (3): 255–269.
Courson, Mike. 2009. "Raw Humanity, Not Contrived 'Reality,' Displayed in Biography Channel's Show *I Survived*." *The Underground* (Missouri State University), August 3. Available at http://www.msu-underground.com/archives/618.
Creamer, Matthew. 2007. "Big Media Blunted by Blacksburg Tragedy." *Advertising Age* 78, no. 17 (April 23): 2.
Crossley, Nick. 1998. "Emotion and Communicative Action: Habermas, Linguistic Philosophy and Existentialism." In *Emotions in Social Life: Critical Themes*

and Contemporary Issues, ed. Gillian Bendelow and Simon J. Williams, 17–38. New York: Routledge.

Cummings, Peter, Thomas D. Koepsell, David C. Grossman, James Savarino, and Robert S. Thompson. 1997. "The Association between the Purchase of a Handgun and Homicide or Suicide." *American Journal of Public Health* 87 (6): 974–978.

Dahmen, Nicole Smith, and Andrea Miller. 2012. "Redefining Iconicity: A Five-Year Study of Visual Themes of Hurricane Katrina." *Visual Communication Quarterly* 19 (1): 4–19.

Davies, Douglas. 1999. "The Week of Mourning." In *The Mourning for Diana*, ed. Tony Walter, 3–18. Oxford: Berg.

Davis, Mike. 1999. *Ecology of Fear: Los Angeles and the Imagination of Disaster*. New York: Vintage.

Dean, Carolyn J. 2004. *The Fragility of Empathy after the Holocaust*. Ithaca, NY: Cornell University Press.

Debord, Guy. 2006. *The Society of the Spectacle*. Oakland, CA: AK Press.

Deppa, Joan. 2007. "Coping with a Killer's 'Manifesto.'" *Chronicle of Higher Education* 53 (36): 64.

Deveau, Vicki, and Gregory Fouts. 2005. "Revenge in U.S. and Canadian News Magazines post-9/11." *Canadian Journal of Communication* 30 (1): 99–109.

Dolan, Mark K., John H. Sonnett, and Kirk A. Johnson. 2009. "Katrina Coverage in Black Newspapers Critical of Government, Mainstream Media." *Newspaper Research Journal* 30 (1): 34–42.

Dovey, Jon. 2000. *Freakshow: First Person Media and Factual Television*. London: Pluto.

Doyle, Don Harrison. 1990. *New Men, New Cities, New South: Atlanta, Nashville, Charleston, Mobile, 1860–1910*. Chapel Hill: University of North Carolina Press.

Drabek, Thomas E. 2010. *The Human Side of Disaster*. Boca Raton, FL: CRC Group.

Dumenco, Simon. 2007. "News Flash: Anything This Graphic Should Never Have a Logo." *Advertising Age* 78, no. 17 (April 23): 34.

Dunn, Robert G. 2008. *Identifying Consumption: Subjects and Objects in Consumer Society*. Philadelphia: Temple University Press.

Durham, Frank. 2008. "Media Ritual in Catastrophic Time: The Populist Turn in Television Coverage of Hurricane Katrina." *Journalism* 9 (1): 95–116.

Dute, Jeff. 2014. "Four Years after Deepwater Horizon Exploded, Long-Term Environmental Impacts from BP Oil Spill Remain Mostly Unknown." Alabama.com, April 18. Available at http://blog.al.com/live/2014/04/four_years_after_deepwater_hor.html.

Duttlinger, Carolin. 2008. "Imaginary Encounters: Walter Benjamin and the Aura of Photography." *Poetics Today* 29 (1): 79–101.

Dwyer, Owen J. 2000. "Interpreting the Civil Rights Movement: Place, Memory, and Conflict." *Professional Geographer* 52 (4): 660–671.

Dwyer, Timothy. 2006. "Groundbreaking for 9/11 Memorial at Pentagon Set." *Washington Post*, June 6. Available at http://www.washingtonpost.com/wp-dyn/content/article/2006/06/05/AR2006060501366.html.

Dynes, Russell R. 1998. "Seismic Waves in Intellectual Currents: The Uses of the Lisbon Earthquake in 18th Century Thought." Newark: University of Delaware Disaster Research Center.

———. 2000. "The Dialogue between Voltaire and Rousseau on the Lisbon Earthquake: The Emergence of a Social Science View." *International Journal of Mass Emergencies and Disasters* 18 (1): 97–115.

Dyson, Michael Eric. 2006. *Come Hell or High Water: Hurricane Katrina and the Color of Disaster*. New York: Basic.

Edy, Jill A., and Patrick C. Meirick. 2007. "Wanted, Dead or Alive: Media Frames, Frame Adoption, and Support for the War in Afghanistan." *Journal of Communication* 57 (1): 119–141.

Eichenwald, Kurt. 2012. "The Deafness before the Storm." *New York Times*, September 10. Available at http://www.nytimes.com/2012/09/11/opinion/the-bush-white-house-was-deaf-to-9-11-warnings.html.

"Eight Years after Columbine." 2007. Editorial. *New York Times*, April 17, A26.

Elliott, Debbie. 2015. "Five Years after BP Oil Spill, Effects Linger and Recovery Is Slow." NPR, April 21. Available at http://www.npr.org/2015/04/20/400374744/5-years-after-bp-oil-spill-effects-linger-and-recovery-is-slow.

Englehardt, Tom. 2007. *The End of Victory Culture: Cold War America and the Disillusioning of a Generation*. Rev. ed. Amherst: University of Massachusetts Press.

———. 2012. "What the Afghan War Has in Common with the Vietnam War." *Mother Jones*, April 10. Available at http://www.motherjones.com/politics/2012/04/afghanistan-vietnam-war-quagmire.

Erikson, Kai T. 1976. *Everything in Its Path: Destruction of Community in the Buffalo Creek Flood*. New York: Simon and Schuster.

———. 1994. *A New Species of Trouble: The Human Experience of Modern Disasters*. New York: W. W. Norton.

Ewen, Elizabeth, and Stuart Ewen. 2006. *Typecasting: On the Arts and Sciences of Human Inequality*. New York: Seven Stories.

Ewen, Stuart. 1996. *PR! A Social History of Spin*. New York: Basic.

"The Faces Emerge." 2001. Editorial. *New York Times*, September 16. Available at http://www.nytimes.com/2001/09/16/opinion/the-faces-emerge.html.

Fahrenthold, David A., and Juliet Eilperin. 2010. "Historic Oil Spill Fails to Produce Gains for U.S. Environmentalists." *Washington Post*, July 12. Available at http://www.washingtonpost.com/wp-dyn/content/article/2010/07/11/AR2010071103523.html.

Fairclough, Norman. 1989. *Language and Power*. New York: Longman.

———. 1995. *Critical Discourse Analysis: The Critical Study of Language*. New York: Longman.

Featherstone, Mike. 1991. *Consumer Culture and Postmodernism*. London: Sage.

Feenberg, Andrew. 2009. "Critical Theory of Communication Technology: Introduction to the Special Section." *Information Society* 25 (2): 77–83.

Fine, Gary Alan. 2001. *Difficult Reputations: Collective Memories of the Evil, Inept, and Controversial*. Chicago: University of Chicago Press.

Fisher, Lucy, and Hugh Porter. 2001. "The Online Community Stands Together." *Time Europe* 158 (13): 22.

Fong, Christina M., and Erzo F. P. Luttmer. 2007. "What Determines Giving to Hurricane Katrina Victims? Experiential Evidence on Income, Race, and Fairness." June 18. Available at http://repository.cmu.edu/sds/36.

Foote, Kenneth E. 1997. *Shadowed Ground: America's Landscape of Violence and Tragedy*. Austin: University of Texas Press.

Foster, Thomas. 2005. "Cynical Nationalism." In *The Selling of 9/11: How a National Tragedy Became a Commodity*, ed. Dana Heller, 254–287. New York: Palgrave Macmillan.

Fox, James Alan. 2008. "Fueling a Contagion of Campus Bloodshed." *Chronicle of Higher Education* 54 (25): A36.

Fox, James Alan, and Jenna Savage. 2009. "Mass Murder Goes to College: An Examination of Changes on College Campuses following Virginia Tech." *American Behavioral Scientist* 52 (10): 1465–1485.

Frangos, Alex. 2006. "An Expensive Memorial Mess on World Trade Center Project." *Wall Street Journal Online*, May 9. Available at http://www.realestatejournal.com/regionalnews/20060509-frangos.html.

Frank, Thomas. 2005. "Katrina Inspires Record Charity." *USA Today*, November 13. Available at http://usatoday30.usatoday.com/news/nation/2005-11-13-katrina-charity_x.htm.

Franks, Suzanne. 2013. "Why Michael Buerk's 1984 Famine Report from Ethiopia Entered Media History." BBC Academy, October 11. Available at http://www.bbc.co.uk/blogs/blogcollegeofjournalism/posts/Why-Michael-Buerks-1984-famine-report-from-Ethiopia-entered-media-history.

Franzosi, Roberto. 1998. "Narrative Analysis—Or Why (and How) Sociologists Should Be Interested in Narrative." *Annual Review of Sociology* 24:517–554.

Freud, Sigmund. (1921) 1959. *Group Psychology and the Analysis of the Ego*. New York: W. W. Norton.

Frosh, Paul, and Amit Pinchevski. 2014. "Media Witnessing and the Ripeness of Time." *Cultural Studies* 28 (4): 594–610.

Fry, Katherine. 2006. "Hero for New Orleans, Hero for the Nation." *Space and Culture* 9 (1): 83–85.

Furedi, Frank. 2007a. *Invitation to Terror: The Expanding Empire of the Unknown*. New York: Continuum.

———. 2007b. "Virginia Tech: A Massacre without Meaning." Available at http://www.frankfuredi.com/index.php/site/article/10.

Gammeltoft, Nikolaj. 2009. "Television Beats Internet as Source for Economic News, Pew Says." Bloomberg.com, July 15. Available at http://www.bloomberg.com/apps/news?pid=20601204&sid=aHgnSLvqgftE.

Gans, Herbert J. 1979. *Deciding What's News.* New York: Pantheon.
Garfield, Gail. 2007. "Hurricane Katrina: The Making of Unworthy Disaster Victims." *Journal of African American Studies* 10 (4): 55–74.
Gay, Jason. 2009. "Subprime Time: The Down-Market Sitcom Returns to TV." *New York Magazine,* April 12. Available at http://nymag.com/news/intelligencer/56018.
Gee, James Paul. 1999. *An Introduction to Discourse Analysis: Theory and Method.* New York: Routledge.
Giddens, Anthony. 1990. *The Consequences of Modernity.* Stanford, CA: Stanford University Press.
———. 1991. *Modernity and Self-Identity: Self and Society in the Late Modern Age.* Stanford, CA: Stanford University Press.
Gillette, Felix. 2009. "The Crying Game: I'm Sad as Hell and I'm Not Going to Take This Anymore!" *New York Observer,* April 7. Available at http://observer.com/2009/04/the-crying-game-im-sad-as-hell-and-im-not-going-to-take-this-anymore.
Gillis, Justin. 2010. "U.S. Finds Most Oil from Spill Poses Little Risk." *New York Times,* August 4. Available at http://www.nytimes.com/2010/08/04/science/earth/04oil.html.
Gilmore, James H., and B. Joseph Pine. 2007. *Authenticity: What Consumers Really Want.* Cambridge, MA: Harvard Business School Press.
Glink, Ilyce. 2012. "Study: Home Modification Program Falls Short." *CBS Moneywatch,* September 13. Available at http://www.cbsnews.com/news/study-home-modification-program-falls-short.
Gonçalves, Diana. 2012. "From Panic to Mourning: 9/11 and the Need for Spectacle." In *Panic and Mourning: The Cultural Work of Trauma,* ed. Daniela Agostinho, Elisa Antz, and Cátia Ferreira, 233–245. Boston: Walter de Gruyter.
Goode, Luke. 2009. "Social News, Citizen Journalism and Democracy." *New Media and Society* 11 (8): 1287–1305.
Goodman, Matthew. 2008. *The Sun and the Moon: The Remarkable True Account of Hoaxers, Showmen, Dueling Journalists, and Lunar Man-Bats in Nineteenth-Century New York.* New York: Basic.
Gotham, Kevin Fox. 2007. "(Re)Branding the Big Easy: Tourism Rebuilding in Post-Katrina New Orleans." *Urban Affairs Review* 42 (56): 823–850.
Goulding, Christina. 2000. "The Commodification of the Past, Postmodern Pastiche, and the Search for Authentic Experiences at Contemporary Heritage Attractions." *European Journal of Marketing* 34 (7): 835–853.
Graham, Leigh. 2012. "Razing Lafitte: Defending Public Housing from a Hostile State." *Journal of the American Planning Association* 78 (4): 466–480.
Graham, Nicholas. 2010. "BP's Profits Far Outweigh the Cost of Cleaning up the Gulf Oil Spill." *Huffington Post,* May 27. Available at http://www.huffingtonpost.com/2010/05/27/bps-profits-far-outweigh_n_591992.html.
Granberry, M. 2013. "Following the Zapruder Film." Video file, *Dallas Morning News,* May 31. Available at http://landing.newsinc.com/shared/video.html?

Gravois, John, and Eric Hoover. 2007. "In Media Res." *Chronicle of Higher Education* 53, no. 34 (April 27): A64.

Grayson, Kent, and Radan Martinec. 2004. "Consumer Perceptions of Iconicity and Indexicality and Their Influence on Assessments of Authentic Market Offerings." *Journal of Consumer Research* 31:296–312.

Green, Rodney D., Marie Kouassi, and Belinda Mambo. 2013. "Housing, Race, and Recovery from Hurricane Katrina." *Review of Black Political Economy* 40 (2): 145–163.

Greenson, Ralph R. 1960. "Empathy and Its Vicissitudes." *International Journal of Psychoanalysis* 40:418–424.

Grimshaw, Allen. 2001. "Discourse and Sociology: Sociology and Discourse." In *The Handbook of Discourse Analysis*, ed. Deborah Schiffrin, Deborah Tannen, and Heidi E. Hamilton, 750–771. Malden, MA: Blackwell.

Groom, Debra J. 2012. "Early News Reports Tell Different Titanic Tale." *Post-Standard*, April 15. Available at http://www.syracuse.com/news/index.ssf/2012/04/early_news_reports_tell_differ.html.

Gross, Daniel. 2010. "Home Equity: How the Gulf Crisis made BP British Again." *Slate*, June 19. Available at http://www.slate.com/toolbar.aspx?action=print&id=2257377.

Grove-White, Robin. 1996. "Environmental Knowledge and Public Policy Needs: On Humanising the Research Agenda." In *Risk, Environment, and Modernity: Towards a New Ecology*, ed. Scott Lash, Bronislaw Szerszynski, and Brian Wynne, 269–286. London: Sage.

Guarino, Mark. 2010. "Gulf Oil Spill Clean-Up: BP's Hayward Out, Dudley In." *Christian Science Monitor*, June 18. Available at http://www.csmonitor.com/USA/2010/0618/Gulf-oil-spill-cleanup-BP-s-Hayward-out-Dudley-in.

Gutman, Matt, and Bradley Blackburn. 2010. "Oil Spill: Government and Researchers Face Off over Estimates." ABC News, August 17. Available at http://abcnews.go.com/WN/bp-oil-spill-researchers-80-percent-oil-remains/story?id=11420557.

Gutman, Matt, and Kevin Dolak. 2010. "Oil from the BP Spill Found at Bottom of Gulf." ABC News, September 12. Available at http://abcnews.go.com/WN/oil-bp-spill-found-bottom-gulf/story?id=11618039.

Habermas, Jürgen. 1975. *Legitimation Crisis*. Boston: Beacon.

———. 2001. *The Structural Transformation of the Public Sphere: An Inquiry into a Category of Bourgeois Society*. Cambridge, MA: MIT Press.

Hagan, Joe. 2005. "CNN's Midlife Midwife." *New York Observer*, January 16. Available at http://www.observer.com/nodes/50342.

Haider-Markel, Donald P., William Delehanty, and Matthew Beverlin. 2007. "Media Framing and Racial Attitudes in the Aftermath of Katrina." *Policy Studies Journal* 35 (4): 587–605.

Halbwachs, Maurice. 1992. *On Collective Memory*. Ed. L. Coser. Chicago: University of Chicago Press.

Hall, L. C. 1902. "Telegraph Talk and Talkers: Human Character and Emotions an Old Telegrapher Reads on the Wire." *McClure's Magazine*, January, 227–231. Available at http://www.telegraph-office.com/pages/Telegraph_Talk-McClure-1902.html.

Hall, Stuart. 1980. "Encoding/Decoding." In *Culture, Media, Language: Working Papers in Cultural Studies, 1972–79*, ed. Stuart Hall, Dorothy Hobson, Andrew Lowe, and Paul Willis, 117–127. London: Hutchinson.

Handmer, John, and Paul James. 2007. "Trust Us and Be Scared: The Changing Nature of Contemporary Risk." *Global Society* 21 (1): 119–130.

Haney, C. Allen and Dell Davis. 1999. "America Responds to Diana's Death: Spontaneous Memorials." In *The Mourning for Diana*, ed. Tony Walter, 227–240. Oxford: Berg.

Hansen, Miriam Bratu. 2008. "Benjamin's Aura." *Critical Inquiry* 34: 336–375.

Hariman, Robert, and John Louis. Lucaites. 2007. *No Caption Needed: Iconic Photographs, Public Culture, and Liberal Democracy*. Chicago: University of Chicago Press.

Harper, Robert S. 1951. *Lincoln and the Press*. New York: McGraw-Hill.

Harris, Chris. 1999. "Secular Religion and the Public Response to Diana's Death." In *The Mourning for Diana*, ed. Tony Walter, 97–109. Oxford: Berg.

Hart, Roderick P., Sharon E. Jarvis, and Elvin T. Lim. 2002. "The American People in Crisis: A Content Analysis." *Political Psychology* 23 (3): 417–437.

Hart, William. 2005. "The Country Connection: Country Music, 9/11, and the War on Terrorism." In *The Selling of 9/11: How a National Tragedy Became a Commodity*, ed. Dana Heller, 155–173. New York: Palgrave Macmillan.

Hayes, R. Allen. 2004. "Habitat for Humanity: Building Social Capital through Faith Based Service." *Journal of Urban Affairs* 2 (3): 247–269.

Heatley, Holly S. 2007. "'Commies and Queers': Narratives that Supported the Lavender Scare." Master's thesis. Arlington: University of Texas.

Hechter, Michael, and Karl-Dieter Opp. 2001. "Introduction." In *Social Norms*, ed. Michael Hechter and Karl-Dieter Opp, xi–xx New York: Russell Sage.

Heller, Dana. 2005. "Introduction." In *The Selling of 9/11: How a National Tragedy Became a Commodity*, ed. Dana Heller, 1–26. New York: Palgrave Macmillan.

Hellström, Tomas. 2008. "Transferability and Naturalistic Generalization: New Generalizability Concepts for Social Science or Old Wine in New Bottles?" *Quality and Quantity* 42:321–327.

Herkenhoff, Kyle F., and Lee E. Ohanian. 2011. "Labor Market Dysfunction during the Great Recession." National Bureau of Economic Research Working Paper. Available at http://www.nber.org/papers/w17313.

Herring, Cedric. 2006. "Hurricane Katrina and the Racial Gulf." *Du Bois Review* 3 (1): 129–144.

Heyer, Paul. 1995. *Titanic Legacy: Disaster as Media Event and Myth*. Westport, CT: Praeger.

Hinton, Laura. 1999. *The Perverse Gaze of Sympathy: Sadomasochistic Sentiments from Clarissa to Rescue 911.* Albany: State University of New York Press.

Hoffner, Cynthia, and Joanne Cantor. 1991. "Perceiving and Responding to Mass Media Characters." In *Responding to the Screen: Reception and Reaction Processes,* ed. Jennings Bryant and Dolf Zillman, 63–103. Hillsdale, NJ: Lawrence Erlbaum Associates.

Horkheimer, Max, and Theodor W. Adorno. (1944) 2002. *Dialectic of Enlightenment.* Trans. J. Cumming. New York: Continuum.

Hotz, Robert Lee. 2010. "Scientists Try to Gauge Potential Long-Term Environmental Impact." *Wall Street Journal,* June 12. Available at http://online.wsj.com/article/SB10001424052748.

Hucheson, John, David Domke, Andre Billeaudeaux, and Philip Garland. 2004. "U.S. National Identity, Political Elites, and a Patriotic Press following September 11." *Political Communication* 21:27–50.

Hulse, Carl, and David M. Herszenhorn. 2008. "House Rejects Bailout Package, 228–205; Stocks Plunge." *New York Times,* September 29. Available at http://www.nytimes.com/2008/09/30/business/30bailout.html.

Hume, David. 1874. *A Treatise on Human Nature and Dialogues Concerning Natural Religion.* Vol. 2. London: Longmans, Green.

Huntress, Keith Gibson. 1974. *Narratives of Shipwrecks and Disasters, 1586–1860.* Iowa City: University of Iowa Press.

Ickes, William, ed. 1997. *Empathic Accuracy.* New York: Guilford.

Illouz, Eva. 2003. *Oprah Winfrey and the Glamour of Misery: An Essay on Popular Culture.* New York: Columbia University Press.

———. 2008. *Saving the Modern Soul: Therapy, Emotions, and the Culture of Self-Help.* Berkeley: University of California Press.

Izard, Ralph, and Jay Perkins, eds. 2011. *Lessons from Ground Zero: Media Response to Terror.* New Brunswick, NJ: Transaction.

Jameson, Frederic. 2002. "The Dialectics of Disaster." *South Atlantic Quarterly* 101 (2): 297–304.

Jeleniewski Seidler, Victor. 2013. *Remembering Diana: Cultural Memory and the Reinvention of Authority.* New York: Palgrave Macmillan.

Jenni, Karen E., and George Loewenstein. 1997. "Explaining the 'Identifiable Victim Effect.'" *Journal of Risk and Uncertainty* 14:235–257.

Jensen, Devon. 2008. "Transferability." In *The Sage Encyclopedia of Qualitative Research Methods,* ed. Lisa M. Given, 886. Vol. 2. Thousand Oaks, CA: Sage.

Jesiek, Brent K., and Jeremy Hunsinger. 2008. "The April 16 Archive: Collecting and Preserving the Memories of the Virginia Tech Tragedy." In *There Is a Gunman on Campus: Tragedy and Terror at Virginia Tech,* ed. Ben Agger and Timothy W. Luke, 29–54. New York: Rowman and Littlefield.

Johnson, M. Alex. 2007. "Gunman in Massacre Contacted NBC News." MSNBC.com, April 19. Available at http://www.msnbc.msn.com/id/18195423/print/1/displaymode/1098.

Johnson, Simon. 2010. "TARP, the Long Goodbye." *New York Times*, September 30. Available at http://economix.blogs.nytimes.com/2010/09/30/tarp-the-long-goodbye/.

Jonsson, Patrik. 2010. "BP 'Top Kill' Live Feed Makes Stars out of Disaster Bots." *Christian Science Monitor*, May 29. Available at http://www.csmonitor.com/layout/set/print/content/view/print/30486.

Jurgenson, Nathan. 2011. "Digital Dualism versus Augmented Reality." *Cyborgology*. Available at http://thesocietypages.org/cyborgology/2011/02/24/digital-dualism-versus-augmented-reality.

Kaplan, E. Ann. 2005. *Trauma Culture: The Trauma of Terror and Loss in Media and Literature*. New Brunswick, NJ: Rutgers University Press.

Kasindorf, Martin. 2005. "Poll, Charities Chart American Outpouring." *USA Today*, January 6. Available at http://usatoday30.usatoday.com/news/world/2005-01-06-poll-usat_x.htm.

Katz, Elihu, and Tamar Liebes. 2007. "'No More Peace!': How Disaster, Terror and War Have Upstaged Media Events." *International Journal of Communication* 1:157–166.

Kellermann, Arthur L., Frederick P. Rivara, Norman B. Rushforth, Joyce G. Banton, Donald T. Reay, Jerry T. Francisco, Ana B. Locci, Janice Prodzinski, Bela B. Hackman, and Grant Somes. 1993. "Gun Ownership as a Risk Factor for Homicide in the Home." *New England Journal of Medicine* 329 (15): 1084–1091.

Kellner, Douglas. 2008. *Guys and Guns Amok: Domestic Terrorism and School Shootings from the Oklahoma City Bombing to the Virginia Tech Massacre*. Boulder, CO: Paradigm.

Kendrick, T. D. 1956. *The Lisbon Earthquake*. London: Methuen.

King, Samantha. 2006. *Pink Ribbons, Inc.: Breast Cancer and the Politics of Philanthropy*. Minneapolis: University of Minnesota Press.

Kitch, Carolyn. 2003. "'Mourning in America': Ritual, Redemption, and Recovery in News Narrative after September 11." *Journalism Studies* 4 (2): 213–224.

Klein, Naomi. 2007. *The Shock Doctrine: The Rise of Disaster Capitalism*. New York: Metropolitan.

———. 2010. "Gulf Oil Spill: A Hole in the World." *Common Dreams*, June 20. Available at http://www.commondreams.org/print/57464.

Kleinman, Arthur, and Joan Kleinman. 1996. "The Appeal of Experience; the Dismay of Images: Cultural Appropriations of Suffering in Our Times." *Daedalus* 125 (1): 1–23.

Klinenberg, Eric. 2002. *Heat Wave: A Social Autopsy of Disaster in Chicago*. Chicago: University of Chicago Press.

Kogut, Tehila. 2011. "Someone to Blame: When Identifying a Victim Decreases Helping." *Journal of Experimental Social Psychology* 47:748–755.

Kohut, Heinz. 1984. *How Does Analysis Cure?* Chicago: University of Chicago Press.

Kosicki, Gerald M. 1993. "Problems and Opportunities in Agenda-Setting Research." *Journal of Communication* 43 (2): 100–127.

Kurtz, Howard. 2006. "The Media's New Orleans Burnout." *Washington Post*, May 7. Available at http://www.washingtonpost.com/wp-dyn/content/article/2006/05/05/AR2006050501744.html.

Landsberg, Alison. 2009. "Memory, Empathy, and the Politics of Identification." *International Journal of Politics, Culture, and Society* 22 (2): 221–229.

Lane, Anthony. 2001. "This Is Not a Movie." *New Yorker*, September 24. Available at http://www.newyorker.com/archive/2001/09/24/010924crci_cinema.

Langer, John. 1992. "Truly Awful News on Television." In *Journalism and Popular Culture*, ed. P. Dahlgren and C. Sparks, 113–129. London: Sage Publications.

Larabee, Ann. 2001. "'Nothing Ends Here': Managing the *Challenger* Disaster." In *American Disasters*, ed. Steven Bielm, 197–221. New York: New York University Press.

Le Bon, Gustave. (1895) 1960. *The Crowd: A Study of the Popular Mind*. New York: Viking.

Leigh, Thomas W., Cara Peters, and Jeremy Shelton. 2006. "The Consumer Quest for Authenticity: Multiple Meanings within the MG Subculture." *Journal of the Academy of Marketing Science* 34 (4): 481–493.

Leiserowitz, Anthony, Edward Maibach, Connie Roser-Renouf, Geoff Feinberg, Seth Rosenthal, and Jennifer Marlon. 2014. "Climate Change in the American Mind: Americans' Global Warming Beliefs and Attitudes in November, 2013." Report. Yale University and George Mason University. Yale Project on Climate Change Communication, New Haven, CT.

Lewis, Lloyd. 1957. *The Assassination of Lincoln: History and Myth*. Lincoln: University of Nebraska Press.

Li, Xigen, and Ralph Izard. 2003. "9/11 Attack Coverage Reveals Similarities, Differences." *Newspaper Research Journal* 24 (1): 204–219.

Liebes, Tamar. 1998. "Television's Disaster Marathons: A Danger for Democratic Processes?" In *Media, Ritual and Identity*, ed. Tamar Liebes and James Curran, 71–84. London: Routledge.

Lincoln, Yvonna S., and Egon G. Guba. 1985. *Naturalistic Inquiry*. Newbury Park, CA: Sage.

Linenthal, Edward T. 2001. *The Unfinished Bombing: Oklahoma City in American Memory*. New York: Oxford University Press.

Lloyd, Robert. 2009. "Walter Cronkite: And That's the Way It Was." *Los Angeles Times*, July 18. Available at http://www.latimes.com/entertainment/news/la-et-cronkite-appreciation18-2009jul18,0,5128038.story.

Lockard, Joe. 2005. "Social Fear and the *Terrorism Survival Guide*." In *The Selling of 9/11: How a National Tragedy Became a Commodity*, ed. Dana Heller, 221–232. New York: Palgrave Macmillan.

Lowrey, Annie. 2011. "Final Arguments: Was TARP a Success or Failure? It Depends on Who You Think It Was Supposed to Help." *Slate*, April 1. Available at

http://www.slate.com/articles/business/moneybox/2011/04/final_arguments.html.
Lubin, David M. 2003. *Shooting Kennedy: JFK and the Culture of Images*. Berkeley: University of California Press.
Lucas, Fred. 2014. "Dem Senator: Not Passing Gun Control Is a 'Stunning Failure of Democracy.'" *The Blaze*, July 16. Available at http://www.theblaze.com/stories/2014/07/16/dem-senator-not-passing-gun-control-is-a-stunning-failure-of-democracy.
Lupton, Deborah. 2013. "Risk and Emotion: Towards an Alternative Theoretical Perspective." *Health, Risk and Society* 15 (8): 634–647.
MacCash, Doug. 2007. "New Orleans Katrina Memorial Is Almost Perfect." NOLA.com, September 14. Available at http://blog.nola.com/dougmaccash/2007/09/new_orleans_katrina_memorial.html.
Mackay, Charles. (1841) 1980. *Extraordinary Popular Delusions and the Madness of Crowds*. New York: Harmony.
Man, John. 2002. *Gutenberg: How One Man Remade the World with Words*. New York: Wiley.
Manovich, Lev. 2001. *The Language of New Media*. Cambridge, MA: MIT Press.
Martin, Patrick, and Sean Phelan. 2002. "Representing Islam in the Wake of September 11: A Comparison of US Television and CNN Online Messageboard Discourses." *Prometheus* 20 (3): 263–269.
Marwell, Gerald. 1964. "Problems of Operational Definitions of 'Empathy,' 'Identification' and Related Concepts." *Journal of Social Psychology* 63:87–102.
Mason, Haydn. 1992. *Candide: Optimism Demolished*. Woodbridge, CT: Twayne.
McCosker, Anthony. 2013. "De-framing Disaster: Affective Encounters with Raw and Autonomous Media." *Continuum* 27 (3): 382–396.
McMurria, John. 2008. "Desperate Citizens and Good Samaritans: Neoliberalism and Makeover Reality TV." *Television and New Media* 9 (4): 305–332.
McRobbie, Angela, and Sarah L. Thornton. 1995. "Rethinking 'Moral Panic' for Multi-mediated Social Worlds." *British Journal of Sociology* 46 (4): 559–574.
Mencimer, Stephanie. 2010. "Glenn Beck's Gold Gurus Charged with Fraud." *Mother Jones*, May 19. Available at http://www.motherjones.com/politics/2010/05/glenn-beck-goldline-weiner.
Mercer, Philip. 1972. *Sympathy and Ethics: A Study of the Relationship between Sympathy and Morality with Special Reference to Hume's* Treatise. Oxford: Clarendon.
Metz, Christian. 1992. "Identification, Mirror." In *Film Theory and Criticism: Introductory Readings*, ed. Gerald Mast, Marshall Cohen, and Leo Braudy, 694–700. 4th ed. New York: Oxford University Press.
Mian, Atif, and Amir Sufi. 2014. *House of Debt: How They (and You) Caused the Great Recession, and How We Can Prevent It from Happening Again*. Chicago: University of Chicago Press.
Miller, DeMond Shondell. 2006. "Visualizing the Corrosive Community: Looting in the Aftermath of Hurricane Katrina." *Space and Culture* 9 (1): 71–73.

Miller, Toby. 2007. *Cultural Citizenship: Cosmopolitanism, Consumerism, and Television in a Neoliberal Age*. Philadelphia: Temple University Press.

———. 2008. *Makeover Nation: The United States of Reinvention*. Columbus: Ohio State University Press.

Moeller, S. D. 1999. *Compassion Fatigue: How the Media Sell Disease, Famine, War and Death*. New York: Routledge.

———. 2006. "'Regarding the Pain of Others': Media, Bias and the Coverage of International Disasters." *Journal of International Affairs* 59 (2): 173–196.

Mogensen, Kirsten. 2008. "Television Journalism during Terror Attacks." *Media, War and Conflict* 1 (1): 31–49.

Monahan, Brian A. 2010. *Shock of the News: Media Coverage and the Making of 9/11*. New York: New York University Press.

Moore, David W. 2003. "Public Little Concerned about Patriot Act." Gallup, September 9. Available at http://www.gallup.com/poll/9205/Public-Little-Concerned-About-Patriot-Act.aspx.

Moser, Barry. 2007. *Ashen Sky: The Letters of Pliny the Younger on the Eruption of Vesuvius*. Los Angeles: Getty.

Moskowitz, Eva S. 2001. *In Therapy We Trust: America's Obsession with Self-Fulfillment*. Baltimore, MD: Johns Hopkins University Press.

Mott, Frank Luther. 1962. *American Journalism: A History, 1690–1960*. New York: Macmillan.

Mrozowski, Daniel. 2013. "From *Hoarders* to *Pickers*: Salvage Aesthetics and Reality Television in the Great Recession." In *The Great Recession in Fiction, Film, and Television: Twenty-First-Century Bust Culture*, ed. Kirk Boyle and Daniel Mrozowski, 189–210. New York: Lexington.

Mulvey, Laura. 1992. "Visual Pleasure and Narrative Cinema." In *Film Theory and Criticism: Introductory Readings*, ed. Gerald Mast, Marshall Cohen, and Leo Braudy, 711–722. 4th ed. New York: Oxford University Press.

Nora, Pierre. 1996. "General Introduction: Between Memory and History." In *Realms of Memory, Volume 1: Conflicts and Divisions*, ed. Pierre Nora, trans. Arthur Goldhammer, 1–20. New York: Columbia University Press.

Nordhaus, William D. 2006. "The Economics of Hurricanes in the United States." December 21. Available at http://nordhaus.econ.yale.edu/hurr_122106a.pdf.

Nunberg, Geoffrey. 2001. "Since Sept. 11, We're Watching Our Words." *Los Angeles Times*, November 4. Available at http://articles.latimes.com/2001/nov/04/opinion/op-65510.

Nuttall, A. D. 1996. *Why Does Tragedy Give Pleasure?* Oxford: Oxford University Press.

O'Hehir, Andrew. 2008. "Heroes of Katrina, Ghost of 'Gonzo.'" Salon.com, January 21. Available at http://www.salon.com/ent/movies/btm/2008/01/21/trouble.

O'Keefe, Ed, and Philip Rucker. 2013. "Gun Control Overhaul Is Defeated in Senate." *Washington Post*, April 17. Available at http://www.washingtonpost.com/

politics/gun-control-overhaul-is-defeated-in-senate/2013/04/17/57eb028a-a77c-11e2-b029-8fb7e977ef71_story.html.

Olenski, Steve. 2014. "Nearly Four Years after Deepwater Horizon, Has BP's Brand Image Recovered?" *Forbes*, January 24. Available at http://www.forbes.com/sites/steveolenski/2014/01/24/nearly-four-years-after-deepwater-horizon-has-bps-brand-image-recovered.

Olick, Jeffrey K. 1999. "Collective Memory: The Two Cultures." *Sociological Theory* 17 (3): 333–348.

Park, Ahran. 2008. "The Right to Know about Violent Images? The Virginia Tech Killer's Gun Points at the Viewer." Paper presented at the annual meeting of the International Communication Association, Montreal, May 22.

Park, Michael. Y. 2006. "'Disaster Tourists' Flock to Lower Ninth Ward." FoxNews.com, March 8. Available at http://www.foxnews.com/story/0,2933,187242,00.html.

Patterson, Troy. 2009. "Save It: Irritating New Budget-Conscious Lifestyle Shows." *Slate*, May 7. Available at http://www.slate.com/id/2217907.

Pellegrino, Charles R. 2004. *Ghosts of Vesuvius: A New Look at the Last Days of Pompeii, How Towers Fall, and Other Strange Connections*. New York: William Morrow.

Peters, Jeremy W. 2010. "Efforts to Limit the Flow of Spill News." *New York Times*, June 9. Available at http://www.nytimes.com/2010/06/10/us/10access.html?_r=1.

Peters, John Durham. 1999. *Speaking into the Air: A History of the Idea of Communication*. Chicago: University of Chicago Press.

———. 2001. "Witnessing." *Media, Culture, and Society* 23:707–723.

Peters, Michael A. 2012. "In a Risk Society, Is Consumption Our Only Tool to Influence the World?" *Truthout*, July 29. Available at http://truth-out.org/news/item/10531-in-a-risk-society-is-consumption-our-only-tool-to-influence-our-world.

Petersen, Jennifer. 2011. *Murder, the Media, and the Politics of Public Feelings: Remembering Matthew Shepard and James Byrd Jr.* Bloomington: Indiana University Press.

Pew Research Center for the People and the Press. 2001a. "American Psyche Reeling from Terrorist Attacks." September 19. Available at http://www.people-press.org/2001/09/19/american-psyche-reeling-from-terror-attacks.

———. 2001b. "Americans Open to Dissenting Views on the War on Terrorism." October 4. Available at http://www.people-press.org/2001/10/04/americans-open-to-dissenting-views-on-the-war-on-terrorism.

———. 2001c. "But Guarded Confidence in Military Success: Military Action a Higher Priority than Homeland Defense." September 27. Available at http://www.people-press.org/files/legacy-pdf/2.pdf.

———. 2001d. "Public Remains Steady in Face of Anthrax Scare." October 15. Available at http://www.people-press.org/2001/10/15/punlic-remains-steady-in-face-of-anthrax-scare.

———. 2003. "Two Years Later, the Fear Lingers." September 4. Available at http://www.people-press.org/2003/09/04/two-years-later-the-fear-lingers.

———. 2005. "Two-in-Three Critical of Bush's Relief Efforts." September 8. Available at http://www.people-press.org/2005/09/08/two-in-three-critical-of-bushs-relief-efforts.

———. 2007. "Widespread Interest in Virginia Tech Shootings. But Public Paid Closer Attention to Columbine." April 25. Available at http://people-press.org/report/322/widespread-interest-in-virginia-tech-shootings.

———. 2008a. "Economic Problems, Especially in Detroit, Absorb Public's Attention." November 20. Available at http://www.people-press.org/2008/11/20/economic-problems-especially-in-detroit-absorb-publics-attention.

———. 2008b. "Small Plurality Backs Bailout Plan." September 30. Available at http://www.people-press.org/2008/09/30/small-plurality-backs-bailout-plan.

———. 2009. "America's Place in the World 2009." December. Available at http://www.people-press.org/files/legacy-pdf/569.pdf.

———. 2010a. "Earmarks Could Help Candidates in Midterms; Palin and Tea Party Connections Could Hurt." August 2. Available at http://people-press.org/report/642/#energy.

———. 2010b. "Health Care Reform—Can't Live with It, or without It." March 18. Available at http://www.people-press.org/files/legacy-pdf/598.pdf.

———. 2010c. "Public's Top Stories of the Decade—9/11 and Katrina." December 30. Available at http://www.people-press.org/2010/12/30/publics-top-stories-of-the-decade-911-and-katrina.

Pitz, Marylynne. 2009. "Groundbreaking Set for Flight 93 Memorial." *Pittsburgh Post-Gazette*, February 21. Available at http://www.post-gazette.com/pg/09052/950745-84.stm.

Postman, Neil. 1985. *Amusing Ourselves to Death: Public Discourse in the Age of Show Business*. New York: Viking Penguin.

Potter, Jonathan. 1996. "Discourse Analysis and Constructionist Approaches: Theoretical Background." In *Handbook of Qualitative Research Methods for Psychology and the Social Sciences*, ed. J.T.E. Richardson, 125–140. Leicester, UK: British Psychological Society.

Prinz, Jesse. 2011. "Against Empathy." *Southern Journal of Philosophy* 49:214–233.

Quarantelli, E. L. 2001. "The Sociology of Panic." In *International Encyclopedia of the Social and Behavioral Sciences*, ed. Neil J. Smelser and Paul B. Baltes, 11020–11023. Oxford: Elsevier.

Quarantelli, E. L., and R. R. Dynes. 1977. "Response to Social Crisis and Disaster." *Annual Review of Sociology* 3:23–49.

Recuber, Timothy. 2013. "Disaster Porn!" *Contexts* 12 (2): 28–33.

Reddy, William M. 2001. *The Navigation of Feeling: A Framework for the History of Emotions*. New York: Cambridge University Press.

Reese, Stephen D. 2003. "Prologue—Framing Public Life: A Bridging Model for Media Research." In *Framing Public Life: Perspectives on Media and Our Un-*

derstanding of the Social World, ed. Stephen D. Reese, Oscar H. Gandy, and August E. Grant, 7–32. Mahwah, NJ: Lawrence Erlbaum.

Reich, Robert. 2001. "How Did Spending Become Our Patriotic Duty?" *Washington Post*, September 23, B1.

Reiff, Philip. 1966. *The Triumph of the Therapeutic: Uses of Faith after Freud*. New York: Harper and Row.

Reinhart, Carmen M., and Kenneth S. Rogoff. 2009. *This Time Is Different: Eight Centuries of Financial Folly*. Princeton, NJ: Princeton University Press.

"Revising 9/11." 2005. Editorial. *New York Times*, September 11. Available at http://www.nytimes.com/2005/09/11/opinion/revising-911.html?_r=0.

Ritzer, George. 1999. *Enchanting a Disenchanted World: Revolutionizing the Means of Consumption*. Thousand Oaks, CA: Pine Forge.

Ritzer, George, and Nathan Jurgenson. 2010. "Production, Consumption, Prosumption: The Nature of Capitalism in the Age of the Digital 'Prosumer.'" *Journal of Consumer Culture* 10 (1): 13–36.

Roberts, Dan, and Spencer Ackerman. 2013. "US Lawmakers Call for Review of Patriot Act after NSA Surveillance Revelations." *The Guardian*, June 10. Available at http://www.theguardian.com/world/2013/jun/10/patriot-act-nsa-surveillance-review.

Robinson, Sue. 2009. "'If You Had Been with Us': Mainstream Press and Citizen Journalists Jockey for Authority over the Collective Memory of Hurricane Katrina." *New Media and Society* 11 (5): 795–814.

Rodríguez, Havidán, and Russell Dynes. 2006. "Finding and Framing Katrina: The Social Construction of Disaster." June 11. Available at http://understandingkatrina.ssrc.org/Dynes_Rodriguez/printable.html.

Rodríguez, Havidán, Joseph Trainor, and Enrico L. Quarantelli. 2006. "Rising to the Challenges of a Catastrophe: The Emergent and Prosocial Behavior following Hurricane Katrina." *Annals of the American Academy of Political and Social Science* 604:82–101.

Rose, Randall L., and Stacy L. Wood. 2005. "Paradox and the Consumption of Authenticity through Reality Television." *Journal of Consumer Research* 32:284–296.

Rose, Steve. 2013. "Abraham Zapruder: The Man behind History's Most Infamous Home Movie." *The Guardian*, November 14. Available at http://www.theguardian.com/film/2013/nov/14/abraham-zapruder-film-kennedy-killing-parkland.

Rousseau, Jean-Jacques. 1997. *The Discourses and Other Early Writings*. Ed. and trans. Victor Gourevitch. New York: Cambridge University Press.

Rozario, Kevin. 2007. *The Culture of Calamity: Disaster and the Making of Modern America*. Chicago: University of Chicago Press.

Rushkoff, Douglas. 2002. "Renaissance Now?" June 13. Available at http://www.rushkoff.com/blog/2002/6/13/renaissance-now.html.

Saad, Lydia. 2004. "Americans Generally Comfortable with Patriot Act." Gallup News Service, March 2. Available at http://www.gallup.com/poll/10858/Americans-Generally-Comfortable-Patriot-Act.aspx.

Sandy, Adam. 2001. "Dreamland." Available at http://history.amusement parks.com/Dreamland.html.
Santino, Jack. 1992. "'Not an Unimportant Failure': Rituals of Death and Politics in Northern Ireland." In *Displayed in Mortal Light*, ed. Michael McCaughan, n.p. Antrim, Ireland: Antrim Arts Council.
———. 2006. "Performative Commemoratives: Spontaneous Shrines and the Public Memorialization of Death." In *Spontaneous Shrines and the Public Memorialization of Death*, ed. Jack Santino, 363–372. New York: Palgrave Macmillan.
"Sarnoff, David: U.S. Media Executive." N.d. In *Encyclopedia of Television*, ed. Horace Newcomb, Museum of Broadcast Communications website. Available at http://www.museum.tv/archives/etv/S/htmlS/sarnoffdavi/sarnoffdavi.htm.
Savage, Kirk. 2006. "Trauma, Healing, and the Therapeutic Monument." In *Terror, Culture, Politics: Rethinking 9/11*, ed. Daniel J. Sherman and Terry Nardin, 103–120. Bloomington: Indiana University Press.
Scanlon, Jennifer. 2005. "'Your Flag Decal Won't Get You into Heaven Anymore': U.S. Consumers, Wal-Mart, and the Commodification of Patriotism." In *The Selling of 9/11: How a National Tragedy Became a Commodity*, ed. Dana Heller, 174–199. New York: Palgrave Macmillan.
Scarry, Elaine. 1985. *The Body in Pain: The Making and Unmaking of the World*. New York: Oxford University Press.
Schudson, Michael. 1978. *Discovering the News: A Social History of American Newspapers*. New York: Basic.
Schwartz, Barry. 1982. "The Social Context of Commemoration: A Study in Collective Memory." *Social Forces* 61 (2): 374–402.
Scott, A. O. 2007. "Drawing a Line from Movie to Murder." *New York Times*, April 23. Available at http://www.nytimes.com/2007/04/23/movies/23movi.html.
Sears, Michael D. 2013. "The Formation of Issue Publics during the Great Recession: Examining the Influences of News Media, Geography, and Demographics." Ph.D. diss. University of Iowa, Iowa City.
Shales, Tom. 2007. "NBC Broadcasts an Eerie Epilogue." *Washington Post*, April 19. Available at http://www.washingtonpost.com/wp-dyn/content/article/2007/04/18/AR2007041802745.html.
Shirky, Clay. 2011. "The Political Power of Social Media: Technology, the Public Sphere, and Political Change." *Foreign Affairs*. Available at http://www.foreignaffairs.com/articles/67038/clay-shirky/the-political-power-of-social-media.
Shrum, Wesley. 2007. "Hurricane Stories, from Within." *Social Studies of Science* 37 (1): 97–102.
Simmons, James C. 1969. "Bulwer and Vesuvius: The Topicality of the *Last Days of Pompeii*." *Nineteenth-Century Fiction* 24 (1): 103–105.
Simon, Art. 1996. *Dangerous Knowledge: The JFK Assassination in Art and Film*. Philadelphia: Temple University Press.

Sirota, David. 2009. "TARP on Steroids." Truthdig, October 29. Available at http://www.truthdig.com/report/item/20091029_tarp_on_steroids#.

Smelser, Neil J. 2004. "September 11, 2001, as Cultural Trauma." In *Cultural Trauma and Collective Identity*, ed. Jeffrey C. Alexander, Ron Eyerman, Bernhard Giesen, Neil J. Smelser, and Piotr Sztompka, 264–282. Berkeley: University of California Press.

Smith, Aaron. 2011. "How Sept. 11 Changed Charity in America." *CNN Money*, September 6. Available at http://money.cnn.com/2011/09/06/news/economy/katrina_donations_911.

Smith, Adam. (1790) 2009. *The Theory of Moral Sentiments*. New York: Penguin.

———. 1869. *The Essays of Adam Smith*. London: Alex. Murray and Son.

Solnit, Rebecca. 2009. *A Paradise Built in Hell: The Extraordinary Communities that Arise in Disaster*. New York: Viking.

Solomon, Jesse. 2010. "Nine Years after 9/11, a Photo Provides Some Peace." CNN.com, September 11. Available at http://www.cnn.com/2010/US/09/10/september.11.photo/index.html.

Song, Felicia Wu. 2004. "Online Communities in a Therapeutic Age." In *Therapeutic Culture: Triumph and Defeat*, ed. Jonathan B. Imber, 137–151. New Brunswick, NJ: Transaction.

Sontag, Susan. 1990. *On Photography*. New York: Anchor.

———. 2003. *Regarding the Pain of Others*. New York: Farrar, Straus and Giroux.

Spigel, Lynn. 2005. "Entertainment Wars: Television Culture after 9/11." In *The Selling of 9/11: How a National Tragedy Became a Commodity*, ed. Dana Heller, 119–154. New York: Palgrave Macmillan.

Spitzer, Eliot. 2010. "Regulators and Risk-Takers." *Slate*, July 14. Available at http://www.slate.com/id/2260470/.

Stanley, Alessandra. 2007. "Ghosts of Abu Ghraib: Abu Ghraib and Its Multiple Failures." *New York Times*. Available at http://www.nytimes.com/2007/02/22/arts/television/22stan.html.

Stearns, Peter N. 2006. *American Fear: The Causes and Consequences of High Anxiety*. New York: Routledge.

———. 2008. "Texas and Virginia: A Bloodied Window into Changes in American Public Life." *Journal of Social History* 42 (2): 299–318.

Steinberg, Jacques. 2007. "Arts, Briefly: Suspect's Video Boosts Ratings for NBC News." *New York Times*, April 25, 2.

Steinberg, Ted. 2000. *Acts of God: The Unnatural History of Natural Disaster in America*. Oxford: Oxford University Press.

Stephen, Andrew. 2007. "The Unmentionable Causes of Violence." *New Statesmen*, April 30, 20–21.

Stephens, Mitchell. 1988. *A History of News: From the Drum to the Satellite*. New York: Viking.

Stewart, Doug. 2006. "Resurrecting Pompeii: A New Exhibition Brings the Doomed Residents of Pompeii and Herculaneum Vividly to Life." *Smithsonian*

Magazine, February. Available at http://www.smithsonianmag.com/history-archaeology/pompeii.html.

Strobel, Warren P. 2008. "Exhaustive Review Finds No Link between Saddam and al Qaida." *McClatchy Newspapers*, March 10. Available at http://www.mcclatchydc.com/2008/03/10/29959/exhaustive-review-finds-no-link.html.

Strom, Stephanie. 2006. "Red Cross Sifting Internal Charges over Katrina Aid." *New York Times*, March 24. Available at http://www.nytimes.com/2006/03/24/national/nationalspecial/24cross.html.

Sturken, Marita. 1997. *Tangled Memories: The Vietnam War, the AIDS Epidemic, and the Politics of Remembering*. Berkeley: University of California Press.

———. 2007. *Tourists of History: Memory, Kitsch, and Consumerism from Oklahoma City to Ground Zero*. Durham, NC: Duke University Press.

Szasz, Andrew. 2007. *Shopping Our Way to Safety: How We Changed from Protecting the Environment to Protecting Ourselves*. Minneapolis: University of Minnesota Press.

Taylor, Charles. 1991. *The Ethics of Authenticity*. Cambridge, MA: Harvard University Press.

Teal, Harvey S. 2001. *Partners with the Sun: South Carolina Photographers, 1840–1940*. Columbia: University of South Carolina Press.

Thomas, Jeannie B. 2006. "Communicative Commemoration and Graveside Shrines: Princess Diana, Jim Morrison, My 'Bro' Max, and Boogs the Cat." In *Spontaneous Shrines and the Public Memorialization of Death*, ed. Jack Santino, 17–40. New York: Palgrave Macmillan.

"Three Shocks Yesterday; Citizens of Charleston Repairing Their Homes." 1886. *New York Times*, September 8, 1.

Thrift, Nigel. 2006. "Re-inventing Invention: New Tendencies in Capitalist Commodification." *Economy and Society* 35 (2): 279–306.

Tierney, Kathleen J. 2007. "From the Margins to the Mainstream? Disaster Research at the Crossroads." *Annual Review of Sociology* 33:503–525.

Tierney, Kathleen, Christine Bevc, and Erica Kuligowski. 2006. "Metaphors Matter: Disaster Myths, Media Frames, and Their Consequences in Hurricane Katrina." *Annals of the American Academy of Political and Social Science* 604:57–81.

Tocqueville, Alexis de. 2000. *Democracy in America*. Trans. G. Lawrence. New York: Perennial Classics.

Toffler, Alvin. 1980. *The Third Wave*. New York: William Morrow.

Torpey, John. 2006. *Making Whole What Has Been Smashed: On Reparations Politics*. Cambridge, MA: Harvard University Press.

Trotter, Wilfred. (1919) 1953. *Instincts of the Herd in Peace and War*. London: Oxford University Press.

"'Trouble the Water' Examines Katrina Aftermath." 2008. *Nashville City Paper*, September 26. Available at http://nashvillecitypaper.com/content/lifestyles/%E2%80%98trouble-water%E2%80%99-examines-katrina-aftermath70446350457530055188070 6526.html.

Turner, Graeme. 2006. "The Mass Production of Celebrity: 'Celetoids,' Reality TV and the 'Demotic Turn.'" *International Journal of Cultural Studies* 9 (2): 153–165.

Turnock, Robert. 2000. *Interpreting Diana: Television Audiences and the Death of a Princess*. London: British Film Institute.

Ulmer, Gregory L. 2005. *Electronic Monuments*. Minneapolis: University of Minnesota Press.

Underwood, Doug. 2001. "Reporting and the Push for Market-Oriented Journalism: Media Organizations as Businesses." In *Mediated Politics: Communication in the Future of Democracy*, ed. W. Lance Bennett and Robert M. Entman, 99–116. New York: Cambridge University Press.

Ungar, Sheldon. 1990. "Moral Panics, the Military-Industrial Complex, and the Arms Race." *Sociological Quarterly* 31 (2): 165–185.

Van Meter, Jonathan. 2005. "Unanchored." *New York Magazine*, September 11. Available at http://nymag.com/nymetro/news/features/14301.

Van Zoonen, Liesbet. 1998. "The Ethics of Making Private Life Public." In *The Media in Question: Popular Cultures and Public Interests*, ed. Kees Brants, Joke Hermes, and Liesbet van Zoonen, 113–123. Thousand Oaks, CA: Sage.

Vattimo, Gianni. 1992. *The Transparent Society*. Baltimore: Johns Hopkins University Press.

Vetlesen, Arne Johan. 1994. *Perception, Empathy, and Judgment: An Inquiry into the Preconditions of Moral Performance*. University Park: Pennsylvania State University Press.

Victor, Jeffrey S. 1991. "The Dynamics of Rumor-Panics about Satanic Cults." In *The Satanism Scare*, ed. James T. Richardson, Joel Best, and David G. Bromley, 221–236. New York: Aldine de Gruyter.

Voorhees, Courte C. W., John Vick, and Douglas D. Perkins. 2007. "'Came Hell and High Water': The Intersection of Hurricane Katrina, the News Media, Race and Poverty." *Journal of Community and Applied Social Psychology* 17:415–429.

Walker, Joyce. 2007. "Narratives in the Database: Memorializing September 11th Online." *Computers and Composition* 24:121–153.

Walt, Stephen M. 2012. "Why Afghanistan Was Obama's Biggest Mistake." Weatherhead Center for International Affairs, Harvard University. Available at http://wcfia.harvard.edu/publications/why-afghanistan-was-obamas-biggest-mistake.

Ward, Patrick S., and Gerald E. Shively. 2011. "Disaster Risk, Social Vulnerability and Economic Development." Paper presented at the Agricultural and Applied Economics Association and Northeastern Agricultural and Resource Economics Association Joint Annual Meeting, Pittsburgh, July 24–26.

Weber, Harry R., and Erin McClam. 2010. "Gulf Oil Spill: BP's Failures Amplified by Numerous Gaffes." *Huffington Post*, June 11. Available at http://www.huffingtonpost.com/2010/06/11/gulf-oil-spil-bp-gaffes_n_609859.html.

Weisbrot, Mark. 2013. "Are Snowden, Greenwald, and Wikileaks Winning?" Alternet, August 7. Available at http://www.files.alternet.org/are-snowden-greenwald-and-wikileaks-winning.

Wellman, Barry, Anabel Quan Haase, James Witte, and Keith Hampton. 2001. "Does the Internet Increase, Decrease, or Supplement Social Capital? Social Networks, Participation, and Community Commitment." *American Behavioral Scientist* 45 (3): 436–455.

Werner, Erica. 2010. "BP Agrees to Show 'Top Kill' Video." ABC News, May 25. Available at http://abcnews.go.com/Business/wireStory?id=10742878.

Wherry, Frederick F. 2006. "The Social Sources of Authenticity in Global Handicraft Markets: Evidence from Northern Thailand." *Journal of Consumer Culture* 6 (1): 5–32.

Wilkinson, Richard G. 1996. *Unhealthy Societies: The Afflictions of Inequality.* New York: Routledge.

Wilkinson, Richard, and Kate Pickett. 2009. *The Spirit Level: Why Greater Equality Makes Societies Stronger.* New York: Bloomsbury.

Williams, Raymond. 1977. *Marxism and Literature.* New York: Oxford University Press.

———. 1985. *Keywords: A Vocabulary of Culture and Society.* Rev. ed. New York: Oxford University Press.

Williams, Susan Millar, and Stephen G. Hoffius. 2011. *Upheaval in Charleston: Earthquake and Murder on the Eve of Jim Crow.* Athens: University of Georgia Press.

Willis, Margaret, and Juliet B. Schor. 2012. "Does Changing a Light Bulb Lead to Changing the World? Political Action and the Conscious Consumer." *Annals of the American Academy of Political and Social Science* 644:160–190.

Wispé, Lauren. 1986. "The Distinction between Sympathy and Empathy: To Call Forth a Concept, a Word Is Needed." *Journal of Personality and Social Psychology* 50 (2): 314–321.

Young, James E. 1993. *The Texture of Memory: Holocaust Memorials and Meaning.* New Haven, CT: Yale University Press.

Zelizer, Barbie. 1992. *Covering the Body: The Kennedy Assassination, the Media, and the Shaping of Collective Memory.* Chicago: University of Chicago Press.

Zinn, Jens O. 2006. "Risk, Affect and Emotion." *Forum* 7 (1). Available at http://www.qualitative-research.net/index.php/fqs/article/view/67/137.

Zinner, Ellen S. 1999. "The *Challenger* Disaster: Group Survivorship on a National Landscape." In *When a Community Weeps: Case Studies in Group Survivorship*, ed. Ellen S. Zinner and Mary Beth Williams, 23–48. Ann Arbor, MI: Brunner/Mazel.

Zukin, Sharon. 2002. "Our World Trade Center." In *After the World Trade Center: Rethinking New York City*, ed. Michael Sorkin and Sharon Zukin, 13–22. New York: Routledge.

———. 2008. "Consuming Authenticity: From Outposts of Difference to Means of Exclusion." *Cultural Studies* 22 (5): 724–748.

———. 2010. *Naked City: The Death and Life of Authentic Urban Places.* New York: Oxford University Press.

INDEX

ABC World News, 100, 108, 113, 114, 117, 121–122
Abu Ghraib, 105
"Accidental Napalm," 60
Activism, 174
AC 360. See Anderson Cooper 360 Degrees
Advertising Age, 5
Afghanistan, invasion of, 99, 104, 106–107, 109, 120–122, 172, 176
Agee, James, 41
Al-Qaeda, 104
Altgens, James, 43
Altheide, David, 113, 122
Altruism, 95
American Airlines Flight 11, 146
American Biograph Company, 36
American exceptionalism, 151
American Morning with Paula Zahn, 108
American Psychiatric Association, 66
American Red Cross, 171
American Social History Project, 137
Anderson Cooper 360 Degrees (AC 360), 60, 81–86, 106, 108, 115; criticism of, 92
Andrejevic, Mark, 79
Anthrax attacks, 99, 107–110, 112, 121
Anxieties, modern, 24
AP (Associated Press), 43, 165, 167

Aristotle, 23
Army Corp of Engineers, 149, 151
Art, 23–24; classical works of, 26, 45
Ashcroft, John, 112–113
Asian financial crisis of 1997–1998, 103
Associated Press (AP), 43, 165, 167
Atomism, 52. See also Individualism
Aura, 16, 21, 25, 36, 48, 52, 57, 177; of digital archives, 161; of disaster consumption, 48–49; in early photographs, 56; in Hurricane Katrina imagery, 56; in September 11 imagery, 56, 126; of Seung-Hui Cho's manifesto, 73, 94; of space shuttle *Challenger* imagery, 51, 56; of the written word, 39; of the Zapruder film, 46, 56
Aurora, Colorado, shootings, 174–175
Authenticity, 7–8, 12–13, 16–17, 21, 24, 25, 70, 126; of camcorder and webcam footage, 74, 88–89; of digital archives, 161; disasters as carriers of, 55, 161, 171; eighteenth-century disasters and, 30; and identifiability of victims, 125; of *I Survived*, 61; of live footage, 166; of memorabilia and images, 47–49; of New Orleans, 175; paradoxes of, 95–96, 171; postmodern critics of, 57; and reality

Authenticity (*continued*)
 television, 79–80, 83; of Seung-Hui
 Cho's manifesto, 70–71, 73, 93–94, 161;
 of space shuttle *Challenger* imagery, 51;
 of the Zapruder film, 46
Authenticity: What Consumers Really Want,
 13
"Autonomous, self-illusory hedonism," 55

Banet-Weiser, Sarah, 13
Baton Rouge, Lousiana, 81
Baudrillard, Jean, 79
Bauman, Zygmunt, 173
Bealer, Paula, 58–59
Bear Stearns, 106, 108, 114–115
Beck, Ulrich, 17, 102–103
Begley, Sharon, 166
Benjamin, Walter, 16, 25–26, 36, 56, 73
Berger, John, 11
Bernanke, Ben, 115, 117–118
Bernays, Edward, 40
Bhopal chemical disaster, 103
Bin Laden, Osama, 112
Biography channel, 60, 74
Birchall, Clare, 47
Blitzer, Wolf, 114, 116, 118
Blunt, Roy, 119
Boltanski, Luc, 77
Box, Gary, 128, 130–131, 154
Box, Helen, 128, 130–131, 154
Box, Judson, 128, 130–131, 154
BP. *See* British Petroleum
Brady, Matthew, 33
Breaux, Helena, 86
Breaux, Tad, 86
British Petroleum (BP), 163–169, 173;
 boycott of, 166–167
Broad, William, 111
Brown, Aaron, 112–113
Brown, Michael, 62
Bulwer-Lytton, Edward, 34–35
Bush, George H. W., 113
Bush, George W., 4, 62, 88, 106–107,
 113, 119, 149; and poor response to
 Hurricane Katrina, 92, 164–165

Cable News Network (CNN), 60, 81–87,
 108–109, 114, 128
CafePress, 166

Camcorders, 60; aesthetic style of, 74
Cameron, James, 39
Campbell, Colin, 54–55
Candide, 29
Cantril, Hadley, 40
Carpathia, RMS, 37
Catharsis, 9, 23, 92, 131, 144, 151
CBS (Columbia Broadcasting System), 98
CBS Evening News, 98–99, 108, 112, 114,
 116–117, 122
Center for History and New Media
 (CHNM), 130, 137–138
Challenger, space shuttle, 24, 50–51, 53
Charitable giving, 9, 64–65, 67, 81, 94, 97,
 169–171, 174
Charleston, South Carolina, 24; earth-
 quake of 1886 in, 33
Chatzky, Jean, 115
Cheney, Dick, 124
Chernobyl, 103
CHNM (Center for History and New
 Media), 130, 137–138
Cho, Seung-Hui, 5, 17, 61, 65–66; multi-
 media manifesto of, 70–74, 80; psycho-
 logical understandings of, 70
Chouliaraki, Lilie, 126
Citizen journalism, 48, 132
Civil liberties, 104–105, 112
Civil Rights Movement, 134, 167
Clark, Candace, 69
Clarke, Richard, 113
Climate change, 127, 176, 178–179
Clinton, Bill, 113
Close reading, 14
Closure, 144–145
CNN (Cable News Network), 60, 81–87,
 108–109, 114, 128
Cohen, Stanley, 40–41
Collective memory, 20, 50, 129–131, 137,
 152, 157, 162
Collins, Coleman, 58–59
Columbia Broadcasting System (CBS), 98
Columbine High School shootings, 9;
 connection to Virginia Tech shootings,
 66, 92
Commemoration: as challenge to elites,
 134, 159; of the dead, 152; digital
 and online forms of, 20, 65, 128–130,
 137–162; and forgetting, 150; pace of,

159; pedagogical forms of, 153; politics of, 135, 152–157; prosumer-oriented, 136; rituals of, 18–19, 134; of space shuttle *Challenger*, 51; therapeutic, 133, 138, 155
Community, 10, 18, 24, 52; African American, 64; desire for, 176–177; disaster-stricken, 19; and grieving, 52; vs. individualism, 155; local, 147; and media technologies, 131, 155; and memorial processes, 135; and misfortunes, 49; and sentiment, 52
Compassion, 31, 68–69, 150–151, 167, 176
"Compassion fatigue," 18
"Concert for Hurricane Relief, A," 64
Coney Island, 35
Conrad, Joseph, 38
Conspiracy theories: around JFK assassination, 46; around September 11 attacks, 47, 137
Consumer culture, 2, 4–7, 9, 12–13, 24, 57, 160; disasters in, 48, 56, 67–68; and first-person footage, 94; and September 11 attacks, 123–124
Consumerism, 20, 48–49; green, 166, 175; psychosocial roots of, 54–55
Consumers, 17, 20–21, 173; ethical, 97; and prosumption, 131–132; and risk, 173
Consumption, 11–12, 17, 25, 54; cathartic, 177; of digital archives, 131; of disaster, 20, 171; empathetically motivated, 94–95; new strategies of, 178; preventative, 20; and September 11 attacks, 123–124
Content analysis, 15
Cook, George LaGrange, 33
Cooper, Anderson, 61, 81–84, 93, 97
Counter-Strike, 66
Couric, Katie, 116–117, 119
Cousin de Grainville, Jean-Baptiste, 34
Crisis of legitimacy, 103
Cronkite, Walter, 43, 83
Cross-counseling, 132, 142; simulated, 154

Dadaist artwork, 36
Daily Show with Jon Stewart, The, 92
Dallas, Texas, 42–43
Davis, Mike, 10
Deal, Carl, 87–88
Dean, Carolyn, 41

Debord, Guy, 79
Deepwater Horizon oil spill, 163–169, 173, 176
DeFazio, Peter, 120
Democracy, 39–40, 60, 106
Dernier Homme, Le, 34
Desire, 13, 30, 54–55
Dewey, John, 40
Diana, Princess of Wales, 24, 52–53
Digital archives, 9, 13, 15, 20, 128–133, 137, 145–146, 152–162
Digital memory banks. *See* Digital archives
Disaster: consumerism or consumption of, 7–9, 12, 18, 21, 160, 169; "disaster capitalism," 119; "disaster marathons," 22, 96, 169; "disaster pornography," 41, 169; joy in, 176; relief for, 3; social science view of, 30; sociologists in the field of, 10; tourism and, 33, 68, 175, 177–178
Discourse analysis, 14–15, 109
Dobbs, Lou, 106
Dodd, Chris, 117–119
Doyle, Arthur Conan, 38
Drabek, Thomas, 10
Dumenco, Simon, 5
Dynes, Russell, 30

Early warning systems, 68
East Grand Terre Island, Louisiana, 165
Elites, 9, 29, 56; authorized to view Zapruder film, 45; inauthenticity of, 125–126; lack of aversion to risk among, 172–173; and struggle to control commemoration, 135; and use of disasters to pursue policy, 124, 127, 175–176, 178
Emergency Economic Stabilization Act, 99–102, 105, 107–108, 114, 120, 125. *See also* Troubled Asset Relief Program
"Emotional regimes," 59
Empathetic gaze, 19, 62, 92, 94–97; and reality television, 78–80; in *Trouble the Water,* 89
Empathetic hedonism, 9, 19, 96, 171
Empathy, 7–9, 19, 21, 48, 59–62, 76, 77, 97, 174–175, 178; and agency, 171; connections to authenticity, 74, 93; connections to risk, 127; definition of, 68–70; "empty," 10, 170; and identification, 125; racial biases and limits of, 80–86,

Empathy (*continued*)
95, 151; and reality television, 79; for Seung-Hui Cho, 71–73, 94; in *Trouble the Water*, 88–91
Enlightenment, 9, 16, 19, 29–30, 57, 59
Erikson, Kai, 10
Ethiopian famine of 1983–1985, charitable giving after, 171
"Ethnographic content analysis," 15
Exploitation, 11, 132
Extreme Makeover: Home Edition, 80
Exxon Valdez, 164

Facebook, 58, 65, 130, 137
Fear, 1–2, 6, 9, 13, 41, 48, 84, 144, 178; connection to empathy, 127; of environmental pollution, 164, 172; fear entrepreneurs, 113; of politicians, 117–118; as social construction, 100–101; of terrorism vs. financial crisis, 99–101, 107–110, 112–114, 120, 122–123, 126–127, 179; and trust, 102, 118–119, 127
Federal Emergency Management Agency (FEMA), 5, 62–63, 151
Film, 14, 16, 26, 36, 38, 42, 48; disaster, 13; documentary, 9, 14, 78, 80; fake documentary, 36
Financial crisis of 2008, 3, 10, 99, 101, 104–107, 109, 114–121, 124–127, 168–169, 173
Firearms, 172, 175
Flight 93 National Memorial, 161
Foreman, Tom, 115
Fortune, 116
Fort Worth, Texas, 86
Fossil fuels, 167, 169, 176
Fox News Channel, 66
Frames, 18, 110
Framing strategies, 20, 56–57
Frankfurt school, 16
Franklin, Benjamin, 28
Freud, Sigmund, 40
Furedi, Frank, 113

Galveston, Texas, hurricane of 1900, 35, 41–42
Garrison, Jim, 45
Genetically modified foods, 103
George Mason University, 130

Ghosts of the Abyss, 39
Gibson, Charles, 117, 119
Gibson, Dorothy, 38
Giddens, Anthony, 17, 102–103
Gilmore, Jim, 13
Glor, Jeff, 116
Good Night America, 45
Government, 17; affinity for crises, 120; anger toward, 143, 149–150, 160; authenticity of, 24; lack of trust in, 46, 100, 123; officials of, 110–113, 121–122, 125–127, 174; praise toward, 143, 148–149; pre-9/11 incompetence of, 105; and rescue efforts during Hurricane Katrina, 63, 67, 88, 149; and risk claims, 18, 102–103, 117–119, 126–127
Graduate Center, City University of New York, 137
Great Depression, 114, 116
Great Recession, 105, 124
Greenspan, Alan, 116
"Greenwashing," 175
Ground Zero. *See* World Trade Center
Gulf of Mexico, 163–165, 168, 173
Gun control, 2, 174–175

Habermas, Jürgen, 31–32
Haiti earthquake of 2010, charitable giving after, 170–171
Halbwachs, Maurice, 156
Halliburton, 4
Hands across the Sand, 167
Hardy, Thomas, 38
Hariman, Robert, 44
Harman, Jane, 111
Harris, Dan, 114–115
Hayward, Tony, 166–167
HBO (Home Box Office), 88
Herculaneum, 26–29
Heroes, 62, 73, 152; news reporters as, 63; and September 11, 105, 143–144, 151
Heroism, 45, 88, 90, 93
Hindenburg, 60
Holocaust, 11, 41
Home Box Office (HBO), 88
Horatio Alger myth, 91
Houston, Texas, 85
Hume, David, 31, 78, 95

Hurricane Digital Memory Bank, 129–130, 138–140, 142–151, 157
Hurricane Katrina, 1, 3, 5, 8, 10, 58, 60–64, 67, 92–95, 129–131, 140–141, 143–151, 155–157, 164, 168–169, 173–174, 177; charitable giving after, 170; debates over media coverage of, 67; memorial devoted to, 161–162; news coverage of, 80–87; online responses to, 136–137; relief efforts for, 63–64; in *Trouble the Water,* 87–92
Hurricane Rita, 64, 130, 145, 147
Hurricane Season, 64
Hussein, Saddam, 104

Iconic images, 44, 48, 158, 165
"Identifiable victim effect," 124–125
Illouz, Eva, 155
Imagination, 8; of another's pain, 171; of audience for digital archive posts, 152; of community, 177; and consumption, 54–55; and empathy, 68; of new terrorist attacks, 110–111
Individualism, 5, 9, 20, 52, 156, 162, 173–174
Individuality, 24, 90
Industrial Revolution, 55, 132
Ineffability of disasters, 9, 26, 47, 53, 56, 74
Inequality, 20, 160–161, 175, 178
Invasion from Mars, The, 40
Iraq, U.S. invasion of, 73, 87, 104, 172, 176
Irrationality, 39–41
I Survived, 60–61, 74–77, 93, 96, 125
Iwo Jima, 41

Jameson, Frederic, 4
Jefferson, Thomas, 28
Jennings, Peter, 121–122
JFK, 45, 47
Johnson, Jack, 38
Johnson, Lyndon Baines, 44
Johnstown, Pennsylvania, flood of 1889, 35
JP Morgan, 106, 108, 115

Kant, Immanuel, 29
Kaplan, E. Ann, 10
"Katrina fatigue," 92, 151

Katz, Elihu, 22
Keith, Toby, 4
Kennedy, Jacqueline Lee, 44
Kennedy, John F., 24, 42–49, 51, 83, 98
King, Larry, 111, 123
Kitsch, 16
Kiyosaki, Robert, 115
Klein, Naomi, 10
Kleinman, Arthur, 11, 170
Kleinman, Joan, 11, 170
Klinenberg, Eric, 10
Koch, Kathleen, 97
Kozik, Frank, 47
Krugman, Paul, 116, 123

Landrieu, Mary, 81–82, 84
Landsberg, Alison, 60
Lane, Anthony, 4
Larry King Live, 108, 111, 115
Last Days of Pompeii, The, 34
Last Man, The, 34
Launch of the H.M.S. Albion, The, 35
Lawrence, Chris, 85
Leadbelly, 38
Le Bon, Gustave, 39–40
Lehman Brothers, 2, 116
Lesar, David, 4
Lessin, Tia, 87–88
Liebes, Tamar, 22
Life magazine, 45–46
Lifting Our Eyes: Finding God's Grace though the Virginia Tech Tragedy. The Lauren McCain Story, 65
Lincoln, Abraham, death of, 43–44
Lippmann, Walter, 40
Lisbon, Portugal, 16; earthquake in, 28–30, 33–34, 53, 176
Looting, 63, 67, 82, 148; depiction of African Americans engaged in, 81, 84–86, 95, 157, 174
Los Angeles, 10
Louisiana National Guard, 87
Lucaites, John Louis, 44–45

Mackay, Charles, 39
Main Street, 100, 117, 120, 123, 126
Malveaux, Julianne, 112
Mass communication, 24, 30, 36, 54–55, 77, 129

210 \ INDEX

Mass culture, 14, 19, 24–25, 59–60; and American meritocracy, 174; and financial crisis of 2008, 124; John F. Kennedy–related, 45; and September 11 terrorist attacks, 123–124
Mass media, 2, 4–7, 11, 14, 18, 20, 23–24, 55, 123, 160; and ethics of representation, 158; technologies of, 9, 25, 32, 41, 57, 178
McAuliffe, Christa, 50
McCain, John, 2, 119
McConnell, Mitch, 119
"Media events," 22
Memorials, 20, 65, 133–134, 146, 152–153, 154, 160
Mental health, 130, 178–179
Merrill Lynch, 116
Mexico City earthquake of 1985, charitable giving after, 171
Middle East, 172
Miller, Judith, 111
Minneapolis, Minnesota, collapse of I-35 bridge, 75
Misfortune, 14, 34, 44, 49, 59
Mitchell, Russ, 114
Modernity, 16, 25–26
Moeller, Susan, 165, 170
Monahan, Brian, 105
Moody's, 100
Moore, Michael, 87
Moore, Stephen, 116
Morrison, Herbert, 60
Morton, Andrew, 52
Moskowitz, Eva, 133
Motion pictures, 36
Mount Pelée, 1902 eruption of, 35
Mount Vesuvius, 26, 34
Mourning, 26, 43–44, 50, 53, 134, 136, 141
"Muckraking," 35
MyDeathSpace.com, 136
MySpace, 65, 130, 136–137

Nagin, Ray, 63, 67
Narratives, 14; and commemoration, 157; in digital archives, 153; of the self, 49; shipwreck, 34; of suffering, 62, 74, 89–90, 155; of survival, 76; traumatic, 93

National Aeronautics and Space Administration (NASA), 50–51
National Broadcasting Company (NBC), 37
Nationalism, 20; and Deepwater Horizon oil spill, 166; and September 11 attacks, 122, 147–148, 150
National Rifle Association (NRA), 174–175
National September 11 Memorial and Museum, 128–129, 161–162
NBC (National Broadcasting Company), 37
NBC News, 5, 108
NBC Nightly News, 60–61, 65, 70–71, 80, 93–94, 108, 112, 114, 116–117
Neoliberal governance, 10–11, 20, 175
New Orleans, Louisiana, 1, 5, 12, 67–68, 144, 147–148, 161–162, 165; *AC 360* coverage of, 81, 84–87; Lower Ninth Ward of, 87; musicians in, 19, 63; problems of reconstruction efforts for, 92, 175; on reality television; in *Trouble the Water,* 88–91
News, 13, 99; criticism of news organizations, 96, 143, 158; print vs. televised, 42; shelf life of news stories, 92; speculative coverage, 38; stories about Hurricane Katrina, 80–87; television, 9, 11–12, 14–15, 25, 61, 101, 107; twenty-four-hour networks, 44, 63
NewsNight with Aaron Brown, 108
Newspapers, 32, 34, 43; coverage of Princess Diana, 52–53; coverage of *Titanic,* 37–39; hoax stories in, 40; as venues for national mourning, 136
Newsweek, 158, 166
Newtown, Connecticut, shootings, 174
New York City, 32, 35, 37, 144–145, 148, 159
New York Sun, 32
New York Times, 7–9, 111, 116; coverage of *Titanic,* 37–39
9/11. *See* September 11 terrorist attacks
9/11 First Capitalizers Act, 4
Nixon, Richard, 42
Nora, Pierre, 160, 162
Norms, 6–7, 9, 13–14, 19; concerning emotional expression, 24, 59; concern-

ing empathy, 62; concerning pace of commemoration, 159; concerning public expressions of fear, 113–114; concerning suffering of others, 97; online, 20; relation to news media, 101
Nostalgia, 156
Nuttall, A. D., 23

Obama, Barack, 2, 69, 116, 119, 163–165, 167–168
Oklahoma City bombing, 10
Oklahoma City National Memorial, 135
Oldboy, 66
Olick, Jeffrey, 157
Onion, The, 3–5, 21
On Photography, 11
Oprah Winfrey Show, The, 67, 79
Oswald, Lee Harvey, 42, 44, 47–48

Pain, 6, 17, 24–26, 154; mass-mediated, 11; of others, 47, 54, 59, 62, 68; physical, 53; psychic, 132; of September 11 attacks, 151
Panic, 18, 40, 101, 109, 110, 112, 115, 120; moral, 40–41
Panopticon, 77
Patriot Act (USA PATRIOT Act), 99–102, 104–105, 107–108, 110, 112–113, 120, 126, 176
Patriotism, 21, 105, 123–124, 148–149
Paulson, Henry "Hank," 118, 120
PBS (Public Broadcasting Service), 165
Pearl Harbor, 149
Pearlman, Russell, 116
Pelée, Mount, 1902 eruption of, 35
Pennsylvania, 8
Penny press, 32
Pentagon, 8, 111, 147
Peters, John Durham, 21, 54
Photography, 11, 16, 26
Pine, Joe, 13
Pity, 73, 158
Plato, 23
Pliny the Elder, 27
Pliny the Younger, 27
"Poem on the Lisbon Disaster," 29
"Political anesthesia," 19, 175
Politics, 2, 5; of commemoration, 135, 152–153, 156–157; of empathy, 91, 97;

and fragmentation, 52; progressive, 176, 178
Pompeii, 16, 24, 26–29, 33, 35
Popular culture, 7, 14, 20–21, 49, 77; breakdown of boundaries between elite culture and, 134; and psychotherapy, 133, 154; surrounding *Titanic*, 38; surrounding Virginia Tech, 65–66; surrounding Zapruder film, 46
Pornography of World War II and Holocaust images, 11, 41
Postman, Neil, 38–39
Prince William Sound, Alaska, 164
Printing press, 9
Prinz, Jesse, 95
Progress, 24
Prosumption, 20, 130–133, 135–136, 156–157
"Pseudo-events," 50
Psychoanalysis, 69; of Seung-Hui Cho, 71
Public Broadcasting Service (PBS), 165
Public Citizen, 166
"Public drama," 168
Public opinion, 5, 8, 101; challenges to mainstream, 159–160
Public sphere, 10, 29, 31–32, 129

Quintanilla, Carlos, 116–117

Racial minorities, stereotypical and unfair depictions of, 63, 67, 81, 84–87, 151
Racial "othering," 84–85
Racial prejudice, 67, 136
Racism, 173–174
Radio Corporation of America (RCA), 37
Rather, Dan, 112
Ratigan, Dylan, 117
RCA (Radio Corporation of America), 37
Real, the, 7, 12–13, 16, 23, 25, 47–48, 56–57, 75; and reality television, 78–79
Reality television, 9, 13–14, 19, 52, 62, 78–79, 90, 94, 124
Reason, 24
Reassurance, 111–112, 118
Religious rhetoric, 142, 152
Repetition: of *Challenger* explosion imagery, 50; of disasters, 8
"Reputational entrepreneurs," 135
Rescue 911, 78

Revolutionary War, 32
Risk, 17–18, 21, 55, 100–103, 108, 118–119, 127, 178
Risk Society, 102
Rivera, Geraldo, 45
Roberts, John, 98
Roberts, Kimberly, 87–91
Roberts, Scott, 87–90
Romantic movement, 30
Ronald, Reagan, 50, 53
Rousseau, Jean-Jacques, 30–31, 73
Rozario, Kevin, 10
Ruby, Jack, 43, 47
Rushkoff, Douglas, 129

San Francisco earthquake and fire of 1906, 36, 42
Sarnoff, David, 37
Savage, Kirk, 153
Scarry, Elaine, 53
Schudson, Michael, 34
Second Life, 130
Security, 3, 6, 9, 21, 99, 102–103, 179; "consumerism of," 76, 124, 172–173
Segregation, 34
Self, the, 23, 49, 174; consumption's meanings for, 54–55; and memory, 162; selfhood of "ordinary people," 79; suffering and, 74, 79, 89–90, 156
Self-help, 20–21, 69, 174; and closure, 145; as form of prosumption, 132–133, 138; and Freudian psychotherapy, 133; as message of *I Survived*, 76–77; narratives of, in American culture, 91–92; and therapeutic commemoration, 131–133, 138, 141–142, 154
Sensationalism, 17, 34–36, 38, 41; in September 11 and Hurricane Katrina news coverage, 143
September 11 Digital Archive, 129–130, 137–151
September 11 terrorist attacks, 1, 3–8, 10, 14, 21, 50, 53, 63, 99, 101–105, 109–110, 114, 121–123, 129, 131, 138, 140–151, 155–156, 165, 168–169, 176–177; charitable giving after, 170; collective trauma of, 126; emotional aftermath of, 122; memorial devoted to, 161; online responses to, 136–137; return to normal television after, 98; unifying themes in news coverage, 63
Serwer, Andy, 116, 123
Shanksville, Pennsylvania, 147
Shaw, Clay, 45
Shaw, George Bernard, 38
Shelley, Mary, 34
Sherman, Brad, 120
Shirky, Clay, 129
Shock, 36, 38, 41
"Shock doctrine," 10
Simon, Art, 47
Situation Room with Wolf Blitzer, The, 108, 118–119
Smart Money, 116
Smart phones, 60
Smith, Adam, 31, 77, 95
Smith, Michael, 51
Snowden, Edward, 105
Social networking sites, 10, 74, 130–131, 136
Solnit, Rebecca, 176
Song, Felicia Wu, 155
Sontag, Susan, 11
Southeast Asian tsunami of 2004, 170
Space shuttle *Challenger*, 24, 50–51, 53
Speaking into the Air, 54
Spectacle, 4, 8, 16, 18, 35, 38, 42, 70, 78–79, 127, 176; of Deepwater Horizon spill, 166; injunction to understand working in tandem with, 72; scholars of, 78; of September 11 attacks, 102, 126; and *War of the Worlds*, 40
Spectatorship: changing notions of, 61; of disasters, 7, 18, 21–22, 56, 178; empathetic, 175; mass media, 17; of others' suffering, 177
Spitzer, Eliot, 172
Spontaneous shrines, 52, 133–134, 146, 158–159
Stearns, Peter, 113
Stephanopoulos, George, 117
Stone, Oliver, 4, 45, 47
Stress, 140
"Structures of feeling," 59
Sturken, Marita, 10
Suffering, 12, 14, 17, 21, 26, 49, 55, 154: authenticity of, 96; Anderson Cooper's

reaction to, 83–84; depoliticization of, 91–92; narratives of, 62, 89–90; of others, 9, 11, 19, 23–25, 30–32, 57, 61–62, 68, 76, 151, 158, 170–171, 174, 177; and reality television, 52; and self-improvement, 95, 155; sharing of, 142
Superdome, 1, 67, 86
Surveillance, 3, 99; opposition to, 104
Survivor, 78
Swonk, Diane, 100
Sympathy, 9, 19, 68, 76; Enlightenment views of, 31, 61, 69–70, 77–78, 87, 91, 95; waning after Hurricane Katrina, 150–151
Syracuse Herald coverage of the *Titanic*, 37
Szasz, Andrew, 19

Tacitus, 27
Tapper, Jake, 119
TARP. *See* Troubled Asset Relief Program
Taylor, Charles, 52
"Teacher-in-Space" program, 50
Telegraph, 32, 34, 37, 43; criticism of, 38–39
Television, 1–2, 5, 8, 9, 11, 14, 19, 22, 42–44, 47, 48; "post-documentary" culture of, 78–79; talk shows, 132, 143; vicarious connections through, 145
Temptation Island, 79, 90
Terrorism, 3, 6, 98–99, 102, 107–108, 112–113, 122, 143, 172, 179
Theodicy, 142–143
Therapeutic culture, 61, 155
Therapeutic dialogue, 132
Therapeutic experience, 7, 78–79, 82, 131
Therapeutic gospel, 133
Therapeutic ideal, 77, 130, 141
Therapeutic monuments, 133, 135
Therapeutic rhetoric, 138, 152
Therapeutic self-help, 20–21, 131, 133
Thomas, W. I., 48
Time Magazine, 21, 50
Times of London, 167
Titanic, RMS, 24, 37–39, 47–48, 50
Tocqueville, Alexis de, 69
Today, 64
Toffler, Alvin, 132

Torpey, John, 155–156
Tracy, Ben, 117
Tragedy, 6, 23, 42, 44, 49, 75, 140
Transferability, 15
Trauma, 10–11, 41, 130; collective, 57; expanding definition of, 49; of Hurricane Katrina, 140; of Kennedy assassination, 45; performance of, 93; and reality television, 78–79; and self-help, 142, 154; of September 11 attacks, 126, 140; of Seung-Hui Cho's manifesto, 72; vicarious, 18, 49, 140
Trotter, Wilfred, 40
Troubled Asset Relief Program (TARP), 100–101, 104–105, 107–108, 117, 119–120, 123, 127
Trouble the Water, 60–61, 87–91, 93, 125
TrueHoop blog, 58
Trump, Donald, 123
Trust, 17–18, 63, 100, 102, 118–119, 166
Twain, Mark, 27–28

Udoji, Adori, 85
Union Square, New York City, 159
United Airlines Flight 93, 147
University of New Orleans, 138
University of Texas shooting, 66, 159
USA PATRIOT Act. *See* Patriot Act
U.S. Coast Guard, 163
U.S. Holocaust Museum, 135

Values, 13–14
Vanity Fair, 21
Van Zandt, Clint, 71
Velshi, Ali, 115
Vesuvius, Mount, 26, 34
Victims, 19, 25, 56–58, 60, 93, 145, 170; blaming of, 151, 173; depictions of white vs. African American, 81, 83, 85–87, 95; expanding definition of, 49; family members of, 152; of hurricanes Katrina and Rita, 64; imagined communion with, 48; political status of, 19; and self-improvement, 95; of Virginia Tech shootings, 66, 71–72, 75–77
Vietnam Veterans Memorial, 135
Vietnam War, 42, 135
Violence, 14

Virginia Polytechnic Institute and State University (Virginia Tech), 19; shootings at, 2, 3, 5, 9–10, 17, 58, 60–61, 64–67, 70–77, 92–94, 96, 130, 136, 159, 168–169, 174, 177
Voltaire, 29–30
Voyeurism, 5, 8, 35, 97; and film theory, 79, 94; and reality television, 77; and sympathy, 77–78

Wall Street, 100, 106, 116–117, 119–120, 123, 126
Wall Street Journal, 116
Warhol, Andy, 47
"War of the Worlds," 40
War on terror, 99, 106, 114, 144, 149
Washington, DC, 145
Washington, George, 28
Washington Post, 61, 164
Waveland, Mississippi, 147; *AC 360* coverage of, 81–83, 85–86, 96–97
Web 2.0, 131
Welles, Orson, 40

West, Kanye, 64
Whitaker, Forrest, 64
White House, 164–165, 167–168
White supremacy, 33
Wikipedia, 130
Williams, Brian, 65, 70–71, 73, 93, 114
Williams, Pete, 72–73
Williams, Raymond, 12
Wispé, Lauren, 69
Witnessing, 20–21, 59
Wordsworth, William, 34
World Trade Center, 1, 5, 8, 98, 111, 121, 140, 146–147, 153
World War II, 11, 41–42
Worst-case scenarios, 113, 164

Yellin, Jessica, 119–120
YouTube and the Zapruder film, 46

Zahn, Paula, 112
Zapruder, Abraham, 45; as "citizen journalist," 48
Zapruder film, 45–48, 74

Timothy Recuber is a Visiting Assistant Professor in the Communication Department at Hamilton College.